SCOTTISH MONASTIC LANDSCAPES

SCOTTISH MONASTIC LANDSCAPES

DEREK HALL

TEMPUS

This book is dedicated to Alice, Kitty and Fergus.

First published 2006

Tempus Publishing Limited
The Mill, Brimscombe Port,
Stroud, Gloucestershire, GL5 2QG
www.tempus-publishing.com

© Derek Hall, 2006

The right of Derek Hall to be identified as the Author
of this work has been asserted in accordance with the
Copyrights, Designs and Patents Act 1988.

All rights reserved. No part of this book may be reprinted
or reproduced or utilised in any form or by any electronic,
mechanical or other means, now known or hereafter invented,
including photocopying and recording, or in any information
storage or retrieval system, without the permission in writing
from the Publishers.

British Library Cataloguing in Publication Data.
A catalogue record for this book is available from the British Library.

ISBN 0 7524 4012 8

Typesetting and origination by Tempus Publishing Limited
Printed in Great Britain

CONTENTS

	Introduction	7
	Acknowledgements	10
1	A land untouched?	11
2	Monastic revolution: agriculture and industry	17
3	Care of the sick	43
4	God's bankers: the military orders in Scotland (Stenhouse and the Knights of St John)	60
5	A future for the past?	80
	Gazetteer of Scottish monastic granges	86
	Appendix 1 List of potential Scottish monastic industrial grange sites	203
	Appendix 2 List of Scottish medieval hospitals	208
	Bibliography	218

INTRODUCTION

A loop in the Forth is worth an earldom in the North. Registrum Cambuskenneth

In today's modern Scottish landscape ruined abbeys and churches stand as mute reminders of the enormous part that the major monastic orders once played in the development and control of society.

The aim of this book is to take a fresh look at exactly what role these orders of holy men played in the development of the nation of Scotland and more importantly what effect they had on the landscape. The idea of adding this book to the growing pile of work on medieval Scotland largely sprang out of the work commissioned by Historic Scotland on Scottish monastic granges and industries and was then given further impetus by the publication of *Monastic Landscapes* by James Bond in 2004.

Bond's book is an exemplary study of the impact of the monastic orders on the landscape of England and Wales but does not cover Scotland. This book is designed to remedy this. As will be seen it has only started to scratch the surface of a vast store of knowledge.

1 St Andrews Cathedral. © *SUAT Ltd*

2 Monks at the dinner table

3 Architectural fragment with crossed crosiers, Drygrange, Scottish Borders. © SUAT Ltd

ACKNOWLEDGEMENTS

The author would like to acknowledge the support of Historic Scotland, in particular Dr Richard Fawcett, throughout all of the monastic gazetteer projects. He would also like to thank his colleagues at SUAT Ltd and in particular Ray Cachart and Catherine Smith and the external authors of gazetteers, especially Charlie Murray, Martin Brann, Mike Middleton, Mike Roy and Graeme Brown. For their support and interest in this subject he would like to thank John Dent, Rory McDonald, Piers Dixon, Strat Halliday, George Haggarty and Richard Oram. The author would also like to thank Peter Kemmis Betty at Tempus for commissioning this work and gently encouraging its completion and submission.

The help and advice of all the local authority archaeologists is also gratefully acknowledged. Except where stated all the photographs and illustrations are the author's own.

1

A LAND UNTOUCHED?

Stet domus haec donec fluctus formica marinos ebibat, et totum testudo perambulet orbem.
May this house stand until an ant drains the flowing sea, and a tortoise walks around the whole world.
(Medieval inscription above doorway to Inchcolm abbey, Fife)

A LAND UNTOUCHED?

In twelfth-century Scotland the countryside was largely untouched and as such offered the opportunity for the exploitation of natural resources such as coal, lead, silver, stone and salt. The monks, in particular the Cistercians, were the first to realise the enormous potential that was available. This was also true as regards the opportunity for agriculture, livestock farming and fishing. In a society where most ordinary people lived in houses that were built out of wood, the appearance in the landscape of large stone-built abbeys and churches must have been very striking.

This is still something that is apparent to the modern visitor to abbeys such as Melrose, Jedburgh, Dryburgh, Sweetheart and Dundrennan where the massive scale of these new buildings is still in evidence. However there are places, like Scone Palace, where an abbey once dominated the landscape where the only evidence that now survives are rockeries full of stone sculpture.

Being a Monk was to be part of a new movement, monasticism, meaning literally 'dwelling alone'. A monk was expected to seek seclusion from worldly life to study and contemplate the word of God.

From a Scottish perspective this explains the location of monasteries like Inchcolm, Iona and Oronsay which are all located on islands. What started in the deserts of North Africa in the fourth century rapidly spread across the western world, but in attempting to escape the world the Monks couldn't help but change it dramatically.

Through their commitment to spirituality they established new ideas on virtuous living, becoming renowned as holy men with supposedly quasi-magical powers. But it was the monastic commitment to learning that was especially useful to the rulers of medieval Britain. Monastic libraries were huge reservoirs of knowledge, through the medium of the written word monks held the power of transmitting and storing information.

Royal patronage was a crucial component of Christianity's success. Scotland's early saints were usually bishops or abbots who founded a monastery with the local king's blessing. From these monasteries they consolidated Christian belief within their local communities and passed it on to others through missionaries. The Scottish cathedrals in the twelfth and thirteenth centuries tended to look to England for their organisation and constitution. For example, both Glasgow and Dunkeld used Salisbury as their model while Moray, probably on account of their bishop, Richard of Lincoln (1187-1203) used Lincoln Cathedral for its constitution. By 1250 churchmen were likely to be servants of royalty or connected to noble families in some way. In the thirteenth century a mixture of Alexander III's favour and the patronage of the Comyns had largely filled the clergy with their favourites, mostly Scots. A series of new religious orders were also introduced during the twelfth century, mostly from France via daughter-houses in England, such as the Cistercians, Augustinians and Premonstratensians. The Tironensians were the only monastic order to come directly from their mother-house, in this case Tiron near Chatres. One of the most successful of these orders was the Cistercians who by 1273 had 11 houses in Scotland. Four of the 15 religious orders in Scotland had warehouses in Berwick, and between them they controlled five per cent of the wool clip. The Augustinians, however, operated differently reaching out to the laity and using their connections to royalty, as seen at Holyrood, near Edinburgh, and Cambuskenneth, near Stirling. In all a total of 64 religious houses belonging to seven separate monastic orders were founded in Scotland from 1113-1353 (see below).

4 Old Scone market cross

Above: 5 Fragment of medieval tomb in rockery at Scone Palace, Perth and Kinross

Right: 6 Gravestone of monk at Oronsay Abbey

King David I of Scotland: the State-building king

David I had grown up in the excitement surrounding the First Crusade (1095-99), which offered a new ideal of Christian knighthood. His mother, Margaret, had a strong and pious influence on him, and from his time at the Norman court of Henry I of England he had seen the Norman fashion of kingship first hand. When he returned to Scotland in 1113 to claim his inheritance from his brother, King Alexander I, he brought with him these new ideas, along with a pack of Norman followers to aid enforcement.

His revolution, which would ultimately reshape the Scottish Kingdom, began in the lands in the south of Scotland – the old ancestral homes of the Angles and Britons. The latest monastic orders were brought in: the Augustinians to Jedburgh; the Tironensians to Kelso; the Cistercians to Melrose; as was a new bishopric, complete with a new cathedral, at Glasgow. After David became King of Scotland in 1124, the reformed orders went on to establish themselves in Scone, St Andrews, Cambuskenneth, Holyrood and the royal centre at Dunfermline.

Granted massive estates by the monarchy, these new institutions gave renewed impetus to the economy and increased trade with Europe. The churches, bishops and abbots formed the king's closest advisors; the monks formed an educated bureaucracy which looked after the king's records and administered Scotland's first systematic, written and recorded government.

It was a revolution from above as far as the local populace were concerned, but it had profound implications for everyday life. The Church extended its role, establishing Scotland's parish system and bringing Christianity to the heart of every community through the local parish priest, who blessed the crops and tended to the spiritual needs and fears of the community. David's revolution also brought the king's law to the people; at Roxburgh he established Scotland's first sheriffdom for the administration of the king's justice. Indeed it was David who introduced the concept of an urban society, a group of like-minded people working for the common good and of course the king. It was the foundation of the Scottish burghs in the twelfth century that also drew the various orders of friars to found houses in many of them and until the Protestant Reformation of 1559 such centres of commerce would have proved ideal sources of finance for such religious institutions.

THE MONASTIC ORDERS IN SCOTLAND (64 HOUSES)

CISTERCIAN	19	DATE OF FOUNDATION
Melrose	Borders	1136
Newbattle	Lothian	1140
Dundrennan	Dumfries and Galloway	1142
Kinloss	Grampian	1150
North Berwick nunnery	Lothian	1150
Eccles nunnery	Borders	1156
Haddington nunnery	Lothian	1159
Saddell	Argyll	1160/1207
Coupar Angus	Tayside	1161/4
Mauchline	Strathclyde	1165
Manuel nunnery	West Lothian	1174
Glenluce	Dumfries and Galloway	1191/92

St Bathans	Borders	12th or 13th century
Culross	Fife	1217
Deer	Grampian	1219
Balmerino	Fife	1227
Inchmahome	Central	1238
Elcho nunnery	Tayside	1241
Sweetheart	Dumfries and Galloway	1273
AUGUSTINIAN	18	
Scone	Tayside	1120
Loch Tay	Tayside	1122–1124
Inchcolm	Lothian	1123
Holyrood	Lothian	1128
St Marys Priory, Trail	Dumfries and Galloway	1138
Jedburgh	Borders	1139
Cambuskenneth	Central	1140
St Andrews	Fife	1140
St Serfs	Fife	1150
Canonbie	Dumfries and Galloway	1160s
Restenneth	Angus	1162
Inchaffray	Tayside	pre 1198
Monymusk	Grampian	1245
Abernethy	Tayside	1272–73
Pittenweem	Fife	13th or 14th century
Blantyre	Strathclyde	13th century
Strathfillan	Tayside	1317/18
Oronsay	Argyll	1353
BENEDICTINE	7	
Dunfermline	Fife	1128
Urquhart	Grampian	1136
Lincluden nunnery	Dumfries and Galloway	1164
Isle of May	Fife	mid 12th century
Coldingham	Borders	pre 1174
Iona	Argyll	1203
Pluscarden	Grampian	1230/31

TIRONENSIAN	7	
Selkirk	Borders	1113
Kelso	Borders	1128
Lesmahagow	Strathclyde	1144
Kilwinning	Strathclyde	1162 x 1189
Arbroath	Tayside	1178
Lindores	Fife	1191
Fogo	Borders	1242
Fyvie	Grampian	1285
PREMONSTRATENSIAN	6	
Dryburgh	Borders	1150
Soulseat	Dumfries and Galloway	Post 1161
Whithorn	Dumfries and Galloway	1177
Tongland	Dumfries and Galloway	1218
Fearn	Highland	1221/1227
Holywood	Dumfries and Galloway	1225
CLUNIAC	3	
Paisley	Strathclyde	1163
Renfrew	Strathclyde	1163
Crossraguell	Strathclyde	1244
VALLISCAULIAN	2	
Ardchattan	Strathclyde	1230/31
Beauly	Highland	1230
KNIGHTS OF ST JOHN	2	
Torphichen Preceptory	West Lothian	1140s
Balantradoch (Temple)	West Lothian	1175-79

2
MONASTIC REVOLUTION: AGRICULTURE AND INDUSTRY

For several years this author and a few colleagues had begun to suggest that David I's introduction of the major monastic orders into twelfth-century Scotland had a major effect on the landscape. With this in mind, and the support of Historic Scotland, a series of fieldwork projects were carried out with the intention of assessing whether it was still possible to find traces of this in the modern landscape.

This began with the first real survey of Scottish medieval hospitals (between 1997-2000) and then moved onto monastic granges and industrial sites (2001-04), in many cases this was the first time that anybody had checked for this sort of evidence.

AGRICULTURE

The monastic orders can be regarded as the architects of the first real agricultural and industrial improvements in Scotland, and the function and types of their granges often reflect this. In England such granges have been divided into roughly five types which include: agrarian farms, bercaries (sheep farms), vaccaries (cattle ranches), horse studs and industrial complexes (ironworking and coal mining) (English Heritage 1997). Documentary evidence for vaccaries and bercaries in Scotland exists for the Border granges of Buckholm and Whitelee and the Lothian grange of Edmundston (*Liber de Melros* nos 107 and 414; *RRS*, ii, no 386).

Many of the groups of cultivation terraces visible in the Scottish Borders are on monastic lands, one of the best examples at Romanno Bridge is on land formerly in the possession of Holyrood Abbey. If it is accepted that these terraces are of medieval date, they would seem to indicate carefully controlled methods of agriculture. Although several articles have been written discussing their function, more analysis needs to be carried out to discover how they were being used (Eckford 1928; Hannah 1931; Graham 1939). This author has always wondered whether some of these might have been using for growing grapes. Some of these terraces certainly face the right way and up until the onset of 'Little Ice Age' of the sixteenth century the climate in Scotland was probably warm enough (Lamb 1995, 219-22).

GRANGES

The grange or estate centre formed the main focus of control for a monastic house on its landholdings. Overseen by a monk with the job of granger these establishments were where farmers and landholders on the monastic estates would bring their crops and livestock for reckoning and further distribution.

7 Summer palace of the Bishops of Caithness, Durness

11 Towerhouse at site of monastic vaccary, Old Buckholm, Scottish Borders. © SUAT Ltd

8 Settlement of Grange, Perth and Kinross. © SUAT Ltd

The place name Grange can still be found in the modern landscape of Scotland. For example it is the origin of the name Grangemouth, better known these days for its oil refinery, and the settlement of Grange in the Carse of Gowrie in Perthshire.

Many of these monastic granges are occupied today by working farms and small holdings and it is only the place name, which remains largely unaltered, which gives some clue to its original function.

Documentary references

Much of the documentary evidence for these granges can be found in the rental books of the various abbeys; many of which were transcribed and published in the nineteenth century. The fifteenth-century rentals of the Cistercian abbey of Coupar Angus in the Perth and Kinross Council Area seem to suggest that at that stage most, if not all, of the landholdings of the various granges were leased to lay folk who had to agree to pay various rentals to the abbey in both money and livestock. For example in 1444 the Grange of Kerso is let to 'the husbandmen dwelling therein, for seven years, in which grange are contained 52 acres' for a rent of 18s an acre and two hens (Rogers 1879, 123), and in 1448/9 the Grange of Kyncrech is let for five years along with the third part of the mills for 11 merks and 30 capons annually (Ibid, 132).

It is harder to find much surviving documentary evidence for the earlier management of the granges as many of the abbeys were burnt in English raids and their documents destroyed. After the Reformation of 1559/60 all the monastic lands were passed onto various Scottish landowners; the *Register of the Great Seal* lists these and can be a useful source for working out the landholdings of the various monasteries.

9 Farmhouse at site of grange at East Tullyfergus, Perth and Kinross. © *SUAT Ltd*

10 Farm at grange site of Nunhope, West Hopes, East Lothian

For example on 28 January 1568 Margaret Hume, Prioress of North Berwick feus to Alexander Hume, son of Patrick Hume of Polwart: 'the lands of Grange of Breich, with mansions, halls, chambers, barns, gardens, houses, buildings and lands both arable and otherwise, for 6 merks of old feu and 3s 4d of augmentation' (*RMS*, iv, no 1920).

Distribution and missing granges

The 192 Scottish granges that it is possible to identify with a specific religious house break down by order as follows: Augustinian 33, Benedictine 22, Cistercian 86, Cluniac 5, Order of St Lazarus 1, Premonstratensian 9, Tironensian 31, Trinitarian 1, Valliscaulian 4. The largest number of granges belonged to Melrose (24), Newbattle (17), Kelso (15) and Coupar Angus Abbeys (10). The lack of obvious grange sites connected to the likes of Fearn Abbey (Premonstratensian) in the Highland Council Area, St Serfs Priory (Augustinian) in Fife, Saddell Abbey (Cistercian), Iona Abbey (Benedictine) and Oronsay Abbey (Augustinian) in Argyll and Bute is quite marked. Whether this indicates the different priorities of the various monastic orders or suggests the complete disappearance of place names that might give helpful clues to the former location of granges is not clear. For example there is a single reference to an Iona grange in the *Register of the Great Seal* in 1616, which refers to the 'grangiam terre lie Stenage in Icolmekill', but Stenage is not in modern usage as a place name and does not appear on early maps (Thomson 1882, no 1386).

Is it possible that some of the isolated medieval chapels and churches that exist in parts of Scotland may have originally been associated with monastic granges? Examples of such sites can be found at St Murdoch's Chapel at Ethie in Angus (NO 7031 4796), the former site of Coupar Angus Parish Church at Bendochy (NO 2184 4145) and St Mary's Chapel, Whitefield of Boysack (NO 6248 4780). In any future search for grange sites the location of such chapels and churches might prove a good starting point.

12 Ruined medieval church, Abbotrule, Scottish Borders. © *SUAT Ltd*

13 Grange Hall, Aberdeenshire. © SUAT Ltd

14 Shambellie Grange, Dumfries and Galloway. © SUAT Ltd

Place name evidence

There are several examples of grange names being applied to houses of Edwardian and Victorian date that actually have no monastic origin at all. In two examples these houses have had their names changed to include the 'grange' element presumably in an attempt to increase the 'grandness' of the building. This can still be seen happening even now when new names for housing developments are being chosen. In Scots Gaelic the word for grange is 'grainnseach' which can also mean a granary or refer to land under cultivation. These alternative meanings should be kept in mind when any attempt is made to trace place name evidence for former grange sites particularly in the Highlands.

Current state of preservation

Of the 309 sites identified in the Scottish grange survey it is possible to isolate a group of 15 that are represented by standing remains, earthworks or cropmarks. Of the group of standing buildings the most impressive and useful survivor is the grange of Penshiel in the Lammermuir hills in East Lothian. The remains of a sizeable stone building still survive with indications of an internal vault on the south side of a well-defined courtyard, which has the remains of at least two other buildings on its eastern side. On the face of it the large building with a vaulted basement can best be regarded as doubling as a both a storage building and on-site accommodation for the granitar (grangemaster). The other buildings around the courtyard are harder to define.

The grange at Shambellie (Dumfries and Galloway) is now represented by an isolated fragment of a building or enclosure wall containing a door or gate arch which survives in the stackyard of the modern farm. This structure may have originally been a large barn or store building. It has been suggested that one of the buildings at the Augustinian monastery on the island of Oronsay (Argyll and Bute) may have originated as a grange before being incorporated into the monastic complex (pers. comm. G. Stell). The possible site of Incholm Abbey's Grange of Barnhill in Fife is occupied by the Monk's Cave (NT18SE 1), which stands on Charles Hill, is entirely artificial and is really the lower storey of a building, probably a ferry-house and warehouse connected with Inchcolm Abbey (NT18SE 7). The building stands on the edge of a low cliff which has been partly excavated; the doorway, of fifteenth-century date, opens into a vaulted cellar. The upper storey has been reduced to the level of the upper surface of the vault supporting it (RCAHMS 1933).

Other surviving buildings, Byres and Southside Castle (both East Lothian), may be examples of small, defended, grange control 'centres', essentially somewhere that the teinds could be collected for the monastery.

This is an assumption on the author's part but it does seem significant that defensible structures of a medieval date should exist on both these grange sites. Barnes Castle (East Lothian) is a remarkable structure that is identified as a 'fortified grange' on the first edition Ordnance Survey map but is also identified as the sixteenth-century house of Sir John Seaton by MacGibbon and Ross (1887, 333-5).

Further clarification of whether this building is a grange of the Cistercian nunnery of Haddington is required. Grange House (Fife) represents the surviving remains of a sizeable stone house which is on a site associated with the nunnery at North Berwick; again it is unclear if the surviving building is directly related to the grange or stands on the same site. Mauchline (North Ayrshire) and Campsie (Perth and Kinross) are good, surviving examples of the sort of accommodation that was provided for the abbots at some of the granges and estate centres.

The best surviving example of what the basic layout out of a grange complex and its associated buildings might have looked like can be found at Moorfoot (Mid Lothian). At this site it is possible to make out a complex of buildings arranged around a courtyard adjacent to the River South Esk, while in another part of the site enclosures and a culverted watercourse survive which may all relate to a former mill complex.

15 Gamelshiel Castle, East Lothian. © SUAT Ltd

16 Interior of Barnes castle vault

17 Grange House, Fife. © SUAT Ltd

18 Cambusmichael, ruined church, Perth and Kinross. © SUAT Ltd

Earthwork evidence may exist for the grange of Nunhope (East Lothian); a field visit by the author as part of the survey identified the remains of a building at the foot of a narrow glen at East Hopes which is not recorded as being related to modern sheep farming. Earthworks also survive at the grange sites of Abbotshall (Aberdeenshire) and Davoch of Grange (Moray). Intriguing cropmark evidence has also been recorded for Coupar Grange and the possible grange of Cambusmichael (both Perth and Kinross). On both sites evidence for their layout and subdivision can be seen. At Cambusmichael the church seems to have been the focal point for this centre.

At Coupar Grange the cropmarks seem to suggest the existence of sizeable sunken buildings in the eastern corner of a sizeable ditched enclosure. Cartographic evidence has also proved useful for identifying former grange sites, and in at least four cases the first edition Ordnance Survey map of the 1860s marks grange sites, at Garvald (East Lothian), East Barns (Fife), New Grange (Fife) and Grange of Rawhill (Aberdeenshire). Two of these, East Barns and Rawhill are now built over by the modern towns of Dunfermline and Peterhead. Nothing survives at the sites of New Grange and Garvald although they have not been built on.

INDUSTRY

References to industrial activities in the granges can also be found, for example the monks of Newbattle Abbey (Midlothian) are granted coal workings (*carbonarium*) at Preston Grange by a charter of Seyer de Quinci, Earl of Winchester, between 1210 and 1216 (Bannatyne Club 1849, 53). This charter grants '*carbonarium et quarrarium*' between the burn of Whytrig and the bounds of the land of Pontekyn (Pinkie) and Inveresch (Inveresk), and in the ebb and flow of the sea.

19 Colpenhope Grange, Scottish Borders. © *SUAT Ltd*

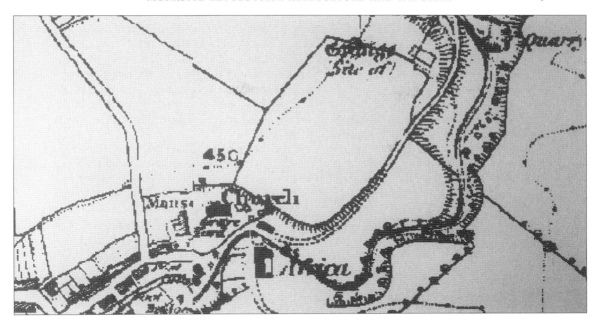

20 Site of grange marked on first edition Ordnance Survey map, Garvald, East Lothian

21 Charleston Limekilns. © *SUAT Ltd*

22 The River Forth at Kincardine. © *SUAT Ltd*

As this document is a reaffirmation of an earlier grant by his father, the coal workings may have been in use from the late twelfth century. A charter of 1291 by Willelmus de Obirwill grants coal workings '*in terra mea de Petyncref* (Pittencrieff)' to the monks of Dunfermline Abbey, thus indicating that this resource was being exploited on both sides of the River Forth (Innes 1842, 218). A later document of 1531 details an agreement between Newbattle and Dunfermline Abbeys regarding their adjacent coal workings at Preston Grange and Inveresk and Pinkie, where the Abbot of Newbattle agrees to ensure that his coal is worked in such a way as to allow water in the Dunfermline workings to escape to the sea, even if this includes the cutting of conduits (Innes 1842, 362). Newbattle Abbey was also lead mining on their lands in Crawford Muir where a mine on Glengonar Water was gifted to them by Sir David Lindsay in 1239 (*The Mining Journal* 1910). A later reference of 1466 refers to a decree against James Lord Hamilton who is alleged to have 'despoiled' 1000 stone of lead ore from Abbot Patrick Madowre of Newbattle (*Bannatyne Club* 1849, xxv).

Salt panning was also being carried out on the Forth, and there are references to '*salina de Preston*', '*salina in Carso*' and '*salinaria in Kalentyr*' (*Bannatyne Club* 1849, 130,131). Indeed, the Newbattle Abbey salt-works in the Carse of Kalentir (Callendar, Falkirk) were leased to the Canons of Holyrood Abbey as is indicated by the settlement of a dispute over the non-payment of rent for these works (*Bannatyne Club* 1849, 131). Documentary evidence for salt panning any earlier than the seventeenth century on the other major river systems is harder to find, but there must be a strong chance that it was taking place in the Tay, Clyde and Solway estuaries and the Dornoch and Moray Firths. Indeed there must be case for arguing that the recorded post-Reformation industries at the likes of Saltcoats (Ayrshire), Methil, St Monance and Culross (Fife) were all based on original monastic workings of this valuable resource. A lot depends on the method of extraction being employed, if it relied on the heating of the pans then it may have only taken place in close proximity to a coal source although evaporation may have still been an option.

SITES BY INDUSTRY

Coal mining

The monks of Newbattle Abbey are well known as the operators of Scotland's earliest coal mining operation at Prestongrange in East Lothian, having been granted the rights to mine from at least the early thirteenth century by the De Quincy family (Innes 1849, 53). The monks of Holyrood Abbey in Edinburgh were granted a tithe by William Di Vipont to dig coal from his Carriden estate, which was then carried to Holyrood in panniers strapped to the backs of their horses; later it was taken to Leith by sailing ship.

Aeneas Sylvius, the future Pope Pius II, visited Central Scotland in 1435 and wrote in his journal: 'the poor, who almost in a state of nakedness begged at the church door, depart with joy in their faces on receiving stones as alms!' This account appears to suggest that although coal was commonly used as fuel in Scotland it was yet unknown in many parts of Europe. This is reinforced as in another account of his visit to Scotland the future Pope wrote: 'A sulphurous stone dug from the earth is used by the people as fuel'. From a search of the available documentary record, coal was also being worked by Culross, Inchcolm and Crossraguel Abbeys.

These mining operations were largely focused in those parts of Scotland that became the location of major coal mines in the early modern period at the likes of Newtongrange and Monktonhall. At Prestongrange it is not only the monks of Newbattle who were working the coal, a charter of 1531 lists Abbot James (of Newbattle) entering into a contract with monks of Dunfermline and agreeing to work his coal of Preston Grange, or to drive conduits through it, in such a manner as to give passage for the water from the Abbot of Dunfermline's coal fields of Inveresk and Pinkie to the sea (Innes 1849, xxvi). It is assumed that these monastic mines were open-cast operations rather than deep mineshafts, there is little description of methods of extraction in the documents.

In the later medieval period there is evidence that mining was conducted with a scatter of bell pits using primitive technology, an exception being the workings at Culross in Fife. There, from 1617 the colliery of George Bruce may have been the first to use a wheel mechanism for drainage (Ewart *et al.* 1996, 1-26). From existing documents of post-Reformation date it seems to be the case that there was a real worry in Scotland that the coal supply was running out. In June 1563 for example, Queen Mary states that: 'na manner or person, stranger nor liege take upon hand to transport, carrie or take furth any coales by schippe, crayer or onie bait' due to the 'exhorbitant dearth and scantness of fewale within the Realme' (Morgan 1929, 111). By 1609 a further Act of Parliament was passed against export of coal as 'the haill coill within this Kingdom sall in a verie schorte tyme be waisted and consumed' (Cochran Patrick 1878, xlvii). Is it possible that this reflects the exhausting of the coal sources that were able to be mined by open-cast methods and predates any deeper mining for coal?

Salt panning

Panning for salt on the Scottish seaboard is certainly well known between the sixteenth and nineteenth centuries and extensive research has been undertaken on the likes of the St Monance saltpans in Fife (Whatley 1987; Lewis *et al.* 1999). Salt produced by boiling brine, often called furnace salt, needs to be drained to remove the 'bittern', that is the various other chemical compounds present in seawater which otherwise render the salt bitter to taste and deliquescent. Scots salt was of a notoriously poor quality from a failure to do this so causing it to 'melt' and was difficult to export by sea as a consequence.

Other salt extraction methods include the practice of 'sleeching' on the Solway Coast, effectively a method of obtaining the salt from the tidal sand by filtering it (Neilson 1899). There has been little or no work on the earlier exploitation of this resource; of the 33 salt panning sites that were identified during the Monastic industrial survey, 13 of them can be definitely identified as being under the control of the monastic houses of Melrose Abbey, Dunfermline Abbey, Culross Abbey, Newbattle Abbey, Holyrood Abbey, Coupar Angus Abbey, Arbroath Abbey, Holm Cultram

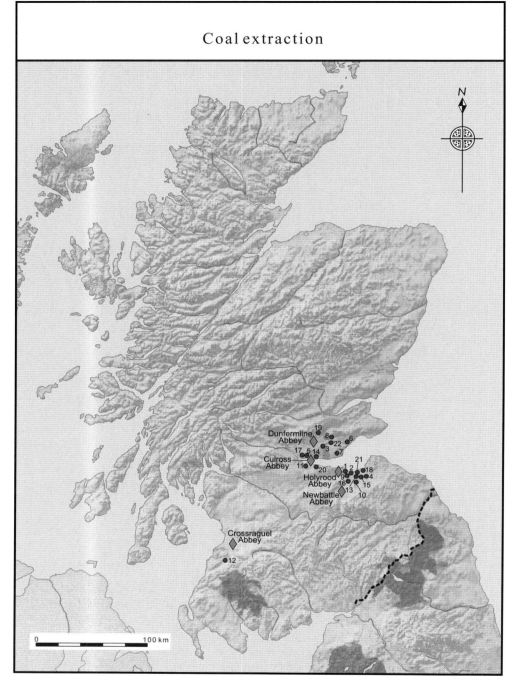

23 Distribution map of monastic coal workings. © *SUAT Ltd*

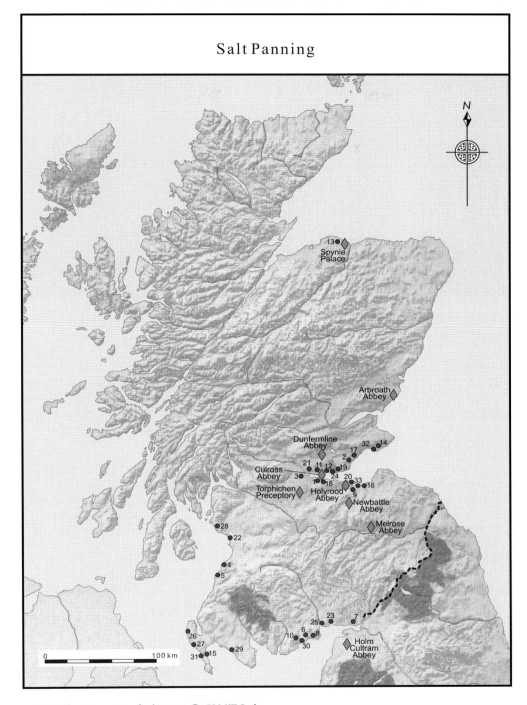

24 Distribution map of salt pans. © *SUAT Ltd*

25 Salt pan at Cockenzie, East Lothian. © *SUAT Ltd*

Abbey (in England), Torphicen Preceptory and Spynie Palace. The remaining 20 sites are well spread across the country in similar locations to the definite monastic ones and it is tempting to wonder if these sites may originate in the medieval period. Some discussion of the way that these pans operated is worth considering here, for most if not all the post-medieval panning sites there is good evidence that they were coal-fired. This may well have been the case for those monastic pans that were situated in the major coal-bearing areas of Scotland but there is good evidence that some of the pans were peat fired, for example the grant of the saltwork of Aldendonech (Aberdeenshire) to the monks of Coupar Angus in 1242 specifically states that it is granted with sufficient peatmoss for making salt (*cum sufficientis petavia ad sal faciendum*) (Easson 1947, 111). Whether evaporation by the sun was ever employed in Scotland as a method of extracting the salt from the seawater is not known but the apparent rock cut pans recorded in Dumfries and Galloway at Saltpan Rocks (NX 892 548) at Dysart in Fife (NT 304 929) and Cockenzie in East Lothian (NT 398 757) may suggest that it was (Cachart, Fyles and Hall 2004).

The importance of this resource in the medieval period is indicated by the battle for ownership that took place over at least one salt pan or pans in the Carse at Grangemouth, they are on record as belonging to Cambuskenneth, Arbroath, Newbattle and Holyrood Abbeys and Torphichen Preceptory at various points (Innes 1849, 134).

Lead, silver and gold mining and iron working
FRIARMURE, SOUTH LANARKSHIRE

The best-documented area of monastic lead and silver mining in Scotland is that of Friarmure (also known as Crawfordmuir) in South Lanarkshire. This land was gifted by the Lindsay family to Newbattle Abbey in 1239 when a mine on Glengonar water is specifically mentioned (*The Mining Journal* 1910). In 1467 David, Earl of Crawford, Lord Lindsay resigns the superiority of Fremure into the King's hands including the minerals and leadmines there (*minera ac plumbifodina*) (Innes 1849, no 292). The next record of mining in this area is in the 1560s when Bevis Bulmer is given licence to mine for silver; it is tempting to wonder if rather than being the first person to discover lead, silver and gold, as he claimed, he was simply using existing monastic knowledge of the resource.

MONASTIC REVOLUTION: AGRICULTURE AND INDUSTRY

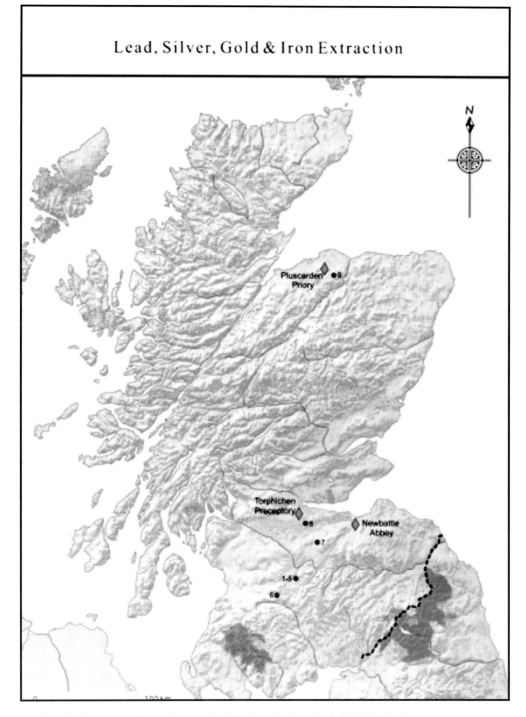

26 Distribution map of lead, silver and gold mines in Scotland. © *SUAT Ltd*

27 Industrial structure at Hilderston mine, West Lothian. © SUAT Ltd

From a field visit to this area there are still substantial surviving remains of mining evidence, the basic problem is the difficulty in dating them. However, the author believes that the workings on Drake Law include structures and features that may be of medieval date. It is clear that at least one of the burns running south down towards the valley of the Glengonar water has been diverted possibly to help the washing and sorting of rocks to extract the ore. The resultant sizeable pile of tailings is still visible and there appears to be a roadway running from this area down to the modern roadway. The features at Drake Law are less than half a mile away from a putative church site at Kirkgill which has been associated with Newbattle Abbey. However, a field visit to this site could identify no definite evidence of a church; any visible structures appear to be either sheep enclosures or byres.

HILDERSTON, WEST LOTHIAN

Silver is on record as being discovered at Hilderston in 1606 and there were at least seven shafts. In 1613 the mine was let to a private firm. The precise date of abandonment is unknown but it must have closed soon after 1614. The lease was renewed in 1870 but the project was abandoned in 1898 (Cadell 1925). A theodolite survey and an assessment of the Hilderston industrial area has been recently carried out by the University of Glasgow (Photos-Jones *et al.* 1999). During the research for the Historic Scotland funded monastic industrial gazetteer the author discovered a reference to silver at Hilderston in an entry in the *Rental of the Knights of St John of Torphichen* dated to 1539-40 (Cowan, MacKay and MacQuarrie 1983, 1). This lists a rental of:

> Villa de Hilderstoun set to tennentis for xx merkis maile in the zeir and xijs' of weddir siluer pait mertimes with uther dewiteis and dew service vsit and wont. (Ibid 1983, 1)

It is not clear whether this reference implies that mining was taking place at this date although the fact that the metal is specifically referred to must make this a very strong possibility and would put the first exploitation of this site at least 60 years earlier than previously noted. All mine workings and structures currently visible at Hilderston appear to relate to the nineteenth-century operations on the site.

LEAD LAW (SILLERHOLES), MIDLOTHIAN

The earliest reference to lead mining at this site is in a 'Summons of the reduction of tack of a Mr Eustachius Roche' dated to June 1592. This document states that Mr Eustachius has:

28 Hilderston silver mines, West Lothian. © *SUAT Ltd*

29 General view of mining remains at Sillerholes in Midlothian

30 Detail view of mine pit at Sillerholes in Midlothian

wrocht the semes of mettelis discouerit and wrocht of auld: To wit the gold in Crawfurd mwre, Hinderland and Tuedis mwre the copper seme in Crawfurd mwrre at the place callit Vamlock heid. The seme of leid at Lyntoun callit <u>Siluerhoilis</u>: And to have enterit ane sufficient number of warkmen: To wit thriescoir men of all sortis of warkmen necessary for ilk same at the leist and to haue biggit houses mylnes furnaces cassin sinkis and mynes.... (Cochran Patrick 1878).

In the autumn of 1993 a new farm pond was created in a low-lying boggy area of this sixteenth-century mining site. As the spoil heaps around the pond weathered during 1994, they were regularly walked and material was recovered from the surface. This includes sherds of medieval pottery, medieval shoes and pieces of textile, as well as bone, slag and ore. The pottery suggests a thirteenth- to fourteenth-century date. All the material was deposited in the conservation laboratory of the National Museum of Scotland (Oakes 1994). Following these discoveries the site was fully surveyed by RCAHMS. From a site visit it is quite obvious that the mining pits do not interfere with either the Roman road or the temporary camp that are located on this site thus allowing the possibility that there may have been lead mining in the Roman period, there is no concrete proof of this as yet.

GOLD MINING
The earliest medieval reference to gold is in a charter of David I, dating to 1124 x 1147, which grants to Dunfermline Abbey 'the whole tenth part of gold [*auro*] which shall come into the king's hands from Fife and Fothrif [West Fife, Kinross and Clackmannanshire]' (Barrow 1999, 120 no 140). Unfortunately this document does not state precisely where the metal is being mined. In James I's Parliament, held in Perth 1424, it was provided that wherever gold and silver mines were discovered within the lands of any lord or baron, if it can be proved that three halfpennies of silver can be produced out of the pound of lead, the mine should, according to the established practice of other realms, belong to the king (*Tytler's History*, vol iii, pp 63, 201).

31 General shot of mine adit at Sillerholes, Midlothian

32 Earthworks associated with gold working, Glengonnar Water, Crawford Moor, south Lanarkshire

Freirmure (see silver and lead mining above) also seems to have been a source for gold; there are records of it being found on the moor in the early sixteenth century. For example in 1511, 1512, and 1513 a number of payments are recorded at Crawford Muir mines to Lebald Northberge, the master miner; Andrew Ireland, the finer; and Gerald Essemer, a Dutchman, the melter. Bevis Bulmer is also said to have recovered gold from panning the Glengonar water, and this still takes place today. Direct monastic involvement in the mining of gold is hard to track down but it seems unlikely that Newbattle Abbey, for one, would not have been involved.

OTHER SITES

Silver was extracted from mines at Alva in the Ochill hills in Clackmannanshire in the eighteenth century, the possibility of earlier extraction should not be discounted. The same is true of another mine at Bridge of Allan in Stirlingshire which is on record as being the source of copper, silver and gold from early in the seventeenth century (Cochran-Patrick 1878).

IRON WORKING

A major difficulty during the survey was to identify and locate any evidence for monastic iron ore mining in Scotland. A charter of David I dating to 1127 x 1131 grants Dunfermline Abbey 'the tenth part of the salt and iron brought (to Dunfermline) for the king's use' (Barrow 1999, 70) but gives no indication where it is coming from. Given the intensity of Cistercian operations in Yorkshire it seems unlikely that they would not have been exploiting this resource in Scotland. The only site identified is at Croy in Moray; this is based on an entry in the National Monument Record of Scotland which claims association with Pluscarden Priory (NJ15NE 2). A site visit was unable to locate anything relating to this site. No documentary evidence for monastic iron working was encountered in the Scottish Bloomeries Project (pers. comm. J. Atkinson and E. Photos Jones).

Further research is required on this important industry.

Tileworks and clay extraction

A recent Historic Scotland funded chemical sourcing project on Scottish redware tiles from monastic houses has suggested that these are likely to have been locally produced rather than imported as has been suggested in recent years (Chenery, Hall, Haggarty and Murray 2004).

The major problem, similar to that of the Scottish medieval pottery industry, is the location of the sites of the kilns. For the gazetteer the site of the only excavated tile kiln at North Berwick priory was included (Richardson 1929) plus a site that had been identified at Darnick in the Scottish Borders as possibly being a tile kiln associated with Melrose Abbey (Talbot 1976).

The North Berwick site is scheduled although a new housing development was built in the vicinity in recent years. A field visit to the Darnick site suggests that there is no evidence for a tile kiln whatsoever and it should be discounted as being one. The third site included in the gazetteer is based on place name evidence alone. The site at Parkfield Farm near Scone was formerly called 'Limepotts' and is referred to in the *Scone Register* as being a property belonging to the abbey. From the author's research on Scottish pottery it is clear that the Scots name for earthenware clay is 'laime' thus suggesting that this place name refers to the existence of pits for digging clay that can be used for the production of ceramics, whether pottery or tile is, of course, unclear (Hall 1998). The manufacture of tiles for the monastic houses of Scotland is a subject that requires further research, in particular the analysis of clay sources in the vicinity of these sites.

Stone quarries

There has, as yet, been no systematic study of the location of the quarries that produced the building stone for the major abbeys of Scotland. For the industrial gazetteer project the best identified examples were associated with Scone Abbey, the quarry at Kincarrathie is identified by name on Pont's map and is now the site of the Quarrymill woodland park. Another quarry of Scone Abbey at Balcormoc was not located.

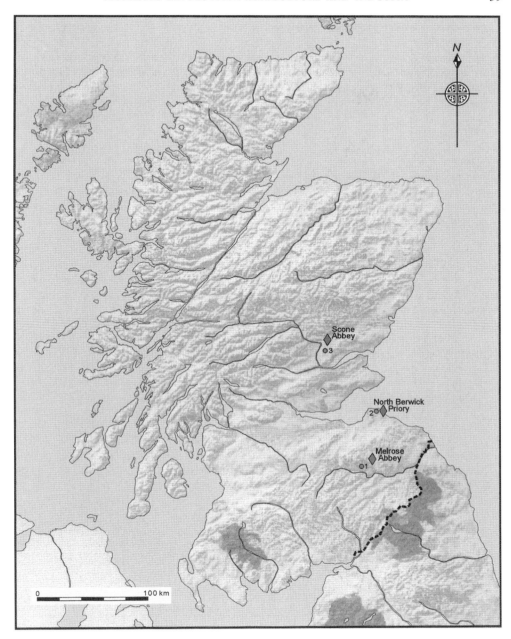

33 Distribution of monastic tile working. © *SUAT Ltd*

In the Scottish Borders the quarry known as 'Bourjo' on the slopes of the Eildon hills has long been identified as a quarry for Melrose Abbey. From a field visit it was noticeable that the gorge occupied by the Malthouse Burn, as it runs north towards Melrose, also seems to have been quarried. A future project concentrating solely on the quarrying and provision of stone for the major Scottish abbeys would seem to be a worthwhile exercise.

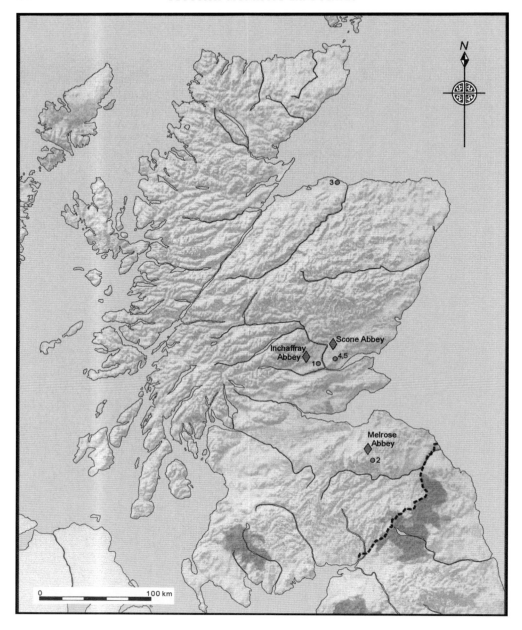

34 Map of potential monastic quarries. © *SUAT Ltd*

CARTOGRAPHIC EVIDENCE
Careful study of Timothy Ponts sixteenth- and seventeenth-century maps of Scotland have proved to be very helpful when searching for saltpans and coal mines that were still operating in that period. For example, many of the saltpans on the south side of the Forth around Grangemouth are still marked, as is the Abbot's Grange, and further north the stone quarries of Kincarrathie and Balcormoc are marked on Pont's map of Scone and area (http://www.nls.uk/pont/). The lead-mining area to the west of Crawford is also indicated on the relevant map sheet but unfortunately in not enough detail to identify individual sites.

35 Bourjo quarry, Scottish Borders

36 Abbey building beside mill pond, Sweetheart Abbey, Dumfries and Galloway

Water management

There has been little or no examination of this subject in Scotland, whereas in England analysis of the subject began in the late 1980s (Bond, 1989).

During the preparation of this book the author came across an intriguing reference in the charters of Coupar Angus Abbey, dating to 1292-6, to the grant of a spring in Kettins (Angus) along with a conduit leading the water to the monastery at Coupar (Easson 1947, 136,137). Kettins is some considerable distance away so, by implication, this must have been a major engineering exercise. There ought to be evidence for land reclamation and water management on Coupar Angus's properties in the Carse of Gowrie. Further careful study of the existing charters may prove beneficial although there is nothing mentioned in an analysis of the economic administration of this abbey between 1440 and 1560 (Morgan 1929). Recent recording and observation on the River Tweed in the Scottish Borders may have also identified features associated with management of the river by Melrose Abbey, this needs further analysis (pers. comm. John Dent).

37 Lade feeding fishpond at Sweetheart Abbey, Dumfries and Galloway

While it is only possible to identify one monastic fishpond, at Newabbey in Dumfries and Galloway, there must have been more? There would also seem to be a good chance that the monks of Inchaffray Abbey in Perth and Kinross managed and straightened the Pow of Inchaffray, a watercourse that runs right by the monastery (Watson 1997).

Routeways and connections

One of the most striking things that comes to the fore in this research is the distance between some of the monasteries and their industrial sites. This would seem to suggest that the road system in medieval Scotland must have been quite good, particularly in those areas south of the Forth where the lines of Roman roads such as Dere Street would have still formed the major routeways. In fact in the *Newbattle Register* that particular road is called '*le Dere Strete*'.

There is another entry in the *Newbattle Register* that indicates how Newbattle Abbey dealt with this problem of distance. The abbey managed to get the various landowners to agree to rights of free passage between their monastery and their lead mines at Freirmur in South Lanarkshire in exchange for a new wagon every year 'such as they manufactured for their own use in Clydesdale' (Innes 1849, xxxviii). In 1225 the monks of Coupar Angus were given a grant for a causeway which they were making, running from the vill of Inchture to their granges in the territory of the Carse (of Gowrie) (Easson 1947, 84). Evidence for such routeways ought to survive either as upstanding remains or cropmarks; a proper review of the true state of the Scottish road system in the Middle Ages would seem to be long overdue.

Distribution of monastic industrial granges

Unsurprisingly the industrial 'granges' that are connected with the major industries of coal mining and salt extraction are located in the same areas that become the focus of the industrial revolution in Scotland in the eighteenth and nineteenth centuries.

From the research that has been carried out for the countrywide gazetteers, this author would suggest that the original industrial revolution in Scotland happened before the Reformation of the 1550s and was led by the major monastic orders, in particular the Cistercians. As far as can be seen it is these monastic operations that are the basis for the later 'new' discoveries of the sixteenth century, made by the likes of Bevis Bulmer at Freirmure and Eustachius Roche at Sillerholes. The author would go on to argue that this is also true of many of the salt panning sites which come to our notice in the seventeenth and eighteenth centuries; they must have monastic origins. In many ways the handing out of various monastic estates to major landowners after the Scottish Reformation of the 1560s can be regarded as a bit like winning the lottery, there was an awful lot of money to be made!

3
CARE OF THE SICK

The best reference work for medieval hospitals in Scotland is Ian Cowan and David Easson's *Medieval Religious Houses: Scotland*, but it suffers from a lack of adequate information regarding site location and survival (Cowan and Easson 1976). This fact, coupled with the limited number of hospital sites that were statutorily protected, led the author to recommend to Historic Scotland that they should fund the preparation of a full gazetteer. The main focus of this project was the preparation of an up-to-date report on the status and condition of the identified sites of these monuments. Historic Scotland and the National Monuments Record in Edinburgh holds the four gazetteers produced by this project and the relevant council areas have been copied to those areas where there is a county council archaeologist in post. It was hoped that these gazetteers could be used to identify hospitals that might justify protection and the individual entries used as 'triggers' to ensure that any proposed development threat could be identified at an early stage in the planning process.

DATE AND DEDICATION

The earliest hospital in Scotland, founded in 1144, appears to have been St Leonard's in St Andrews, which initially functioned as a hospice for pilgrims and travellers. Another possible candidate for an early foundation is the hospital at North Queensferry which may represent one of the 'dwellings' built by Queen Margaret for pilgrims and the poor; a land endowment to this institution could be a grant of either Malcolm III of 1085 x 1093 or Malcolm IV of 1153 x 1165 (Cowan and Easson 1976, 189). Although the dedication for this hospital is not known there must be a very strong chance that it was connected with the Chapel of St James (patron saint of travellers) whose ruins are still visible in Helen Place. Although Cowan and Easson list St Nicholas, St Andrews as an 1128 foundation, the author believes this to be a mistake and from his research; 1178 is the first definite record of this leper hospital (Hall 1995, 48). The greatest number of documented foundations appears to be in the fifteenth century when 52 hospitals come into existence. This sudden increase may reflect a variety of factors, including an apparent decline in the climate, poor harvests and possibly the effects of the plague (Lamb 1995, 205). Whether the number of hospitals founded in the fifteenth century confirms that this century was one of decline and disorder is open to debate (Brown 1977).

Where it is possible to identify the dedication of the hospital, the most popular designation appears to be to the Virgin Mary (15) and Saints Leonard (12) and John (10), with St Mary Magdalene (6) also well represented. Amongst the most unusual hospital dedications are those to St Germain in East Lothian and to St Cuthbert in both East Lothian and the Scottish Borders. Only one Scottish hospital, in Dunkeld, is dedicated to St George, a saint who was a very popular protector for the leper hospitals of Scandinavia (Richards 1977, 8-9).

HOSPITAL TYPE AND DISTRIBUTION

The four year's fieldwork and data collection involved in this project produced a final list of 178 medieval hospitals in Scotland, an increase of 24 when compared with the list published by Cowan and Easson (Cowan and Easson 1976, 163-8).

This figure represents almshouses, bedehouses (almshouses for bedesmen or women), poorhouses, leper hospitals, hospices for travellers and pilgrims, hospitals for the care of the sick, and a sizeable group whose function is no longer identifiable. The three most common types of hospital in medieval Scotland appear to have been poorhouses (39), almshouses (26) and leper hospitals (23).

Poorhouses

The earliest hospital that can be classified as a poorhouse is the one at North Berwick which is first recorded in 1154. This must be qualified by the fact that it also helped travellers and given that it is located on the main pilgrimage route to St Andrews from the south this may have been its main function. Parliamentary legislation in Scotland concerning the poor began in the fifteenth century. Early statutes were mostly for the suppression of idle beggars, but gradually two important principles emerged. All parishes were to be responsible for their own poor, but only certain categories of poor were proper objects of poor relief. A statute of 1579, which remained the basis of the poor law until 1845, firmly established these rules. Its twin aims were that 'the puyr aiget [aged] and impotent personis sould be as necessarlie prouidit for', and that 'vagaboundis and strang beggaris' should be 'repressit'. Those entitled to relief through age, illness or otherwise, were to go to the last parish in which they had lived seven years, or failing that the parish of their birth (1579, *c*.12, APS, iii.139). The latest poorhouse for which there is documentary evidence is at Culross in Fife (1637).

Almshouses

Almshouses were, and still are in some parts of Britain, essentially charitable housing that was provided to enable people (typically elderly people who can no longer work to earn enough to pay rent) to live in a particular community. They were often targeted at the poor of a locality, at those from certain forms of previous employment, or their widows, and were generally maintained by a charity or the trustees of a bequest. Almshouses were a European Christian tradition, alms being monies or services donated to support the poor and indigent. The earliest almshouse recorded is at Lauder (1175 x 1189) in the Scottish Borders and the latest in Stirling (1637).

Leper hospitals

Leper hospitals are first documented in Scotland in the twelfth century, with Adniston in the Scottish Borders possibly being founded in 1177, and the hospital of Greenside in Edinburgh being the last documented foundation in 1591 (Cowan and Easson 1976). As late as 1427 an act of the Scottish parliament restricted begging by lepers to their own premises and to outlying districts; they were forbidden to beg in church, churchyard, or in the town. And at the end of the following century, the lepers at Edinburgh were only permitted to beg at the gate of their hospital, a task that they undertook turn and turn about. This is of interest, as the excavations at St Nicholas Farm, St Andrews located a gateway in one of the hospital boundary walls which would have led out onto the old road to St Andrews from Crail, an ideal location for a 'begging' gate (Hall 1995, 58).

As late as 1530, an Act of the Scots Parliament indicated stipulated that:

> no manner of Lipper persone, man nor woman, fra this tyme forth, cum amangis uther cleine personis, nor be nocht fund in the kirk, nor fleshe merket, nor no other merket within this burghe, under the payne of burnyng of their cheik and bannasing off the toune. (Richards 1977, 69).

CARE OF THE SICK

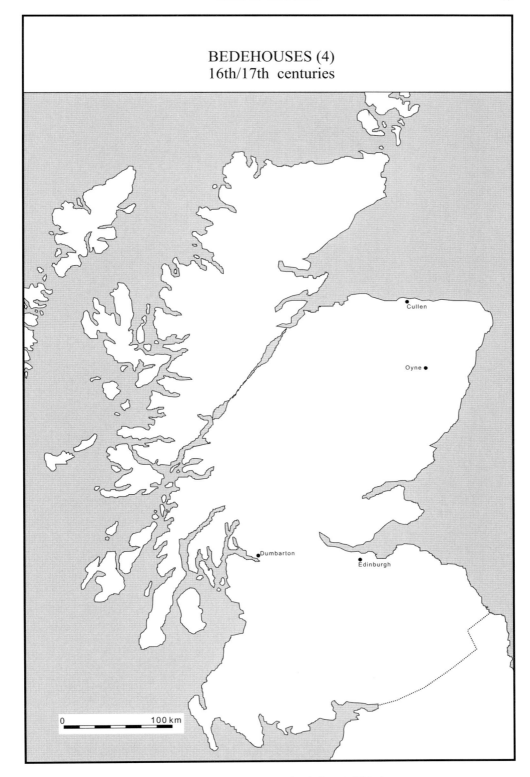

38 Distribution map of medieval bedehouses in Scotland. © *SUAT Ltd*

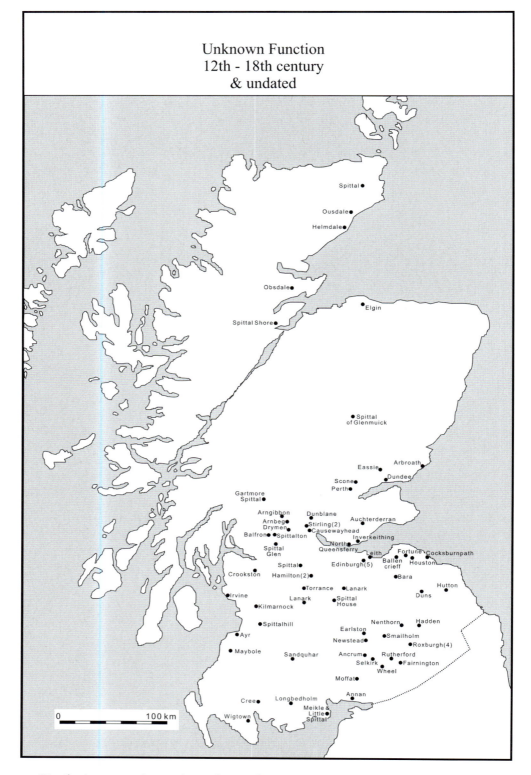

39 Distribution map unknown hospital types. © SUAT Ltd

CARE OF THE SICK 47

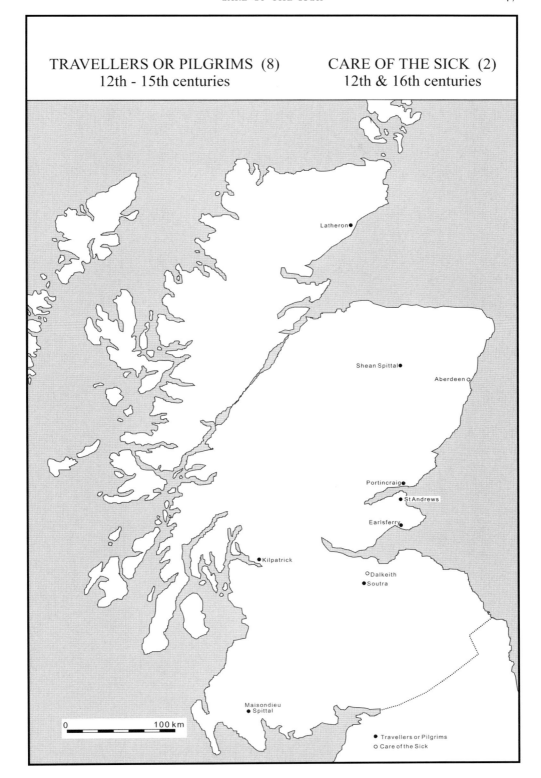

40 Distribution map of hospitals for travellers, pilgrims and the sick. © *SUAT Ltd*

41 Distribution map of medieval poorhouses in Scotland. © SUAT Ltd

CARE OF THE SICK

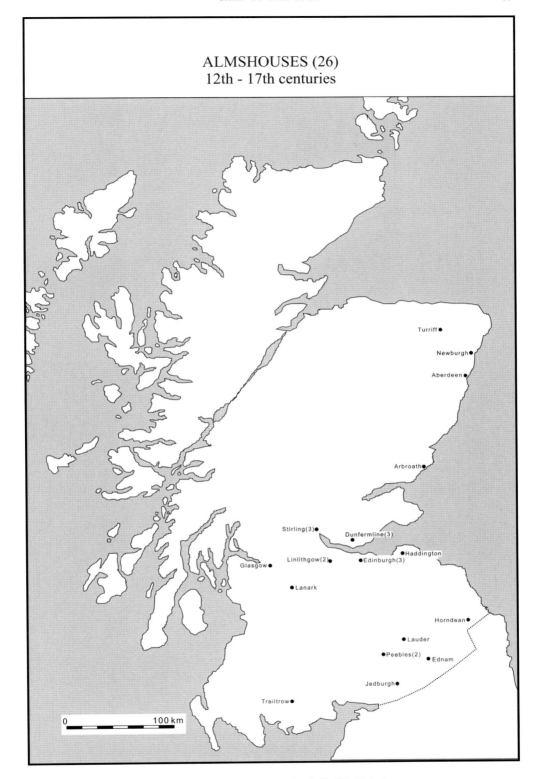

42 Distribution map of medieval almshouses in Scotland. © *SUAT Ltd*

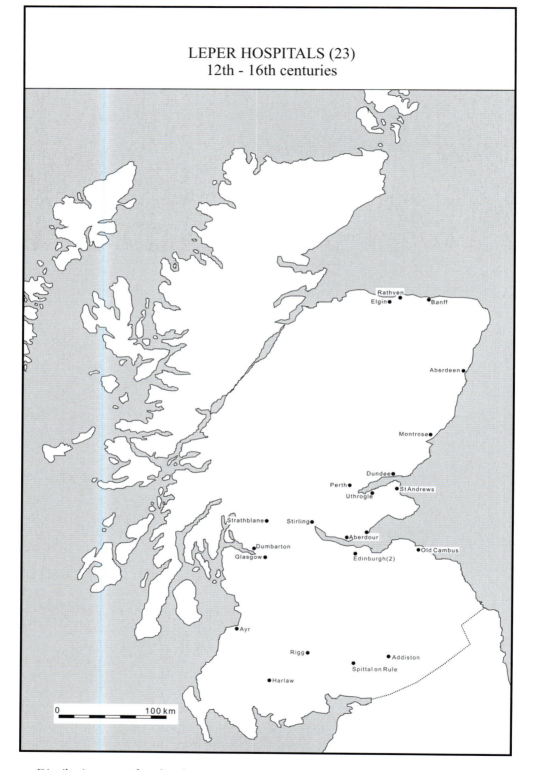

43 Distribution map of medieval Leper hospitals in Scotland. © *SUAT Ltd*

44 Potterhill flats, Perth, site of Leper hospital. © *SUAT Ltd*

It is still a matter of some debate whether many of the inmates of these hospitals actually had leprosy; there would seem to be a good chance that any disease that affected the skin would have been diagnosed as such.

PLACE NAME EVIDENCE

The most obvious place name element that is usually assumed to indicate the former location of a medieval hospital is 'Spittal'. Of the 178 potential hospitals listed in Scotland, 23 of them have this place name element and 12 of these are sites where it is not obvious that a hospital ever existed. In the case of Spittal at Auchterderran in Fife there is existing documentary evidence that indicates that land in this parish was once owned by Trinity hospital in Edinburgh, and Cowan and Easson state that no other evidence for a hospital can be found (see below). The same is true of Spittalfields in Perth and Kinross where the lands were once owned by the seventeenth-century King James VI hospital in Perth. The authors of the gazetteers would advise that this place name element should not always be automatically used to identify these sites and that it always requires further research. The same may often be the case in the use of the name 'Maison Dieu'.

In an urban setting it is often possible to recognise street names that relate to the former location of some of these hospitals. To take Perth as an example, St Catherine's hospital is recorded as both a street name and a new retail park, St Leonard's by a street and a bus station, and St Paul's by a close off the Old High Street and a nineteenth-century inscription above the '101 chip shop'!

CARTOGRAPHIC AND PICTORIAL EVIDENCE

Blaeu's seventeenth-century atlas of Scotland has proved to be useful for those hospitals that were still apparently operating at that date. In the Scottish Borders, for example, the hospitals of Ancrum and Ednam are both marked as 'Spittell' on the maps of Lauderdale and Berwickshire, while the hospital and mill at Uthrogle in Fife are marked on the relevant map again as 'Spittell' and 'Spittel Mill'. Of most interest on Blaeu's map of Fife is the place name of 'Colheuch Spittel', as this seems to correspond with the farm of Spittal at Aucherderran and may suggest that Cowan and Easson are mistaken in their assertion that there was never a hospital at this site. This is backed up by a reference in the *Fife Court Book* to the 'lands and spittal at Dundonald' (pers. comm. Simon Taylor). Pont's earlier sixteenth-century maps of Scotland have not proved to be as useful when checking for hospital locations. Slezer's *Theatrum Scotiae* includes two views of Dundee that show the later version of the hospital on the Nethergate.

DOCUMENTARY EVIDENCE

The documentary evidence included in the hospital gazetteers is all based on the information provided by Cowan and Easson, this is then backed up with any relevant new information that has been discovered during the survey. Scottish hospitals largely figure in documents that record the foundation of the institution or the payment of sums of money to it. Sometimes there are indirect references to the occupants of the hospitals such as the use of a leper at a sixteenth-century witch trial in Elgin to implicate the accused, one Marjory Bisset:

> Then suddenly there was ane motion in ye crowd, and ye peopel parting on ilk syde, ane Leper came down frae ye Hous [the leper house] and in ye face of ye peopel bared his hand and his haill arm, ye which was wythered and covered over with scurfs, most piteous to behold, and he said 'At ye day of Pentecost lat past, thys womyan did give unto me ane shell of oyntment, with ye which i annoynted my hand to cure ane imposthume which had cum over it, and behold from that day furthe untyll thys, it hath shrunk and wythered as you see it now.' (Richards 1977, 71).

The latter is an intriguing example of the exploitation of someone with a disease that most people did not understand and more importantly would presumably have stayed well away from. More often than not, one has to use the available secondary source materials, although some of these, such as Robert Scott Fittis' *Ecclesiastical Annals of Perth*, seem to be reliable sources of information (Fittis 1885). The continuing publication of documents from the Vatican archives has also proved to be a valuable source of evidence for Scottish hospitals (Kirk, Tanner and Dunlop 1997).

CURRENT STATE OF PRESERVATION

Standing remains of hospital buildings are few and far between in Scotland as a whole. The remains of St Magnus Spittal in Caithness can still be traced as grass-covered wall lines and are protected as a Scheduled Ancient Monument (SAM no 5413).

The best surviving example of a maisondieu can be found at Brechin, and there is a surviving fragment of arch from the hospital of St John at Arbroath built into the inside face of one of the bay windows on the ground floor of Hospitalfield House. SUAT's survey of the Scottish Borders revealed that the farmhouse of St Leonards near Lauder includes a stone built into its southern wall with an inscription that reads:

> *Deus est fons vitae*
> I thirst for the vater of lif

There must be a strong chance that this stone originates from the hospital that formerly stood on the site. The survey of the Lothians has indicated that many hospital sites may now occupied by churches and graveyards, and the potential for surviving remains on these sites must be fairly high.

45 Surviving standing wall of Maison Dieu at Brechin. © *SUAT Ltd*

46 Soutra Aisle, Scottish Borders. © *SUAT Ltd*

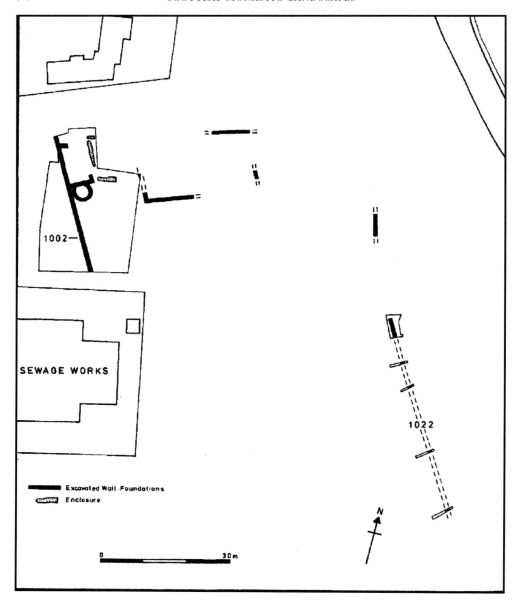

47 Ground plan of excavated building at St Nicholas leper hospital, St Andrews, Fife. © SUAT Ltd

Good cropmark evidence exists for the hospitals of Arrat in Angus and Soutra in Midlothian, and when these are combined with the excavated evidence from St Nicholas Farm, St Andrews, it is possible to get a very good idea of what the layout of some of the larger hospitals was like. The apparent large size of both St Nicholas and Soutra must be due in some part both to their proximity to major routeways – Soutra, for example, was used as a way station by the invading English army – and to the apparent self-sufficient nature of both communities.

48 General view of building excavated at Leper hospital of St Nicholas, St Andrews, Fife

PRESERVATION, PROTECTION OR EXCAVATION?

A large percentage of Scottish medieval hospital sites are now situated on the edges of modern towns and as such are very susceptible to large-scale developments such as retail parks, supermarkets and housing schemes. At a Society of Antiquaries of Scotland seminar 'Building on the Past' (held May 2001) the author argued that this very fact means that schemes of mitigation may prove difficult to implement and that targeted scheduling may not provide the ideal solution. It would appear that the most constructive way of tackling this problem is to ensure that any threatened sites are quickly identified and that a programme of excavation is properly designed and undertaken. For this to work there appears to be a need for the formulation of carefully designed research frameworks, very much along the lines of the Monument Class Descriptions produced by English Heritage, to ensure that any opportunity for archaeological excavation is properly targeted.

One of the intentions behind the Scotland-wide gazetteer was to identify those hospital sites that warranted statutory protection, and from two scheduled hospital sites in 1996 the number for the country as a whole now stands at eight (May 2006).

CONCLUSIONS

The four-year Scottish medieval hospitals gazetteer project has laid the foundations for the continuing study of this under-researched facet of medieval life in Scotland.

The limited excavations of such sites have providing tantalising glimpses of the sort of information that might be recovered. The intriguing work of Dr Brian Moffat at Soutra on blood-letting and other medical practices still requires corroboraion from work at other important Scottish hospital sites but is an important reminder of the sort of evidence that might be present (Moffat 1989, 10). More importantly, the final gazetteers will hopefully prove to be useful tools in the development control process.

49 Standing building at hospital site, Earlsferry, Fife. © *SUAT Ltd*

50 Hospitalfield House, Angus. © *SUAT Ltd*

51 Inscription marking site of St Mary's Hospital, Scotlandwell, Fife. © *SUAT Ltd*

52 Site of St Cuthbert's hospital, Dumfries and Galloway. © *SUAT Ltd*

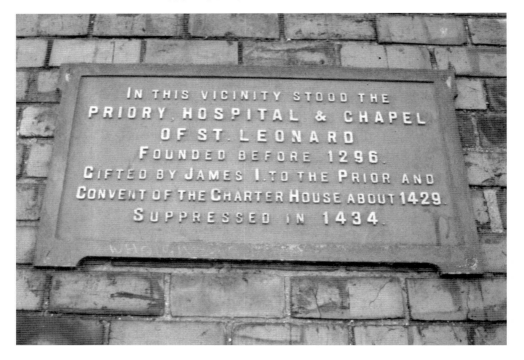

53 Plaque marking site of St Leonard's Hospital, Perth. © *SUAT Ltd*

54 Site of St Paul's Hospital, Perth. © *SUAT Ltd*

55 Site of hospital at Trailtrow, Dumfries and Galloway. © *SUAT Ltd*

The lack of substantial standing remains in Scotland and the absence of adequate surviving documentary evidence mean that the sort of analysis that has been carried out on the likes of St Leonard's Hospital at York, in England, cannot be undertaken (Cullum 1993, 11-18). Whilst continuing development pressure will allow for further excavation of medieval hospital sites in Scotland, it may be the case that a properly designed and funded research excavation is the only way of making substantial progress.

4
GOD'S BANKERS: THE MILITARY ORDERS IN SCOTLAND (STENHOUSE AND THE KNIGHTS OF ST JOHN)

Perhaps the most unusual of the various religious orders are the so-called Military Orders or *Milites Christi*, this new type of monasticism came into being in the twelfth century on the back of conflict in the Holy Land between the East and West. In Britain the Order of St John was the best represented with two distinct groups, the Knights Templar who fought in the Crusades and the Knights Hospitaller whose avowed aim was to protect pilgrims on the way to the Holy Land and to provide a more charitable function. Following the suppression of the Knights Templar by Pope Clement V in 1312 their lands and properties were passed on to the Hospitallers. The Order of St John was based on the Cistercian rule and wore white robes emblazoned with red crosses if Templar and white ones if Hospitaller. The order is best known in modern times as the St John's Ambulance organisation.

In recent years particularly with the publication of *The Da Vinci Code* a lot of nonsense has been written about the orders of Knights Templar and Hospitaller and this chapter will aim to review what little physical evidence exists and offer a more considered view. Despite the vast number of sites in Scotland that claim association with the Knights of St John there are only three, at Temple and Torphichen in West Lothian and Maryculter in Aberdeenshire for which it is possible to find any evidence for a definite link. The order was certainly gifted lands in most of the major Scottish burghs but probably only ever rented these out to tenants (Cowan *et al.* 1983). So far there has been little opportunity for any archaeological work at sites connected with any of the military orders; however during the post-excavation work on an unpublished excavation from the 1950s a possible connection with the Knights of St John was identified.

Sand quarrying by the Carron Iron company in the mid-1950s revealed the remains of pottery kilns on a site in Stenhousemuir (Falkirk Council) which lay within the policies of the mansion of Stenhouse (NS 8804 8314). The Carron Iron Company reported this find to the late Doreen Hunter, who was then the curator of the Dollar Park Museum, and she undertook rescue excavation which continued on separate occasions until 1962. In 1978 in advance of further development of part of the area for housing, some trial excavation was carried out by Marjorie Kenworthy. Apart from abortive attempts in the late 1970s, no report has ever been produced on either the excavation or the important corpus of medieval pottery. SUAT Ltd were commissioned by Historic Scotland to catalogue the whole assemblage and produce the following report.

SITE LOCATION

The Carron Iron Company's sand quarries were located due north of the mansion of Stenhouse, which was erected in 1622 by Sir William Bruce, second son of Sir Alexander

Bruce of Airth. This fine house fell into disrepair and was finally demolished in the late 1960s prior to the building of the local authority housing estate, which now occupies the site. An attempt has been made by the author to accurately locate the kilns that were recorded by Doreen Hunter using compass bearings given in her site notes. As only one of her reference points, the church spire, now survives at Stenhouse, a copy of the relevant 1950s OS sheet was used as a base map (NS8783SE). Following this exercise all the kilns except one, J, were located due north of the mansion of Stenhouse, within the location of the sand quarries. The bearings for kiln J appear to be erroneous and should be discounted.

HISTORICAL BACKGROUND

The place name of 'Stenhouse' possibly refers to 'Arthur's Oven', a stone-built circular structure resembling a kiln, of uncertain origin but generally regarded as a Roman temple. This structure formerly stood to the south of the mansion of Stenhouse, but was removed by the landowner, Sir Michael Bruce, to build a dam for a nearby meal mill in 1743. Despite its destruction, it continued to be represented on plans of the second half of the eighteenth century. This building is mentioned as *furnum Arthur* in a charter to Newbattle Abbey (Midlothian) in 1293, a reference which indicates that its origins were unknown and already ancient at that time.

Stenhouse itself belonged to the Morham family and was originally part of the barony of Dunipace (Falkirk). It should not be confused with Stenhouse, near Liberton, Midlothian, belonging to the Melvilles and inherited through a Melville heiress by the Lords Ross of Halkhead or with Stenhouse in Lanarkshire. Sir Adam de Morham granted the mill of *Stanhus* to the Cistercian monks of Newbattle Abbey in the thirteenth century, a grant confirmed by his son, Thomas, Lord of Morham. In addition, in 1293 William Gurlay granted to the monks of Newbattle:

> one pond on his land for the work and use of their mill of *Stanhus*, which is situated beside Arthur's Oven, within the barony of Dunipace, together with half an acre of his land, if so much is lying between the old course of the water flowing from the said pond and the new waterlead from that pond to the said mill.

Gurlay's charter was witnessed by Sir Thomas de Morham. Alexander II (1214-49) or Alexander III (1249-86) confirmed Thomas de Morham's grant in the thirty-second year of his reign, and Pope Gregory X's confirmation to Newbattle Abbey in 1273 refers to 'the mill of *Stanhus* with watercourses and all its entries and exits'. However, despite these royal and papal confirmations, the abbey seems to have been deprived of the mill of Stenhouse in a 'false assize' in 1325, by judgement of Sir Alexander Seton in favour of Reginald More, who had repossessed the watercourse before the assize and may have transferred it to someone else (there is a gap in the text); the monks were fined £10 for 'spuilzie of the water'. The basis of More's claim is not recorded. More is perhaps the same individual as the Reginald More who was administrator of the estates of the Knights Hospitallers in the early fourteenth century and a colleague of Seton in the fermes of the burgh of Berwick (Northumberland).

In 1322 a later Sir Thomas de Morham was liferented in all the lands and tenements in the barony of Dunipace resigned by Thomas Randolph, Earl of Moray, as well as in his own lands and tenements in the baronies of Morham and Duncanlaw (East Lothian); on Morham's death the estates were to pass to Morham's son-in-law and daughter, Sir John Gifford and Euphemia. Moray was presumably Morham's neighbour in the barony of Dunipace, although the exact nature of their feudal relationship is unclear.

In addition to the grant by the Morhams to Newbattle of the mill of Stenhouse, they may have granted land there to the Knights Hospitaller, or to the Knights Templar before their dissolution in 1312, when their lands were transferred to the Hospitallers. Land in Duncanlaw was described as Templar land, and the Hospitallers owned land in Morham and Stenhouse in the sixteenth century. They seem to have owned two parcels of land in Stenhouse in 1539: one leased to the Bruce laird (see below) of Airth (Falkirk) for 10 merks (£6 13s 4d) yearly, the other with a rent of 6d from the laird of Dalderse. The Hospitallers' land in Stenhouse was not listed in 1564 among the possessions of the Order of St John granted as a heritable barony to James Sandilands, Lord St John, the last Preceptor of Torphichen, who became Lord Torphichen, and no later record seems to exist among the Torphichen records of Stenhouse as a former property of the Hospitallers.

Gifford must have succeeded to Morham's estates under the agreement of 1325, as David II (1329-71) confirmed a grant to John Douglas, son of James, Lord [of] Douglas, by Hugh Gifford of Yester of his baronies, including Morham, Duncanlaw and Herbertshire. The identity of this John Douglas is unknown: if his description as son of James, Lord of Douglas is correct, then he must have been an otherwise unrecorded natural son of the 'Good Sir James', Robert I's companion-in-arms (died 1330), in addition to 'Archibald the Grim', afterwards Third Earl of Douglas. In 1388 this Archibald, Third Earl of Douglas granted the barony of Herbertshire to his own natural son, William Douglas of Nithsdale, and in 1407, Archibald, Fourth Earl of Douglas granted it to William's son-in-law, Henry Sinclair of Roslin (Midlothian), Second Earl of Orkney. In 1482 Henry's grandson, the Second Lord Sinclair renounced his interest in Roslin and Herbertshire in favour of his brother, Oliver. Herbertshire seems to have been the successor to the barony of Dunipace as, by 1510, Stenhouse was part of the barony of Herbertshire, which belonged to Oliver Sinclair of Roslin. Stenhouse itself, or half of it, was a tenandry of the Bruces of Airth from at least 1491, the other half being retained by the Sinclairs; the Bruce holding was separate from their lease of the Hospitallers' land. Also forming a tenandry within the barony of Herbertshire was Quarrell, now Carronshire, a place name implying a quarry, though whether for sand, gravel or clay is unclear.

In 1608 William Sinclair of Roslin resigned the barony of Herbertshire to Alexander Livingston, First Earl of Linlithgow; included in the grant was the superiority over the lands of Quarrell held by Lord Elphinstone and the lands of Stenhouse held by Sir John Bruce of Airth. Linlithgow resigned the lands and barony of Herbertshire and other lands to Sir John Blackadder of Tulliallan in 1632, retaining only the superiority of Stenhouse and Quarrell. In 1637 the lands of Slammananmuir, including half of the town and lands of Stenhouse with the manor-place, mills, fishings, feu-fermes, tenants, etc., apprised from the Second Earl of Linlithgow in 1636, were granted to John, Lord Hay of Yester (East Lothian), who transferred them to James Livingstone, First Earl of Callendar (Stirling) in 1642, when they were united to the latter's lands and barony of Callendar, which he had previously acquired from his brother, the Second Earl of Linlithgow. Thereafter Stenhouse continued to be a part of the barony of Callendar, whose owner was superior of the Bruces of Stenhouse. The last Earl of Linlithgow and Callendar was forfeited after the 1715 Jacobite rebellion, his estates being acquired by the York Building Company in 1720, from whom they were purchased by William Forbes of London in 1783.

From a local corruption (Stanners) of the place name Stenhouse, it is evident that the teinds of the lands of Quarrell and Stanners/Stenhouse, or part of them, had been granted to the Augustinian Abbey of Cambuskenneth (Stirling), which had been included in the temporal lordship of Cardross (Argyll and Bute) in 1604 and 1606 in favour of John Erskine, Earl of Mar. In 1621 Mar's successor resigned the teinds of the lands of Dunipace (Falkirk) and Larbert (Falkirk), including Quarrell and Stannor, to David Livingston of Dunipace.

The mansion of Stenhouse was built in 1622 by Sir William Bruce, second son of Sir Alexander Bruce of Airth, and his descendants, the baronets of Stenhouse, continued as owners into this century. Latterly the mansion was owned by the Carron Company, housing some of its workers.

56 Excavated pottery kiln at Stenhouse. © *SUAT Ltd*

No references to a pottery industry were found in the course of the research into Stenhouse, although the industry there probably dates to the fifteenth and sixteenth centuries, when the Sinclairs of Roslin were the landowners. In view of the similarity of a facemask sherd at Ravenscraig Castle (Fife) to Stenhouse material, it may be no coincidence that in 1470 William Sinclair, Third Earl of Orkney (in the kingdom of Norway) and First Earl of Caithness (in the kingdom of Scotland) resigned his Orkney estates to James III, receiving in return the castle of Ravenscraig and lands around it in Fife.

THE EXCAVATIONS

Eight of the eleven kilns and a hearth which Doreen Hunter and her team recorded during quarrying operations were designated A (1954), B, C, D, E, F (1959), G (1961) and J (1962), the remaining three are only referred to in passing. Kilns B and G are only recorded in the photographic archive, there are no plans. It is not clear why letters H and I are missing from the designation. The record which follows was clearly made in very difficult conditions, and it was not possible to illustrate all the kilns. Nevertheless, Stenhouse is one of only two redware production sites known in Scotland, and the account reproduced here includes extensive and detailed descriptions of the kilns.

1954: Kiln A

During 1954, members of the Field Group of the Falkirk Archaeological and Natural History Society carried out first salvage during pipe-laying, and later excavation, on a medieval kiln site. A kiln, drying hearth and fireplace were discovered, in addition to pits and scattered deposits of waste material, and minor unexplained features. Another kiln and drying hearth were probably broken up by the pipe trench; from the latter were recovered three jars, the only complete specimens found during the excavation. No trace of a building was found, and it is highly probable that the site extends much further.

The kiln was built in a pit. A low wall of unmortared stones had apparently supported a domed, renewable roof of clay and twigs. The floor (which was highest in the centre of the kiln, and was laminated in a way that suggested patching or renewal) had been laid after the walls. There was a stokehole at the west end and a flue opposite; the whole forms an irregular rectangle measuring $c.2 \times 0.9$m, with a stokehole measuring $c.0.6 \times 0.4$m. There was a small, much-burnt pit in front of the stokehole, and another (unexcavated) beyond the flue. Some evidence was found of a floor between fire and pottery, supported presumably on stones (or bricks) that were not set into the kiln floor. This kiln is not the oldest on the site, as sherds were found in the making of the floor. It is probable for various reasons that there was a group of small kilns working on the site, not necessarily all synchronous. The finds, almost all wasters, were considerable.

1959

During the summer of 1959 a sandpit was extended over the greater part of the field where the 1954 excavations had taken place. Several pits of pottery were found, and the topsoil and topsand were said to have produced a great quantity of pottery. Subsequent partial excavation of a pit and surface collecting, however, produced no substantial pieces, with only one or two pieces showing slight variations from forms already known from the site. In addition to the pottery, the machines turned up one stony patch, and, from the descriptions given, it is likely that the area then quarried included at least one kiln and one hearth.

In mid-August an attempt was made to excavate two structures. One was in the face of the quarry, and had partially been cut away. A curved setting of small boulders, one course high, lay approximately 1ft below the surface of the sand, topsoil having been removed. It bounded the remains of a floor of baked clay, with some burnt material over it. On the other side of this, a similar setting of smaller stones (with a few stones of a second course) curved towards the first, but did not meet it; there was no trace of a built stokehole or flue. A setting of four boulders diverged from this line, possibly in a wider curve, but was not pursued. Destruction of this structure took place before further work was done. In the light of the structure of kiln C, however, it is possible that the remains represented an original, smaller kiln partially incorporated in a larger one subjected to damage at plough depth; but the absence of a higher floor is against this.

Kiln C

Kiln C lay further north under a temporary lorry-road which had been levelled and consolidated; the depth below present surface (0.20m) is not significant. The kiln was, just like the first, a pointed oval just over 1.8m long of single boulders. At the southern end there was a well-made stokehole $c.0.30$m wide, with, at the northern end, a fluehole, and at the north-west side a possible small subsidiary flue. Outside the stokehole there was a pit containing clay, baked clay pieces, sherds and burnt material with some earth in the upper part. The western and southern edge of the pit were not excavated, but probing indicated a line making an oval extending south-west, oblique to the kiln. The mass that filled the pit continued behind the stones of the kiln half way along its western edge; here it contained stones ('fist to head' size) and formed a kind of backing for the wall. No similar packing was found on the east side. The pit could not be excavated in the time available, although enough was removed to clear the stokehole.

The main flue was at the northern end. It was slightly narrower than the stokehole, and lacked a floor slab; the clay floor sloped downwards towards that of the kiln, and the sides were rounded into the floor, unlike those of the stokehole which were squared off. When found it was full of black carbonised matter. There were stones at the inner end which may have been laid there to close it. There were pits outside both the flue and the stokehole of this kiln. The curve of the west edge of the pit outside the flue appears on the plan; the east edge was not located. This pit was not excavated; it certainly contained a high proportion of clay (which had

1 Surviving gateway to Scone Abbey, Perth and Kinross

2 Chemical refinery at Grangemouth. *Courtesy of Emerson Process Management*

3 Surviving house at Grange of Drumpellier, North Lanarkshire. © *SUAT Ltd*

4 Romanno Cultivation Terraces, Scottish Borders. © *Scottish Borders Council*

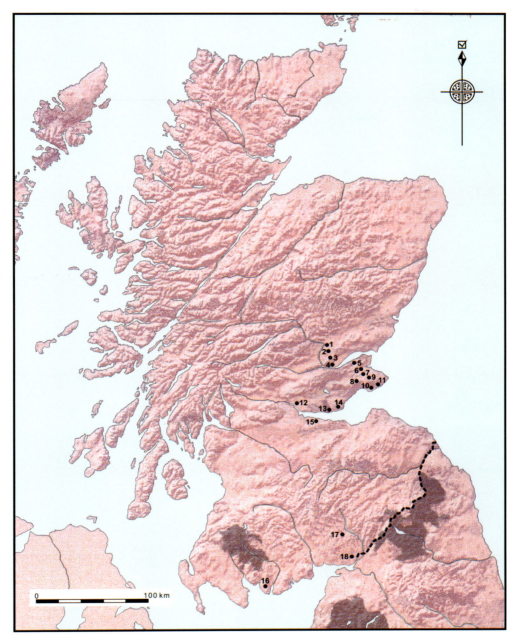

5 Distribution map of Augustinian granges: 1. Cambusmichael (Scone Abbey), 2. Scone (Scone Abbey), 3. Limepots (Scone Abbey), 4. Hole of Clene (Scone Abbey), 5. Easter and Wester Friarton (St Andrews Priory), 6. Strathkinness (St Andrews Priory), 7. Balone (St Andrews Priory), 8. Drumcarro (St Andrews Priory), 9. Grange (St Andrews Priory), 10. West Grangemuir (St Andrews Priory), 11. East Grangemuir (St Andrews Priory), 12. West Grange (Cambuskenneth Abbey), 13. Grange of Donibristle/Barnhill (Inchcolm Abbey), 14. Grangemyre (Inchcolm Abbey), 15. Abbotsgrange (Holyrood Abbey), 16. Grange (Trail Priory), 17. Abbotrule (Jedburgh Abbey), 18. Wolfelee (Jedburgh Abbey). © *SUAT Ltd*

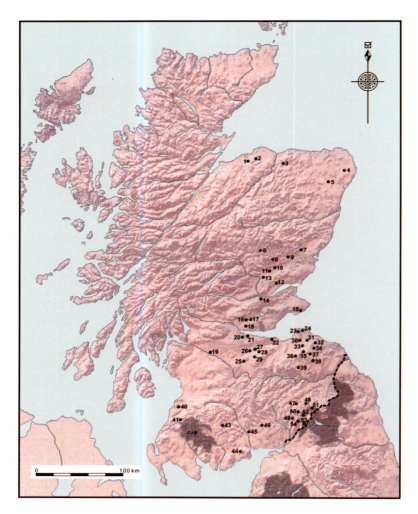

6 Distribution map of Cistercian granges: 1. West Grange (Kinloss Abbey), 2. East Grange (Kinloss Abbey), 3. Davoch of Grange (Kinloss Abbey), 4. Grange of Rawhill (Deer Abbey), 5. Abbotshall (Kinloss Abbey), 6. Drimmie (Coupar Angus Abbey), 7. Grange of Kincreich (Coupar Angus Abbey), 8. Grange of Aberbothrie (Coupar Angus Abbey), 9. Grange of Airlie (Coupar Angus Abbey), 10. Coupar Grange (Coupar Angus Abbey), 11. Balbrogie (Coupar Angus Abbey), 12. Carsegrange (Coupar Angus Abbey), 13. Keithick (Coupar Angus Abbey), 14. Grange of Elcho (Elcho Nunnery), 15. Grange (North Berwick Nunnery), 16. Middle Grange (Culross Abbey), 17. Easter Grange (Culross Abbey), 18. Wester Grange (Culross Abbey), 19. Drumpellier (Newbattle Abbey), 20. Culross Grange (Culross Abbey), 21. Grange of Carriden (Culross Abbey), 22. Prestongrange (Newbattle Abbey), 23. Grange of Haddington (Byres) (Haddington Nunnery), 24. Grange of Haddington (Barnes) (Haddington Nunnery), 25. Grange of Breich (North Berwick Nunnery), 26. Romanno Grange (Newbattle Abbey), 27. Southside Castle (Newbattle Abbey), 28. Moorfoot (Newbattle Abbey), 29. Dalhousie Grange (Newbattle Abbey), 30. Bearford (Newbattle Abbey), 31. Hartside (Melrose Abbey), 32. Friardykes (Melrose Abbey), 33. Newlands (Grange of Nunland) (Haddington Nunnery), 34. Grange of Edmonston (Melrose Abbey), 35. Garvald (Haddington Nunnery), 36. West Hopes (Nunhope) (Haddington Nunnery), 37. Grangemure (Melrose Abbey), 38. Penshiel Grange (Melrose Abbey), 39. Drygrange (Melrose Abbey), 40. Grange of Maybole (Melrose Abbey), 41. Mauchline (Melrose Abbey), 42. Dalmellington (Vaudey Abbey then Melrose Abbey), 43. Carsphairn (Vaudey Abbey), 44. Shambellie Grange (Sweetheart Abbey), 45. Friarscarse (Melrose Abbey), 46. Watcarrick (Melrose Abbey), 47. Whitelee (Melrose Abbey), 48. Blainslie (Melrose Abbey), 49. Colmslie (Melrose Abbey), 50. Darnick (Melrose Abbey), 51. Gattonside (Melrose Abbey), 52. Grange (Melrose Abbey), 53. Hownam Grange (Melrose Abbey), 54. Eildon (Melrose Abbey). © *SUAT Ltd*

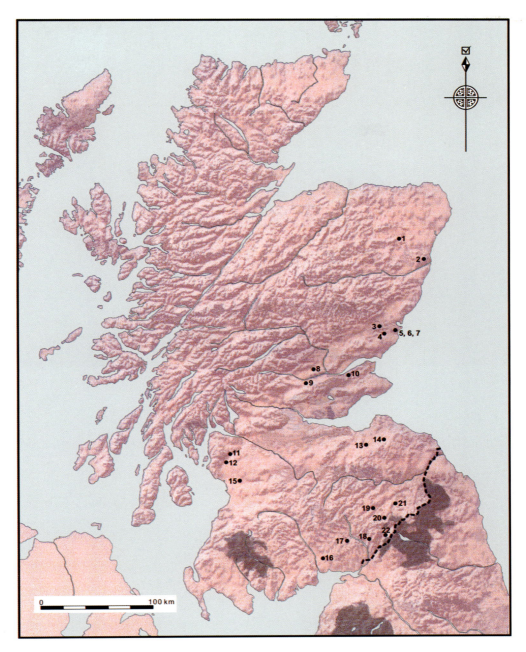

7 Distribution map of Tironensian granges: 1. Hatton of Fintray (Lindores Abbey), 2. Torry (Arbroath Abbey), 3. Grange of Conon (Arbroath Abbey), 4. Newgrange (Arbroath Abbey), 5. Nether Grange (Arbroath Abbey), 6. Over Grange (Arbroath Abbey), 7. Ethie (Arbroath Abbey), 8. Ecclesmagirdle (Lindores Abbey), 9. Braco (Arbroath Abbey), 10. Grange of Lindores (Lindores Abbey), 11. Grangehill (Beith) (Kilwinning Abbey), 12. Grangehill (Kilwinning Abbey), 13. Humbie (Kelso Abbey), 14. Spartleton (Kelso Abbey), 15. Grange (Kilwinning Abbey),16. Whitmuir Hall (Kelso Abbey), 17. Whitlaw (Kelso Abbey), 18. Newton (Kelso Abbey), 19. Faldonside (Kelso Abbey), 20. Holydean (Kelso Abbey), 21. Redden (Kelso Abbey), 22. Elliesheugh (Kelso Abbey). © *SUAT Ltd*

8 Close up of vaulted building at Penshiel Grange, Midlothian, looking south

9 General view of surviving building at Penshiel Grange, Midlothian, looking north-east

10 Small defensive structure at Gamelshiel, East Lothian, near the Kelso Abbey grange of Spartleton

11 Grange House in Fife, a later Georgian house on the site of the grange of North Berwick nunnery

12 Artists reconstruction of Penshiel Grange. *By D. Munro SUAT Ltd*

13 Standing building at Byres Farm in East Lothian looking west

14 Earthworks of Kelso Abbey grange of Colpenhope at Witchcleugh Burn, Scottish Borders. © *SUAT Ltd*

15 General view of building at Barnes castle, East Lothian

16 External view of vaults at Barnes Castle, East Lothian

17 Bishop Hunters tower at Mauchline in Ayrshire. © *SUAT Ltd*

18 River erosion cutting through site of church at Moorfoot in Midlothian

19 Surviving earthworks at Moorfoot Grange in Midlothian

20 Surviving earthworks at Moorfoot Grange in Midlothian

21 Earthworks at Nunhope, East Lothian

22 Salt pan, Dumfries and Galloway

23 Surviving mound of mine tailings at Crawford Moor, South Lanarkshire

26 Saltpan on seashore at Cockenzie, East Lothian

Opposite above: 24 Monastic fishpond for Sweetheart Abbey, Newabbey Dumfries and Galloway

Opposite below: 25 Greenan Castle, Ayrshire, which stands above the site of saltworks belonging to Melrose Abbey

Above: 27 Temple Church, Midlothian. © SUAT Ltd

Left: 28 Green man decoration on pottery from Stenhouse production site

been rammed hard by the passing of vehicles above) and before drying-out was a rich black and red, the red predominating towards the centre. This extended a short distance outside the east side of the kiln, just beyond the gap which may represent a subsidiary flue.

The kiln floor was of baked clay, approximately level and unpatched; in this, and with fewer signs of use, it differed from Kiln A. The walls stood to a one level course above it. On the west side the wall was of large boulders with clay filling and (probably) an inner clay lining; however this contained sherds and was not easily distinguished from the clay of the central filling, though the latter was softer, less coloured and contained a quantity of stones. On the east side the stones were smaller, and a larger proportion of the wall was made up of clay packing. The 'subsidiary' flue may therefore be questioned, though it was a stoneless gap larger than any other; there was no construction here. The walls on both sides showed considerable traces of burning and stone-flaking, especially near the flue.

The deposit within the kiln was an almost earthless mass of glutinous clay, containing (especially at its base) a quantity of sherds and (especially in the northern half) lumps and streaks of baked daub. In the north-western quarter of the kiln the relative position of daub and pottery suggested the collapse of the roof onto the kiln contents, but this was not apparent elsewhere. At no point was there any trace of a pot-floor, or supports for a floor.

Excavation was, unfortunately, abandoned at this point, there being no time to excavate the pits. A few days later children broke up the kiln floor, and it was seen that the floor did not lie directly on sand. Under a deposit of earth (not clay) probably laid to level the ground for the upper floor, there was a deposit which included baked daub, sherds, two complete pots, and much black ashy material, over a hard ashy floor. At one end enough of this deposit remained *in situ* to describe the section; 1) black deposit on white ashy floor; 2) red daub, both in lumps and as a thick streak projecting from one side; 3) grey soft friable earth, with few sherds. The floor was markedly concave, and though hard, had not been laid, and only at the north-west corner did the kiln wall come low enough to touch it, though the clay packing of the east wall lay only a few inches higher. The whole resembled a hearth rather than a kiln. There was a lower 'stokehole' at the southern end, but it was more roughly formed than that of the upper floor, and lacked a stone sill. At the northern end there was a steep, much blackened slope upwards to the main flue passage; it is unfortunate that the junction could not be excavated. Outside the stokehole on the north, at a lower level than the lower floor, and just above the bottom of the pit, there were traces of a floor bounded by stones (not boulders) on two sides, but this also could not be pursued. It did not reach the west edge of the pit.

The upper and lower floors of the kiln were 0.20m apart at the north end, where both survived, and the boulder sides varied from 0.20-0.30m above the lower floor. The two complete pots were found mouth downwards in the north-east and south-west corners; they and the sherds show considerable signs of 'overfiring'.

It is possible that the upper floor was a 'pottery floor', and that the lower took the fire; it is also possible that the curve of burnt daub seen in section extending from the east side is the remains of a first-stage pottery floor. The former is improbable for several reasons; there was stone flaking and other evidence of heat on the boulders above the upper floor, and blackening in the upper stokehole; and the upper floor was not appreciably interrupted in front of or over the flue. It would also have been difficult to rake out fuel and ash from the lower compartment when the upper was in position (though in favour it must be admitted that there was burnt material in the lower compartment, but not on the upper floor). It would also be difficult to account for the debris, and the whole pots, in the lower part. The second suggestion is attractive, but the streak was only seen at one point, and it is difficult to understand the construction of such a kiln, the fire space being too small and low. It is more likely that the lower stage represents the remains of a drying hearth rather than a kiln (the clay streak, which is not daub from a dome, being either a part of its construction or a part of the kiln furniture from a later stage, but not *in situ*). No similar example was found and fully excavated.

Kiln D

This kiln appeared as a tumble of stones on the sand, after the removal of topsoil; there was slight pre-excavation damage to the north-west side and southern flue; and it is possible that a structure similar to that at the north end may have been destroyed, but there was no direct evidence (such as the presence of dislodged boulders) for this.

There was about 11cm of loose sand and disturbed clayey soil above the kiln and the north pit. The kiln had been built hard up against the sand on the west side of the pit into which it was set, but on the east side there was a packing of earth and sherds, narrowing downwards. The kiln was a pointed oval *c*.2.07m long internally with a gap at each end closed by a sill stone, and on the north (and probably at the time of use on the south end) by an 'arch' of two stones. The bottom and second course of the walls were built of large, smooth boulders, carefully laid and set in clay; those on the west being set with particular care. The upper part was of smaller stones, also clay-mortared; this, in places (especially on the north-east), became a packing of clay and stones, with sherds also embedded in the clay. On the east side the wall was unstable, and showed signs of collapse when the filling between it and the rest of the pit was removed. There was a line of stones immediately within it on the kiln floor, at first thought to be the wall itself which was possibly inserted to support it. The stones at the south end of the kiln, and especially those immediately east of the flue, were cracked and very much fire reddened – the upper stones much more than the lower. At the north end there was little structural damage, though there was reddening and flaking for a short distance from the flue. The floor was uneven, and showed signs of patching; it rose towards the centre and both thinned and fell towards the ends of the kiln, though curved up at the edge to join the kiln walls. Under the floor the sand was reddened, and in places bleached, though quite clean, but there was no lower or earlier floor, though at the south end the patching was so extensive (and at one point 6-8cm above the main floor) as to give that appearance. The clay of the floor contained a few small sherds of pottery.

Within the kiln the upper part of the fill was earthy, containing both sherds and clay, and disturbed by roots. The fill contained, and indeed was largely composed of, large and small stones, some very burnt; there would have been sufficient for at least five courses of kiln walling. The lowest layer of this filling (20-30cm above the floor) was clean, dry and very much reddened; here also roots had penetrated and reduced many sherds to a mass of flakes. There was also a quantity of baked daub, including one large piece of (presumably) the kiln roof, found at the centre of the west side, tilted upwards towards the centre. There was, however, no continuous layer of this.

In the north pit the upper part of the fill was markedly sticky; below 15cm the centre of the pit was soft, yielding and of fine soil. Sherds and daub were present in quantity and size sufficient to maintain voids in the fill where the soil had been unable to penetrate. At the top, the sides of the pit were lined by an inch or two of soft, clean earth, containing carbon layers and patches increasing towards the lower part of the pit. The figure-of-eight shape which the pit made with the kiln did not continue downwards; the eastern side was a steep-sided, shallower, flat bottomed subsidiary pit or shelf. At its base there was a layer of 'clean' clay, and beneath it a carbonaceous layer varying in thickness from 2cm to a skin of colouring.

This black layer (but not the 'clean' clay layer above it) continued irregularly under the clay packing on the east side of the kiln which, though irregular, was of closely similar depth to the shelf or subsidiary pit. There was also another similar shelf or step with a steep side that must have been cut shortly before re-filling; on this there was a quantity of white burnt sand.

The bottom of the main pit was below the level of the kiln; it was probably pointed, though as a result of disturbance during excavation the exact shape is unknown. It contained a high proportion of carbonised matter and a quantity of sherds. It underlay a significant feature of the kiln; a mass of clay and stones, little affected by heat, which lay between the pit fill and the kiln mouth, and which rested not on the pit floor but on a mass of carbonised matter. Embedded in the west side of the pit, close to the kiln, there was a well-built wall of stones (fist and two-fist size) from which the clay-and-stone mass sprang. Although there was no comparable 'wall' on the other side of the pit, and though the mass did not quite touch the sill of the flue, it would seem likely that this was a blocking of the kiln mouth made after firing.

In the southern pit the shelf or subsidiary pit was lacking, and the pit itself consisted of a number of rough 'steps', not freshly cut before filling. The fill was less clayey than in the northern pit, and contained less pottery. There were a few large stones on the fill, and, on the east side, runs of sand near the top of the pit. As in the north pit, there was no change in the nature or the content of the fill above and below these streaks.

As in the case of the north pit, there was a clay-and-stone mass springing from the west side of the pit (though not from the wall) and crossing the kiln mouth (with which it was in contact) to a slightly lower level against the east wall. This mass was of compact yellow clay (that on the north was the grey soft clay almost universal on this site) and contained less stone (but more sherds) than the first. Though hard it showed no heat reddening. Like the other it rested not on the bottom of the pit but on a carbonised mass containing sherds.

The floors of both flues were covered by several inches of carbonised matter, continuous with that in the pits outside (though this fell lower) and the north (and possibly on the south) end. It extended also under the sole of the flue. This matter was smooth, earthy and fibrous (it had possibly been penetrated by deep roots) and contained small sticks, but no other lumps; small brushwood (or peat?) was a likely fuel, though coal outcropped at no great distance, and appears as small patches of dirty coal in the natural sand.

Site E, hearth

Burnt stones were seen in the sand and the surface within a 5m square was cleaned and pared down to a level 25cm below the surface as found, in search of the stones of a kiln. All that appeared was a roughly rectangular mass of burnt stones, with some surface disturbance, lightly bound together by clay. Deep gaps between them contained earth and black matter; it seemed likely that fire had been lit on the (formerly level?) surface. Beside the stone mass there was a scallop-edged pit of dark soil, and beyond this there extended dark strips and ovals in the surface of the sand.

There were a few sherds embedded in the clay that bound the 'hearth' and a scatter of soil about it. The stones were found to rest on the filling of a pit, approximately 25cm deep; this was of near-sterile sandy soil, with some traces of heat, containing only a few small sherds. The fill of the scalloped pit (which proved to be two oval pits, in contact only at the surface) was a uniform dirty sand; there were no finds. Immediately south-west of the hearth (and extending for at least 1m but disturbed and largely inaccessible) there was a patch of heat-hardened sand covered by a black deposit, apparently charcoal. There were no traces of habitation debris or tread round the 'hearth', but this may have been destroyed by the striping of topsoil; the dark patches and streaks (one of which was cut by the pit edge) appeared to have no pattern or certain shape, and were probably natural.

Site F, corn drying kiln

In early August 1960, a funnel-shaped group of stones was observed in the same sandpit somewhat to the north of the previous finds.

The main structure was near-circular, 2 x 2.4m at the sand surface, with a funnel-shaped slightly curved 'entrance' approximately 2.3m long, 0.45m wide internally at its junction with the circle, and 0.7-0.8m at the outer end; the doubt is due to the removal of the north-east entrance stone during the stripping process that uncovered the site. Outside the 'entrance' there was an irregular burnt patch, roughly circular and 1.06m in diameter.

Within the circle, and immediately below the surface as found there was a clay layer 10-15cm thick, at the west end appearing to overlie the structure, but possibly only merging with one of the occasional patches of clay mortar between stones. The top surface of the funnel and the adjacent part of the circle were disturbed, but there was no trace here of an overlying clay layer. Within this funnel the fill consisted of unstratified dark sand, overlying a 5-6cm black layer single at the inner end but interleaved with burnt clayey material at the outer. This black layer came nearer the current surface, and formed a bowl-shaped hearth (the patch 1.06m in diameter) outside the funnel, but this was destroyed before excavation was complete. The base of both the funnel and circle (neither had a floor) was 0.75m below the current surface; the outermost stones of the funnel being set slightly higher.

The lowest course within the circle was of much larger stones than the rest (as were those of the funnel). Clay mortar was more apparent between the upper stones; clean sand appeared in the larger gaps below. The stones appeared to be laid against the walls of the pit, without intermediate packing.

Within the circle, the filling was curious. The greater part consisted of black sand, not homogeneous but not stratified, containing dark patches of carbonised matter. Some of these were natural, resembling the lumps and streaks in the natural sand at this site. A few sherds, including parts of the base of a large vessel and a small sherd of thinner and harder ware, were found in this fill, one at the base almost embedded in the natural sand. The rest of the fill consisted of soil and clay, mainly the latter. On the northern part of the circle this deposit reached the base, but on the southern part it overlays the sand; the very bottom of the northern deposit was of homogeneous clay. Both sand and clay-and-earth deposits were almost entirely free of stones, though in the clay layer at the top of the structure there were embedded three large heat-crumbled stones, much reddened on the under side.

Other finds from the circle were: a piece of slate, containing a peghole, found in the sand near the entrance; much decomposed fragments of bone, including a vertebra and long bone of a large animal (horse or cow?); and a long bone with a worked point, also found in sand on the north-west side. A small fragment of very recent pottery was an overnight insertion; it is less likely that this was the case with the slate fragment, though it looks modern. Decomposed bone was also found near the inmost stone of the funnel, on the north side, and small amorphous medieval sherds were also found in sand within the funnel. Built into the lowest course of the kiln wall on the north-west side, there was a much worn grindstone, 40-45cm in diameter and 15cm thick. Among disturbed stones above the kiln was a whetstone-like object, but it showed no sign of use.

North of the kiln there were two hollows and a pit, containing dark homogeneous sand. The two hollows were barren; the pit (which contained recent as well as medieval sherds) was not fully cleared, but exceeded 5cm in depth and was approximately 1m in diameter. The eastmost hollow was possibly connected with the hearth outside the kiln; but this area was disturbed by roots and rabbits.

The filling of the pit, which was recent, (possibly a sheep burial, though no bones were seen) closely resembled the clay and soil deposit within the kiln, and both may be recent. The sherds in the latter do not differ from those found scattered in topsoil throughout the site. The axis of the kiln was at 260.5° north.

In the late summer of 1961 a stone structure, partly cut away by the quarry face, was visible in the face of the sandpit at Stenhousemuir. There was no time for excavation or drawing. An approximately longitudinal section was visible in the quarry face and the surviving eastern half of the structure suggested an oval kiln 2 x 1.5m internally; allowance must however be made for some disturbance at the south end, and for the fact that the width of the presumed flue is unknown. There was no break in the curve found; the stones were closely fitted together with no trace of clay mortaring, and with no attempt to form a good face on the inside. In this it resembled the pottery kilns, but not the corn kiln. The walls stood to a maximum of 1m high at three and four courses, the top being 0.35m below the current sand surface. There was only slightly outward flare to the walls. Two of the stones had pecked markings, apparently irrelevant to their place in this structure. None showed signs of heat, or even of prolonged exposure to smoke and dirt. An approximately longitudinal section was cut back into the quarry face. The fill was of dark, earthy sand, with some clay near the surface. There were two streaks of black, carbonised material, both dipping towards the centre, one on the bottom of the structure and one a few inches higher. Both were about 7-8cm thick at the centre and thinning irregularly towards the sides. The structure had no floor; the bottom was of soft sand unmarked by heat, dipping slightly towards the centre.

Medieval sherds, of the same general kind as were found everywhere on the site, were found at all levels in the filling. There was one small base sherd; but nothing else of definable form. There was a slight clustering of sherds immediately above the upper black layer.

Near, but not on, the bottom of the structure was a small socket stone, or possibly fragment of a larger stone, the upper surface of which was much reddened. It could have held in position a light roof support, which would otherwise have gone deep in the soft sand, but no more.

Kiln J

This was excavated in May 1962. The axis of the kiln, which was much wrecked, was north-west to south-east. The 'arch' over the flue at each end had collapsed in antiquity, though at the northern end the stones were present; at the southern end no large stones remained; the fire passage may here have been of a different kind from those already excavated. The walls were roughly coursed; the boulders of the lowest course were long and flat, the three upper courses of smaller stones, diminishing in size to the top course.

The plan was made when the top of the kiln and pits only was exposed. Severe damage was done before the excavation was complete, and only the kiln was planned at a later stage. The southern pit was steep sided, with one shelf near the bottom, and a short 'arm' of filling outside the west side of the kiln; the northern pit was larger, with a wider 'arm' down the west side of the kiln. Its upper part was cut away on the north side to a depth of 1ft by a later and probably recent pit, but there is no reason to think that this had destroyed any shelf, such as was found in the corresponding pit at kiln D. Both pits at this kiln had a pointed base immediately in front of the fire passage and some inches below it, though in the absence of a sill stone or surviving floor the exact depth is uncertain. In neither pit was there any trace of blocking at the kiln mouth, nor of any wall or mass of stones set into the side of the pit for it to be keyed on; this was probably due to non-recent disturbance.

The sequence in the northern pit of this kiln resembles that in the north pit of kiln D, and the deposit also resembles this pit in the quantity and 'interlocking' of large sherds. It was not possible to section the southern pit; it was steep-sided, shelving near the base; the lower half of the fill and especially the pointed base producing the most pottery. There had been considerable natural silting into this pit, especially on the south and west sides.

The kiln was of inferior construction to kiln D, and probably also to others on the site. Like kilns A and D, it was built in a pit, hard up against the side, but with considerable packing outside it on the west. The stones, except of the lowest course, were smaller than in kiln D and the structure less stable; a revetment had been built within the kiln on the east side, supporting it and narrowing the kiln as in A and D. In the upper 20cm of the fill, which consisted of stones and topsoil, two large and several small lumps of slag were found. These do not appear to be bloomery waste, and may be the result of later (but not recent) activity in the neighbourhood. The kiln filling below this was unstratified, though there was more clay, and more sherds, in the lower part; there was no clean deposit at the bottom as in kiln D. There was no floor, but this does not appear to have been the result of damage or weathering, as a few inches of undisturbed burnt material spread inwards from the fire passages, and a small quantity for some distance along the walls. Some displacement, however, and the presumed removal of the long stones forming the 'arch' over the fire passage, appears to have taken place before the date of the current damage.

East of the kiln, and within the area of a former hollow in the field there was an oblong pit with rounded corners cut into the sand with steep sides and near flat base. On its floor were brown stains strongly suggesting a slatted base (or less probably a woven lining) to the pit. Although the stains were marked, especially at the edges of the pit, there were no organic remains. The fill was sandy soil, barren except for some amorphous medieval sherds near the top, possibly due to recent disturbance. There was no report, during subsequent quarry operations, of a corn kiln resembling Site F near at hand, but this is not conclusive.

Trial excavations 1978

Prior to redevelopment of a part of the site for local authority housing in 1978, a proton magnetometer survey was carried out by Edinburgh University. A trial excavation was carried out over the centre of an anomaly located by this survey which proved to be a layer of vitreous slag probably dating to the nineteenth century. Below this a tumble of stone associated with a concentration of medieval pottery may have been derived from a possible kiln up the hill.

THE KILNS AND OTHER STRUCTURES

There are plans of five kilns from the excavations at Stenhouse, A, C, D, F and J. All the kilns apart from F are Musty's Type 2a with two opposing flues, external stoke pits and no internal structure. The floors of A, C and D are recorded as being made of clay, F had a sand floor and J had no floor at all. It would appear that all the Stenhouse kilns were of the open-topped variety and were covered during firing with temporary covers. The finds assemblage from the excavations includes fragments of fired clay and straw daub which appear to come from these temporary domes, but unfortunately virtually all this material is unmarked so its original location is not known. The superstructures of all the kilns were built of up to two or three courses of stones and kilns D and J had stone 'arches' at at least one of the flue entrances. Kiln F resembles a corn drying kiln rather than a pottery kiln, with a long flue connected to a circular chamber. Indeed, this kiln had a reused quern built into one of its walls. It therefore seems curious that broken kiln furniture was recovered from kiln F, and this may imply that it was used for both purposes.

As well as the kilns, Doreen Hunter's text describes 'drying hearths' which she presumably interpreted as forming part of the pottery making process prior to firing in the kilns. Interestingly enough on two of the three occasions these structures are mentioned they are described as containing complete pots. Three of these vessels are presumably the possible syrup collecting jars from kiln, the other three are not easily identifiable. Another feature described and photographed to the east of kiln J is a square pit that may have been wood lined, its function is unclear. No trace of any buildings or any other structures associated with these kilns was recorded.

THE POTTERY ASSEMBLAGE

Introduction

Following Doreen Hunter's work at Stenhouse, the pottery assemblage was divided between Falkirk museum and the National Museum of Scotland in Edinburgh. The vast proportion of the material was held in Falkirk Museum's store in Grangemouth (Falkirk), the National Museum's material being largely made up of bodysherds in store in Port Edgar (City of Edinburgh). SUAT Ltd catalogued all the material held by Falkirk Museum which includes the material excavated by Marjorie Kenworthy in 1978. The assemblage, excluding the material still in the possession of the National Museum, numbers some 10,304 sherds.

Method

All the pottery held by Falkirk museum has been catalogued and identified using the standard SUAT pottery recording sheet. All vessel forms are described using the terminology in 'A guide to the classification of Medieval Ceramic Forms'. All the analysis and identification has been undertaken by eye.

THE FABRICS

Kiln wasters

Most of the catalogued material from Stenhouse probably represents pottery that never got beyond the kiln site. This is most obvious from those sherds that have glaze running over the edges or are very badly warped after firing in the kiln. So although the vessel types represented in the assemblage are a valuable indication of the products of the kilns, most if not all of them were probably never used.

Stenhouse ware

Fifteen years of archaeological excavations in the Scottish east coast burghs have identified a fabric type now called 'Scottish Redware' as forming a tradition of native pottery production apparently dating from the thirteenth to the fifteenth century. Virtually all the fabric from the excavations at Stenhouse represents variations of this fabric type; it is almost exclusively orange brown in colour with a sandy matrix and no obvious inclusions. The internal and external surfaces are commonly coloured purple. It is not clear whether this represents an applied purple wash or is caused by the leeching of material from the clay during firing. This now a commonly identified characteristic of Scottish redwares, although it is not apparent on the redwares from the kilns at Rattray (Aberdeenshire) (pers. comm. C. Murray). This pottery is probably being made using the Carse clays that are readily available in the Forth valley. There are two unfired fragments of a thumbed base in a blue grey dried clay that is very light and pumice like.

Scottish White Gritty Ware

Recent archaeological excavation has identified three potential production centres for this fabric in Lothian, Tweeddale and Fife. Recent ICPMS analysis by the British Geological Survey has suggested that this tradition might be more widespread than previously thought, with every sample submitted apparently coming from a different kiln. White Gritty Ware in the Scottish Borders has been dated by thermoluminescence to 1065+/-140 and 1175+/-120 AD respectively. It is most commonly highly fired to a white or grey colour and contains quartz inclusions. Cooking pots appear to be the most popular vessel type in this fabric although glazed jugs are also being produced. Its presence at Stenhouse is surprising although, as there are only 10 sherds in the whole assemblage, it seems more likely to have been imported than manufactured on site.

THE VESSEL FORMS

Jugs

The most common vessel being produced by the Stenhouse kilns is the shouldered jug. These vessels are normally glazed green with a simple undecorated strap handle. There are a few examples of twisted-rod handles, including one which has a pierced loop attached to its top surface presumably for suspension.

Some of the Stenhouse jugs have very simple facemasks attached directly to their rims, and on a couple of occasions to their bodies. These facemasks are of a very distinctive 'alien' appearance, being made of three thumbed pads which are then decorated with two ring and dot symbols for eyes and a simple slash mark for the mouth. These facemasks were included in a paper by Lloyd Laing and Norman Robertson in 1970 and dated to the fifteenth century.

The facemasks attached to the vessel body have more incised detail added to represent hair and beard, and it has been kindly suggested that these may be representations of the 'green man' (by S. Moorhouse). The complete jug from Linlithgow Palace (West Lothian) has a facemask which also appears to be a representation of the 'green man', this is particularly evident in the beard which is made of separate strands of clay which have been twisted in and out of each other. The shoulder of this vessel is also decorated with ring and dot and incised foliage similar to that present of some of the bodysherds from the excavation. There are two facemasks from an unstratified context which are modelled on spouts and may be of an earlier date.

All the kilns were producing versions of shouldered jugs with a bridge spout that is fixed to the rim with very well-defined thumb marks. The jugs from kilns A, C, D and G all possess frilled bases and may be attempting to copy Rhenish stoneware vessels which have this style of base. A very distinctive style of tubular spout is also represented from kilns D and A. This spout has been modelled very tightly against the body of the vessel and has deep thumb marks along its length. There is a single very unusual example of this type of tubular spout that is attached to the outside of a strap handle and it is tempting to consider whether this may either be from a puzzle jug or a trial piece. A rimsherd from one of these bridge spouted jugs has a handle junction in such a position to suggest that the vessel appears to have had at least three handles.

Beakers

There are four complete examples of these small, single-handled vessels which are glazed dark green on a purple background. The complete beaker with the wider mouth was found in kiln D, two of the other beaker sherds are from contexts associated with Kiln A, the remainder are unmarked and it is not known where they were found on site. Such vessels are not thought to be in general use until the late medieval period (late fifteenth/sixteenth century) and are probably copying imported Rhenish stoneware drinking vessels.

Urinals

There are two virtually complete examples of this vessel type with looped handles. Parallels for these vessels are best represented in the Melrose Abbey (Scottish Borders) collection and would seem to imply some monastic link with this assemblage.

Jars

Kilns A and C are also producing double-handled jars that possess very well-defined thumbed lug handles. There is a reconstructed single handled jar from context PT.

Vessels with bungholes

There are two bodysherds from these distinctive vessels which would have held liquid. The bungholes were designed to hold a spigot or a tap to enable the contents to be drawn from the vessel.

Cooking pots

There are only eight sherds from Kiln C that may be from cooking pots, but it would appear that this vessel type was either being supplied in another fabric (White Gritty Ware?) or at a later date may have been produced in metal.

Open vessels

There are small numbers of bowls present from all the kilns, and fragments of three, small rod-handled ladles, one from kiln A and the others from unlocated contexts. There is also a small drinking bowl from kiln A and a dish from an unlocated context.

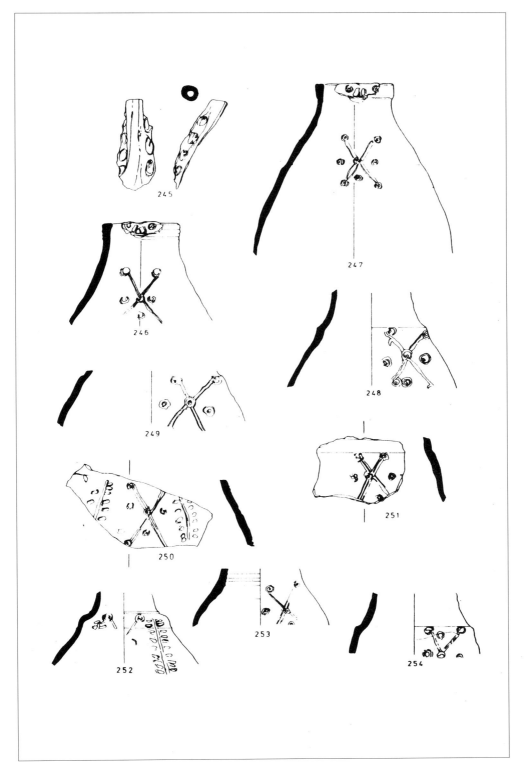

57 Pottery decorated with Saltire crosses and facemasks from Stenhouse. © *SUAT Ltd*

58 Jug from Stenhouse with Maltese Cross on the front

Dripping pans
This very distinctive vessel type is present from kilns A and C. These vessels begin arriving in Scotland from the Low Countries in the mid-fourteenth century and local redware copies have been recovered from excavations in Perth.

Skillets
These ceramic 'frying pans' are present in kilns A and D. A handle from context DN (kiln D) is of the very distinctive folded type that has been found in excavations at Eyemouth (Scottish Borders), Stirling Castle, Linlithgow (West Lothian) and Dunbar (East Lothian). This form is dated to the sixteenth and seventeenth century.

Pirlie pigs
These small, ceramic money boxes are only present from kiln A. These objects are usually dated to the fifteenth to seventeenth century, and there are good parallels in the assemblages from the kiln site at Throsk, Stirling Council, from excavations at the Tron Kirk in Edinburgh and from Melrose Abbey in the Scottish Borders.

Syrup-collecting jars?
Kiln C contained three complete vessels of an unknown function. These are unglazed, very tall and have no handles and have traces of slight internal and external smoke blackening. The closest parallel may be a syrup-collecting jar that was used in the sugar refining process.

Tile
There are three pieces of glazed ceramic tile in this assemblage. One of these is from kiln A but the other two are unlocated. Such a small group of material cannot be used to argue that some of the Stenhouse kilns were also making tile.

Decoration
4.5 per cent of the pottery assemblage from Doreen Hunter's excavations exhibit some form of either incised decoration or facemask. The most common form of decoration on the vessels from Stenhouse is a mixture of ring and dot and incised lines. This is often employed to create a 'saltire' design on the vessel and in at least one example such a decorated vessel also has a facemask. Incised lines are also used on a few occasions to create 'floral' patterns on both vessel bodies and handles. It seems likely from comparison with the complete vessel from Linlithgow Palace (West Lothian) that these incised decorations all relate to the depiction of the 'green man' on many of the vessels that were manufactured at the Stenhouse kilns.

Two vessels from this assemblage are decorated with Maltese crosses. The best example of this is a bodysherd from an unstratified context that has a very well-drawn Maltese cross incised into its surface that has four 'dots' above each arm. Research in the site archive has revealed that these sherds were formerly part of an almost complete reconstructed jug with a frilled base that was then broken up for unknown reasons. The other example is from a warped jug and is a much simpler design.

Historical research has indicated that the Knights of St John (Hospitallers) owned land at Stenhouse in 1539-40 and, as it was only this order that used the Maltese cross (pers. comm. P. Willis), it is worth suggesting that vessels from this kiln site were being made specifically for the Knights at Torphichen preceptory (Midlothian). This may have been done as a form of rental payment to the Hospitallers, or it might even be that the kiln site was set up by the knights in the first place.

59 Green man jug from Linlithgow Palace. © *Historic Scotland*

GOD'S BANKERS: THE MILITARY ORDERS IN SCOTLAND

Above: 60 Details of jug from Linlithgow Palace. © *Historic Scotland*

Right: 61 Knight jug from Stenhouse

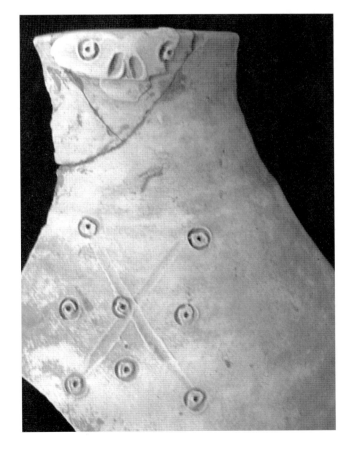

62 Ravenscraig Castle

KILN FURNITURE

During the cataloguing of this material, fragments of kiln stands were found from kilns C, D and F. These objects are of the distinctive conical 'cooling tower' shape that has also been recovered from the kiln sites of Colstoun (East Lothian), Rattray (Aberdeenshire) and Throsk (Stirling Council).

DISCUSSION

Work on Scottish medieval ceramics in the late 1990s concentrated on trying to source and identify the kiln sites that were supplying the medieval burghs. Although a programme of ICPMS (chemical) analysis by the British Geological Survey has proved that it is possible to identify different local wares using physical means, the field search for new kiln sites has yet to bear fruit. This is why it is so important to finally be able to report on all the results of Doreen Hunter's work at Stenhouse.

The kilns excavated at Stenhouse resemble those from Rattray (Aberdeenshire) and two of the kilns from Colstoun (East Lothian). Comparison with the experimental kiln at Barton-on-Humber (North Lincolnshire), which measured 1.4m in diameter and 0.5m deep, indicates that the Stenhouse kilns may have held up to 50 vessels at a firing. Only three of the kilns, C, D and F, contained pieces of kiln furniture, but this may be due to the level of recovery rather than differences in technology. From Doreen Hunter's field notes there is a suggestion that these kilns had clay 'pottery floors' and some of the fired daub present in this assemblage may actually be from such surfaces.

It would appear that the kilns at Stenhouse may have been only producing pottery for a very localised market. From excavations in the Scottish East coast burghs there has been no discovery of any redware that can be identified as being from Stenhouse, the only exception to this being a vessel from Ravenscraig Castle which may possess one of the distinctive facemasks, and a bridge spout from Linlithgow Palace which appears to be a Stenhouse product. The complete vessel rediscovered in the stores of Historic Scotland also appears to be a product of the Stenhouse kilns. Interestingly enough its find spot is also indicated as being Linlithgow Palace although a precise site location is not given.

It is unfortunate that there has been little opportunity for excavation at Torphichen, as the Knights may have been using pottery from Stenhouse. The only pottery from Torphichen is a small box that was recovered from site clearance works in the 1980s and examination of this small assemblage by the author did not identify any material from Stenhouse.

Perhaps the most interesting thing about the Stenhouse pottery is the distinctive styles of decoration used on the vessels. As already suggested the two Maltese crosses appear to suggest a link between the Knights Hospitallers at Torphichen and the Stenhouse potters. The use of the Saltire as a decorative style may also hint at another chivalric link, perhaps reflecting the late fifteenth-century revival of the cult of St Andrew (pers. comm. M. Lynch). Alternatively, the use of this style of cross on jugs with facemasks may suggest that these anthropomorphic vessels were supposed to represent a human figure wearing a tabard with a cross on its front. If this figure was supposed to represent a crusader then there might be an argument to suggest that the decorative style on the Stenhouse vessels is a reflection of the sixteenth-century Scottish revival of the crusading movement which the preceptory of Torphichen was heavily involved in.

There may be another link to Torphichen as this assemblage includes three vessels for which it has not been possible to find a Scottish parallel. All three are recorded as coming from kiln C and may be connected with the sugar refining process. However, the limited work that has been done on this industry in Scotland indicates that the first reference to it is in 1619 and that it is not until between 1667 and 1701 that it really takes off in Glasgow and Leith. As the Hospitallers are known to have been planting sugar cane at Acre (Israel) when it fell to the Saracens in 1291 and European sugar production was developed as a result of the Crusades, is it possible that, if this industry was taking place at Stenhouse, it was very localised, and was being done specifically for the Knights of St John at Torphichen?

The best parallel for some of the Stenhouse decoration comes from excavations at Sandal Castle (West Yorkshire) from levels associated with Richard III's rebuilding in the fifteenth century. One of the jugs at Sandal is decorated with a facemask and incised wavy lines very similar to a vessel from Stenhouse, and is described as being in a coarse redware fabric. Another jug bodysherd also exhibits a similar mix of ring and dot and incised line to that found at Stenhouse.

It is difficult to date the start and finish of pottery production at Stenhouse accurately, but to judge from vessel form and style there would not seem to be any material earlier than the late fifteenth century. The kilns would seem to have ceased production prior to the production of the Reduced Greyware fabrics like those produced at Throsk (Stirling Council). Many of the vessel types being produced appear to be copying imported vessels from France and the Rhineland that would date to the fifteenth or sixteenth centuries. This is particularly evident in the forms of the jugs with narrow necks and those with frilled bases.

As already stated, Stenhouse is important as it represents one of only two redware kiln sites to be investigated in the whole of Scotland. Following the cataloguing and illustration of its products, an attempt now needs to be made to identify pottery from Stenhouse in other excavated assemblages; this may need to wait for the opportunity for excavations in either medieval Falkirk or at the preceptory of the Knights Hospitaller at Torphichen. The suggested link between the pottery production centre at Stenhouse and the Knights at Torphichen is also a subject that seems worthy of further exploration. This is further highlighted by the fact that the Knights of St John also owned land directly adjacent to the Scottish White Gritty Ware production centre at Colstoun in East Lothian.

5
A FUTURE FOR THE PAST?

PRESERVATION, PROTECTION OR EXCAVATION?

It is clear from the fieldwork elements of these various projects that several sites exist that justify protection, and with this in mind a list was provided to Historic Scotland identifying where these were. The relevant local authority elements of the various gazetteers were also passed on to the local authority archaeologists for inclusion in their Sites and Monuments Records. The damage (in August 2003) of the 'grange' buildings at Campsie Linn (Perth and Kinross) is a perfect example of how fragile this monument type is (this site was scheduled in 2005). In this particular case the site was not protected and its function and importance were not recognised by the developer who was improving an existing roadway that ran across the site. As always the solution to this problem has to be a combination of education, adequate protection and sensible planning control by the local authority.

From the fieldwork undertaken for the various monastic gazetteers it is clear that it is often difficult, if not impossible, to date any of the standing remains that are encountered on any of these sites. In most cases any structures or buildings are more likely to date to the later early modern use of the site. However there would seem to be strong argument for protecting those sites for which there is good evidence for early activity, Lead Law (Sillerholes, Midlothian), Hilderston (West Lothian) and some of the sites on Drake Law, South Lanarkshire (Friermure) would seem to be worthy of scheduling and further research.

It is clear to the author that the question of monastic involvement and promotion of extractive and other industries in medieval Scotland is a vastly unexplored area. Without a doubt the Cistercian monks of Newbattle Abbey were at the forefront of coal and lead working in Scotland and it is clear from the records that the Scottish crown realised this early on and made sure that it was able to take advantage of 'God's Treasure House'.

This Historic Scotland-funded research has increased the number of potential monastic grange sites by at least six times. It is very striking how little work has been done in Scotland on these buildings and estate centres, which represent the first proper agricultural revolution in Scotland since the Neolithic. As well as the agricultural aspect the author has been considering the possibility that several other industrial activities, aside from the documented ones, may have also been undertaken at some of these grange sites. The manufacture of pottery in Scotland seems to be a good candidate for something that may have been carried out on a grange; it is striking that many of the Perthshire grange sites are in close proximity or even on some of the major clay resources in the area. In England there is evidence for this happening on at least two of Fountains Abbey's granges in England so any Scottish evidence may rely on future excavation or chance finds (Bond 2004, 340). There is no physical proof for monastic pottery production so far, but a monastic origin for Scotlands earliest medieval pottery industry, the Scottish White Gritty Ware was suggested as long ago as 1984 (Haggarty 1984).

63 Remains of fishtrap, Mersehead, Dumfries and Galloway

It is worth stressing that most if not all of the excavation work that has taken place so far on either monastic sites or hospitals has been in advance of redevelopment, in other words rescue archaeology. This was never more striking than at the first series of excavations at St Nicholas Farm, St Andrews where there was a very limited opportunity to excavate a large part of this leper hospital prior to the construction of a new leisure centre.

Strategic thinking is required to design and implement new controlled research excavations of such sites, the problem as always being who will pay? Southern Ireland has taken the bull by the horns and instituted 'The Discovery Programme' a new, lottery-funded research programme which is also tied into the tourist industry, maybe Scotland ought to consider doing something along similar lines?

In the interim the following research priorities can be suggested for the further understanding of the Scottish granges and monastic landscapes:

1. Proper analysis and historical research of the existing monastic cartularies and rental books to identify the way that the granges functioned.
2. The cataloguing of all the industrial sites that are referred to, and by a combination of fieldwork and research, the production of a priority list of those sites that should be protected.
3. Controlled excavation of part of a monastic grange to elucidate its layout and function. One of the cropmark sites (Coupar Grange or Cambusmichael) would seem to be an ideal candidate as excavation would also allow for some analysis of ongoing attrition by ploughing.

64 Excavation of precinct wall at Arbroath Abbey. © *SUAT Ltd*

65 Building remains at St Nicholas Farm

66 New leisure centre under construction at St Nicholas Farm, St Andrews

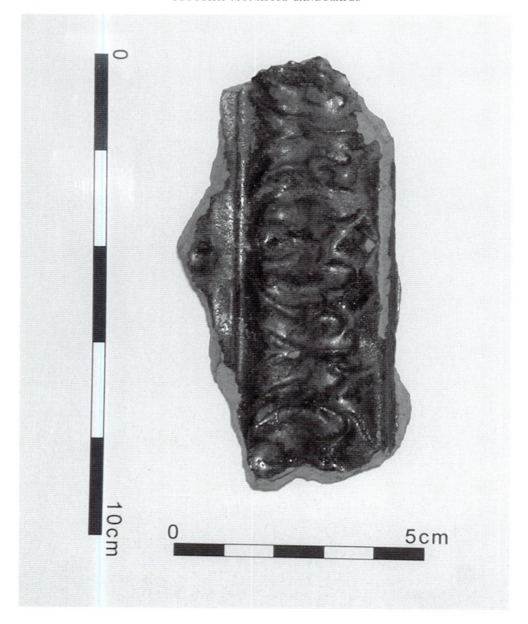

4. Ensure that all grange sites that have standing structures are properly recorded (by RCAHMS threatened buildings section?).
5. Proper research on the form and function of Scottish cultivation terraces involving excavation and environmental analysis to elucidate how they were being used, when they were being used and what they were being used for.
6. There should be further research into evidence for monastic iron extraction in Scotland.
7. Further research and field study is required into the location of the stone quarries associated with the major monastic houses.
8. Further research on the medieval road system would be valuable.
9. It would be useful to source the lead used in the glazing of Scottish medieval pottery and tiles.

Opposite: 67 North German stove tile fragment from excavations at the site of the new Scottish Parliament, Holyrood, Edinburgh. © *SUAT Ltd*

Right: 68 North German stove tile fragment from excavations at St Giles Cathedral, Edinburgh. © *SUAT Ltd*

Below: 69 Carse of Gowrie looking south-east. © *SUAT Ltd*

10. There should be continuing research into the possibility of monastic pottery production.
11. Monastic involvement in the control and management of forestry requires research.

The monastic grange deserves to be regarded as a major element in both the industrial and agricultural evolution of Scotland.

With this in mind, every opportunity should be taken to educate local authorities, the Scottish Parliament and the general public about this important monument type. The research in this book has only scratched the surface of a forgotten period of Scotland's medieval past but has hopefully put it back onto the research agenda.

GAZETTEER OF SCOTTISH MONASTIC GRANGES

You would take these granges not for the living quarters of lay-brothers but for monastic cloisters were it not that ox-yokes, ploughs and other farm implements betray the inhabitants status, and that no books are opened there.

Anonymous twelfth-century monk 'A description of Clairvaux'

FORMAT OF GAZETTEER

Each site entry indicates, where possible, the abbey and order responsible for the grange, and has a brief historical summary and an overview of the archaeological evidence. Where a field visit has been possible the site is described as it existed at the time of this gazetteer (2001 and 2002). Note that most sites are on privately owned land and you should, if possible, always ask permission to visit them. Full bibliographic references are available from the author via email: dhall@suat.co.uk

CENTRAL REGION GRANGES (15)

M. Roy

NMRS NO	NMRS NAME	TYPE OF SITE	MONASTERY	SAM/ LISTED
NS89NW NS 838 951	Blackgrange	Grange?	Cambuskenneth?	
NS88SE NS 87 82	Carron Grange			
Not located	East Grange	Grange?	Cambuskenneth Abbey (OSA)	
Not located	East Grange of Alloa	Grange?		
NT08SW 14	Grange House	Mansion; Grange	Culross Abbey (OCist)	

NS98SW NS 918 841	Grange of Bothkennar	Grange	Crown land (part of the lordship of Stirling)	
NS98SW NS 911 816	Grange Manor Hotel, Grangemouth	Grange		
NS98SW 1	Grangemouth, Zetland Park ALTERNATIVE: Abbotsgrange	Grange or moated homestead	Holyrood Abbey (OSA)	
NS97NW NS 936 793	Inchyra Grange Hotel	Grange?		
NS89SW 18 NS 8345 9292	The Kennels	Castle or grange?	Cambuskenneth Abbey?	
Not located	Kerse	Grange?	Holyrood Abbey (OSA)	
Not located	Newton of Granges (Bothkennar)	Grange?		
Not located	The Grange	Grange	Torphichen Preceptory	
NS89SW NS 814 946	West Grange	Grange?	Cambuskenneth Abbey (OSA)	
Not located	West Grange of Alloa	Grange?		

CENTRAL REGION

Grange　　　　Blackgrange
Abbey　　　　Cambuskenneth?
Order　　　　Cistercian
Parish　　　　Alloa
Council　　　Clackmannanshire
Location　　　The site of Blackgrange lies to the east of Tullibody, on the south side of the A907. The area is relatively flat pasture, with a bonded warehouse to the south. Beyond this warehouse, closer to the River Forth, is Haugh of Blackgrange
NGR　　　　NS 838 951
NMRS site　　No entry
Site visits　　17 September 2001

History
No historical references to this possible grange have been discovered.

Archaeology
The Clackmannanshire Council Sites and Monuments Record records an RAF aerial photograph of 1946 which shows faint rig cultivation in the vicinity of Haugh of Blackgrange

(B72 3255-6). A coastal survey by GUARD in 1996 indicates that although ploughed out this rig is still visible as a cropmark on aerial photographs of 1988.

Current State
At present there is no building at Blackgrange itself, the location of the former farm being covered in rough grass and trees. The area around Blackgrange is under pasture, with some cultivation to the north. A bonded warehouse occupies the land to the south, beyond a railway line. At 'Blackgrange Crossing' or Blackgrange Cottage, on the railway line, there is now no standing building, and the area is overgrown. Haugh of Blackgrange is occupied by a working farm.

Grange	Carron Grange
Abbey	not applicable
Order	not applicable
Parish	Larbert
Council	Falkirk
Location	Lies to south of Stenhousemuir. Area is mainly built up, with landfill site to south. Area lies around River Carron
NGR	NS 87 82
NMRS site	No entry
Site visits	20 September 2001

History
Carron Grange has no monastic connections whatsoever. This 'B' listed building was built for the manager of the Carron Iron Works in the eighteenth century. It is now the headquarters of a company called Scottish Building.

Grange	East Grange
Abbey	Cambuskenneth Abbey
Order	Augustinian
Parish	Unknown
Council	Unknown
Location	Not located

Grange	East Grange of Alloa
Abbey	Unknown
Order	Unknown
Parish	Alloa
Council	Clackmannan
Location	Not located

Grange	The Grange
Abbey	Torphichen Preceptory
Order	Knights Hospitallers
Parish	Unknown
Council	Falkirk
Location	somewhere between Bo'ness and Blackness

History
There is a single entry in the rental of the Knights of St John for 1539-40 that reads 'Item the grange vs'Vjd'. This entry is listed between entries for Blackness and Kinglasse (Cowan *et al.*

1983, 24). The exact location of this grange is unclear but could potentially be at Grange of Carriden (see below).

Grange	Grange House
Abbey	Culross Abbey
Order	Cistercian
Parish	Bo'Ness and Carriden
Council	Falkirk
Location	Residential area in Bo'Ness
NGR	NT 008 813
NMRS site	NT08SW 14
Site visits	20 September 2001

History
During the twelfth century Philip d'Eu granted some of his lands to Culross Abbey, directly opposite on the north side of the Forth. The lands, called the 'granary' of the Abbey, retained the name after they were secularised, and passed to the Hamiltons.

Grange House (NT08SW 1) was built in 1564, but on a site to the East was an older mansion-house (MacDonald 1941, 29). *Grange of Carriden* in the sheriffdom of Linlithgow belonged to Culross Abbey (*RMS*, v, no 1675).

Archaeology
Grange House, which was demolished in 1906, was built in 1564 for Sir John Hamilton. It was a long rectangle on plan, with a square projection near the centre of the south side, containing a staircase (MacGibbon and Ross 1887-92). No monastic remains are visible. A sandstone dovecot/winding house (NT08SW 13), lacking a roof, is located to the south of Old Grange House.

Current State
The site of Grange House (NT08SW 14) is now occupied by late nineteenth- or early twentieth-century sandstone housing, in a residential area of Bo'Ness. To the east the apparently unconnected site of 'Old Grange House' (NT08SW 33), has been converted into a nursing home. This is a large sandstone house of probable nineteenth-century date. Between the two buildings are streets called Grange Loan and Grange Terrace, and it is possible that the former grange incorporated a large area of the present town. To the south of Old Grange House stands a roofless dovecot, apparently converted from a winding house of perhaps eighteenth- or nineteenth-century date. Further south lies a farm surrounded by pasture.

Grange	Grange of Bothkennar (Orchardfield)
Abbey	Crown land (part of the lordship of Stirling)
Order	Not applicable
Parish	Grangemouth
Council	Falkirk
Location	To the east of the A905 and north of the River Carron
NGR	NS 918 841
NMRS site	No entry
Site visits	19 September 2001

History
There are references in the *Registrum Monasterii de Cambuskenneth* to 'firmarum nostrarum de Bothkenner' in 1317 (Fraser 1872, 61 no 41) and to 'sex celdras frumenti de Bothkenner' in 1344 (Fraser 1872, 61 no 42). This grange is listed as part of the Crown lands of the lordship

of Stirling, the earliest reference being in 1375-6 (*RMS*, i, no 565; iii, nos 581, 634, 886, 1125, 1389).

Archaeology
No archaeologically significant remains are visible.

Current State
This area is currently under cultivation. The farm at Orchardhead consists of several buildings, probably of nineteenth-century date, with modern concrete and metal sheds.

Grange	Grange Manor Hotel, Grangemouth
Abbey	Unknown
Order	Unknown
Parish	Grangemouth
Council	Falkirk
Location	This hotel lies near the M9, on the western outskirts of Grangemouth
NGR	NS 911 816
NMRS site	No entry
Site visits	19 September 2001

History
There are no documentary references to confirm that this place name reflects the former existence of a grange.

Archaeology
No archaeologically significant remains are visible.

Current State
The site consisted of a large nineteenth-century residential building (now a hotel) with twentieth-century additions and modifications. To the east stands a sandstone coach-house, which has been converted into a restaurant, with much concrete and sandstone infilling of former openings. The land around the hotel is built up. To the east lies a factory development, beyond an area of woodland. There is pasture to the north.

Grange	Grangemouth, Zetland Park (or Abbotsgrange)
Abbey	Holyrood Abbey
Order	Augustinian
Parish	Grangemouth
Council	Falkirk
Location	This site is located within a public park in Grangemouth, surrounded by modern housing
NGR	NS 929 814
NMRS site	NS98SW 1
Site visits	19 September 2001

History
The earliest reference to this site is on 16 July 1543 when 'Thomas Levingstoun' in *Abbottisgrange* is mentioned (*RMS*, iii, no 2935). On the 24 August 1565 there is a feu confirmation 'to Alexander Chalmer of *the lands called Abbotis-grange* [occupied by Thomas Levingstoun and David Kincaid and others], with the mansion thereof, meadow, yards, gardens, houses, buildings, with garbal teinds included, in their barony of Carse and the sheriffdom of

Stirling; Rendering £46 13s 4d as old ferme and 20s as augmentation, with customary services; together with services in the three head courts at the burgh of Canongate, and in the courts of justiciary and chamberlain of the said monastery when they should happen; with doubling of ferme at entry of heirs; Moreover the commendator and convent incorporate all the said lands into one tenandry, so that one sasine at *Abbotis-grange* should stand for all, 5 August 1560' (*RMS*, iv, no 1662).

By the 9 May 1586 the property is described as the '*lands of Abbotts-grange of Kers*' (*RMS*, v, no 987). And as late as 31 July 1646 there is a confirmation to Robert, Earl of Roxburgh, Lord Ker of Cessford and Caverton, [all his estates including] *the lands of Grange called Abbottisgrange* and others with towers and manor places in the sheriffdoms of Linlithgow and Stirling (*RMS*, ix, no 1696).

Archaeology
There is an area of uneven, undulating land, under grass, to the west of a public paddling pond. The mounds appeared much eroded, with many large trees growing on them, probably causing sub-surface damage to any archaeological features. The site has also been partially levelled. This site has also been identified as a moated site (Coleman *et al.*, 2000).

Current State
The possible grange site has probably been partially levelled, and only several grass-covered mounds remain. There are many large trees in the area, causing subsurface damage. The surrounding land has been much damaged by the insertion of park features such as pools, a carting track, etc.

Grange	Grangeview
Abbey	Unknown
Order	Unknown
Parish	Grangemouth
Council	Falkirk
Location	The site is located in farmland to the north-west of Grangemouth
NGR	NS 914 831
NMRS site	NS98SW 32
Site visits	19 September 2001

History
It has not been possible to find any documentary evidence for this possible grange.

Archaeology
One unroofed complex-shaped building, annotated as ruin and lying within an incomplete enclosure, is depicted on the first edition of the OS 6in map (Stirlingshire 1865, sheet xxiv). The unroofed building is partially marked on the current edition of the OS 1:10000 map (1993). Information from RCAHMS (SAH) 2 July 1999.

Current State
This site consists of farm buildings surrounded by cereal cultivation.

Grange	Inchyra Grange (Hotel)
Abbey	Unknown
Order	Unknown
Parish	Grangemouth
Council	Falkirk

Location	The site lies to the south-east of Grangemouth, in a landscaped area surrounded by roads and modern residential and industrial development
NGR	NS 936 793
NMRS site	NS97NW 46.07
Site visits	19 September 2001

History

It has not been possible to find any documentary evidence for this possible grange.

Archaeology

To the south of this site stands a sandstone church building (Polmont Old Parish Church) of possibly nineteenth-century date, with a large graveyard. Within the graveyard, and to the south-east of the church stands a ruinous rubble building. This functioned as a vault for graves, but was formerly Polmont, Old Church (*NMRS No* NS97NW 7). This church was built in 1732, and several gravestones are of eighteenth-century date, predating the existing church building.

Current State

A sandstone mansion of probable late nineteenth-century date overlies the site. It functions as a hotel (Inchyra Grange Hotel), and is surrounded by landscaped lawns, woodland and car park areas. To the north is a smaller sandstone house. A farm lies on high ground to the east, while to the south stands a church (Polmont Old Parish Church) within a large graveyard. To the north and east of the hotel lies undulating pasture.

Grange	The Kennels
Abbey	Unknown
Order	Unknown
Parish	St Ninians
Council	Stirling
Location	The site lay in farmland to the north of Fallin and south of the River Forth
NGR	NS 8345 9292
NMRS site	NS89SW 18
Site visits	17 September 2001 (proprietor not present so rapid visit only)

History

Edward I had planned to build a castle on each bank of the Forth a little below Stirling, one at Tullibody (see NS89SE 15) and the other at Polmaise. Sites were obtained for this purpose in 1304-5, but neither castle was completed. It is uncertain how much work was done at Polmaise, but, with the possible exception of an otherwise unexplained ditch at Lower Polmaise (NS 834 925) no visible remains of any castle exist there today.

This ditch, 30ft wide and with a maximum depth of 3ft 6in, runs across the north-east end of the former walled garden of Old Polmaise, beyond which it extends for a distance of some 80yds in a north-west direction (RCAHMS 1963).

Archaeology

The ditch mentioned above is still visible running south-east to north-west across the north-east end of a former walled garden (Old Polmaise), and beyond it to the north-west. This ditch is around 90m long by up to 15m wide by less than 1m deep and lies in a field which is currently lying fallow (2001).

Current State

A ruinous walled garden, constructed of brick, lies at the western end of this field. Within the walled garden there are trees and undergrowth which are causing damage to the south-east end of the surviving ditch. To the south of this field stands The Kennels Farm, which is surrounded by pasture. The farm buildings are of eighteenth- or nineteenth-century date, and of sandstone build, often in a poor state. There is also some modern concrete build.

Grange	Kerse
Abbey	Holyrood Abbey
Order	Augustinian
Parish	Unknown
Council	Unknown
Location	Unlocated

History

There are references to this grange in April 1315 when a grant is made to Walter, Steward of Scotland of lands including an annual rent from *Cars Stryuillyn*, which the abbot and convent of the monastery of Holyrood of Edinburgh held from the king (*RRS*, v, no 391). A further confirmation of 16 July 1363 refers to letters by Robert, Steward of Scotland and Earl of Strathearn to Holyrood Abbey, granting [a relaxation from a rent due by them to him from lands of Kerse in the sheriffdom of Stirling; and, because in the time of Robert I, the canons of Holyrood possessed *the demesne lands of the Carss, with manor, grange and pertinents within the grange and with the one meadow called the Dubet* in their own hands, leased annually on account of 32 merks sterling, in which the said King Robert and his predecessors, kings of Scotland, were held to pay annually from their coffers to the canons, as is more fully contained in their charters and instruments between the late kings of Scotland and the canons, – granting that the foresaid *demesne lands of the Carss with manor, grange and pertinents within the grange and with the meadow called the Dubet*, remain and be converted in future to the use of the foresaid religious men freely, fully and peacefully, 2 February 1362/3 (*RRS*, vi, no 298). And finally on 1 October 1552 Holyrood Abbey grants in feu ferme to James, Duke of Chatelherault, Earl of Arran, Lord Hamilton etc, *the lands of the lordship of Kerse* in the sheriffdoms of Stirling and Linlithgow, except the fishery of their *lands of Grange* and any fisheries whatever previously leased in empiteusis (*Holyrood Liber*, App 2, no 37).

Recommendations

Further documentary research should be undertaken to try and accurately locate this grange.

Grange	Newton of Granges (Bothkennar)
Abbey	Unknown
Order	Unknown
Parish	Grangemouth
Council	Falkirk
Location	Not located

Grange	West Grange
Abbey	Cambuskenneth Abbey
Order	Augustinian
Parish	Logie (Stirling)
Council	Stirling
Location	West Grange and Haugh of West Grange lie on the northern side of the River Forth to the north-east of Cambuskenneth Abbey

NGR NS 814 946
NMRS site No entry
Site visits 17 September 2001 (short visit only as proprietor not located)

History
It has not been possible to find any documentary references to this grange.

Archaeology
No monastic remains were visible.

Current State
Several rubble-built stone farm buildings of probable thirteenth- to nineteenth-century date stood on the site, some were in a ruinous state, while others formed private residences. The surrounding land was under pasture with cereal cultivation to the west.

Grange West Grange of Alloa
Abbey Unknown
Order Unknown
Council Clackmannan
Location Not located

TAYSIDE GRANGES (19)

C. Smith and R. Kaye

NMRS NUMBER	NMRS NAME	TYPE OF SITE	ABBEY	COUNCIL	SAM/LISTED
NO24SW 54	Balbrogie	Grange	Coupar Angus Abbey (OCist)	Perth and Kinross	
NO13SW 30	Cambusmichael ALTERNATIVE(S): Cambusmichael Church	Grange	Scone Abbey (OSA)	Perth and Kinross	
NO22NE 18	Carsegrange	Grange	Coupar Angus Abbey (OCist)	Perth and Kinross	
NO13SW 10 NO 1243 3394	Campsie Linn	Farm and Abbots House	Coupar Angus Abbey (OCist)	Perth and Kinross	
NO12SE 5	Glencarse House ALTERNATIVE(S): Clene	Religion	Scone Abbey (OSA)	Perth and Kinross	
NO24SW 74	Coupar Grange	Grange (Possible	Coupar Angus Abbey (OCist)	Perth and Kinross	SAM 7237
NO15SE 33	'Drummie' ALTERNATIVE(S): Drimmie	Farming and Fishing	Coupar Angus Abbey (OCist)	Perth and Kinross	

NO64NE 32 NO 656 494	Grange House (Inverkeilor)			Angus	
NO24SW 51	Grange of Aberbothrie	Grange	Coupar Angus Abbey (OCist)	Angus	
NO35SW	Grange of Airlie		Coupar Angus Abbey (OCist)	Angus	
NO53SW NO 532 346	Grange of Barry		Balmerino Abbey (OCist)	Angus	
NO54SE NO 580 445 NO 581 440 NO 599 450/ NO 593 447	Grange of Conon, West Grange of Conon, East Grange of Conon		Arbroath Abbey (OTiron)	Angus	
NO 142 212	Grange of Elcho		Elcho Nunnery (OCist)	Perth and Kinross	
NO44NE NO 48 47	Grange of Lour			Angus	
NO23NW 40	Keithick ALTERNATIVE(S): Keithside	Grange	Coupar Angus Abbey (OCist)	Perth and Kinross	
NO 442 449	Grange of Kincreich	Grange	Coupar Angus Abbey	Angus	
NO64NW 91 NO 624 456	Letham Grange	Residential/Country House		Angus	
NO43SE 27	Monifieth Grange ALTERNATIVE(S): Castle of Grange	Residential	Barony of Grange	Angus	
NO24NW NO214 488 (West Tullyfergus) NO219 492 (East Tullyfergus) NO 218 481 (South Tullyfergus)	Tullyfergus	Grange	Coupar Angus (OCist)	Perth and Kinross	

TAYSIDE: ANGUS COUNCIL

Grange   Grange of Barry
Abbey   Balmerino
Order   Cistercian
Parish   Barry
Council   Angus

Location	North-west of Barry
NGR	NO 533 347
NMRS site	NO53SW 10
Site visits	26 September 2001

History
Campbell states that 'At Barry the monks had another Grange, from which their lands situated there, or the chief portion of them, would also be cultivated by the lay brothers and hired servants under a Master' (Campbell 1899, 206). On 29 November 1557 an action was raised in the Court of Session against the Abbot of Balmerino and his convent alleging that they wrongly claimed possession of 'twa part' of Grange of Barry (Campbell 1899, 249). Between 1573 and 1582 there is a reference to 'The two part of Grange of Barrie 10s. land of ye same 9 aikers of badihill … ' (Campbell 1899, 620).

Archaeology
There is a possible motte at Grange of Barry *c.*8-12m high measuring 13-14m in circumference at its top. There is no record of any archaeological work having taken place on this site.

Current State
There does not appear to be a farmhouse at Grange of Barry, although there is a row of inhabited cottages. The farmer at Balhungie now runs the farm at Barry. There is an extensive complex of modern buildings associated with a piggery and potatoes are also grown. There is what appears to be an artificial mound (motte) to the west of the modern cottages, otherwise there are no visible remains. None of the farm workers was aware of any historical connections with Barry Grange.

Grange	Grange of Conon
Abbey	Arbroath
Order	Tironensian
Parish	Arbroath and St Vigeans
Council	Angus
Location	Located at farm of same name
NGR	NO 582 446
NMRS site	NO54SE 1
Site visits	26 August 2001

History
The only references to this grange are in the *Register of the Great Seal* where it is listed as one of the possessions of Arbroath Abbey at the time of the dissolution of the abbey lands. In 1588-9 there is a reference to '*villas et terras de Auchmuthe et de Grange de Connan, cum decimus garbalibus de Grange inclusis*' (*RMS* V, 555). There is a further reference to *Grange de Connane* in 1608 (*RMS* VI, 754).

Archaeology
St Vigeans Chapel stands in the field to the east of the settlement at Grange of Conon and has been the subject of some antiquarian excavations in the late eighteenth-century (Miller 1860, 125). It seems likely that this chapel may have functioned as the chapel for the Grange of Conon. There are no other standing remains that may belong to the grange.

Current State
A modern farmhouse and large complex of farm out-buildings, with two associated groups of cottages currently represent the settlement at Grange of Conon. The remains of St Vigean's

chapel lie to the south of a duck-pond (this is shown as a 'well' on OS map, and may be a holy well?). Remains appear as overgrown mound, with thistles, some mature trees and stumps of felled trees. One tree is partially uprooted, possibly because of buried stonework close to surface. The farmer indicated he is not permitted to deep-plough in area of mound. The adjacent fields currently under cereal and potato crops.

Grange	Grange of Kincreich
Abbey	Coupar Angus
Order	Cistercian
Parish	Inverarity
Council	Angus
Location	Around settlements of Gateside, Inverarity and Kincreich
NGR	NO 442 449
NMRS site	No reference to grange
Site visits	20 August 2001

History
In 1198 x 1214 David Ruffus of Forfar grants the whole land of Kinefe to the monks of Coupar Angus (*Cupar Rental* I, 344). The first reference to the *Grange of Kyncreff* is in 1450 and there are numerous rental entries until 1562 (*Cupar Rental* I and II).

Archaeology
Former mill buildings are visible at Grange Mill (NO 447 447) and East Grange (NO 449 445). There are no standing remains visible at the current settlement of Kincreich (NO 435 445).

Current State
Grange Mill farm is still being farmed. The mill buildings are very dilapidated. At East Grange the mill has been demolished although its former site is still visible. A large mill weir constructed of massive stonework is visible in the wood opposite Grange Mill.

Grange	Grange of Lour
Abbey	Unknown
Order	Unknown
Parish	Inverarity
Council	Angus
Location	On the north side of the Vinny Water
NGR	NO 482 473
NMRS site	No entry
Site visits	20 August 2001

History
There are no definite references to a Grange of Lour. All references that exist refer to the barony of Lour and are to the Grange of Kyncreff (see previous entry).

Archaeology
There are no standing remains relating to this possible grange.

Current State
The building marked on the ordnance survey map at Grange of Lour has been demolished.

Grange	Letham Grange
Abbey	Arbroath Abbey

Order	Tironensian
Parish	Arbroath and St Vigeans
Council	Angus
Location	Site now occupied by country house and hotel called Letham Grange
NGR	NO 624 456
NMRS site	NO64NW 91
Site visits	26 August 2001

History

According to Warden, Letham Grange was formerly called Newgrange. The name was changed when the estate was bought by John Hay in 1822 (Warden 1885, 134). The lands and town of Newgrange are mentioned in an entry in the *Register of the Great Seal* for 1601 at the time of the dissolution of the abbey lands (*RMS* VI, 416). Ponts map of the late 1500s shows Newgrange as a separate settlement from Letham (Pont sheet 26).

Archaeology

The first edition Ordnance Survey map of 1856 shows what appears to be a moated enclosure due south of the house of Letham Grange. This feature appears to have been preserved in the modern landscape as a walled garden which contains a building. There are no other visible remains predating the nineteenth century.

Current State

The site is now occupied by a substantial mansion house built in 1884. The house is now run as a hotel and golf club.

Grange	Monifieth Grange
Abbey	Arbroath Abbey
Order	Cistercian
Parish	Monifieth
Council	City of Dundee
Location	North side of Monifieth to north of Airlie Drive
NGR	NO 489 329
NMRS site	NO43SE 27
Site visits	26 August 2001

History

King Robert I granted 'the whole land of Monyfeth which is called *Grange of Monyfeth* together with the mill therof' to Sir William de Dunolmia in May 1321 (*RRS* v, no 186). In 1322 the grange came into the possession of the Durham family who later erected a castellated mansion on the site.

Archaeology

The mansion, known as the 'Castle of Grange' was demolished in 1829 and the current house built in 1879. At the time of the construction of the nineteenth-century house workmen are said to have uncovered the foundations of the earlier building a little to the west.

Current State

The nineteenth-century mansion is now subdivided into rented flats. A club building at the rear is closed due to recent fire damage. To the rear of this building is a grassy mounded area that drops steeply to the west and east. Blocks of worked masonry lie on top of this mound. In the wooded area to the south of the mansion house are the remains of two massive stone gate pillars, reputed to date to 1650 and associated with the Marquis of Montrose. To the east of these pillars are the remains of rough, mortared stone work.

PERTH AND KINROSS COUNCIL

Grange	Arthurstone
Abbey	Coupar Angus
Order	Cistercian
Parish	Coupar Angus
Council	Perth and Kinross
NGR	NO 261 429
NMRS site	NO24SE 57
Site visits	N/A

History
Arthurstone was not a grange in its own right, but formed part of the grange of Balbrogie (see next entry).

Grange	Balbrogie
Abbey	Coupar Angus
Order	Cistercian
Parish	Coupar Angus
Council	Perth and Kinross
Location	Focused on and around Balbrogie farm on east side of River Isla
NGR	NO 239 424
NMRS site	NO24SW 54
Site visits	16 August 2001

History
The lands of Balbrogie were granted to Coupar Angus Abbey by King Malcolm IV between 1159 and 1165 (Barrow 1960, 281). There are detailed records of the leaseholders of Balbrogie in the *Cupar Rental book* from 1465 until 1542 (*Cupar Rental I*, 143-187; *Cupar Rental* II, 47-48, 187-188, 207 and 215-216).

Archaeology
A fragment of a sundial (bearing the numerals x, xiii) is incorporated into the fabric of a barn (2m above ground level, 27.8m from the east end of the north wall) at the centre of the steading complex at Balbrogie. In reuse at ground level at the west end of the south wall of the old steading (NO 2401 4255) there is a lintel, wrought with a mitred chamfer, which is possibly of seventeenth-century date. A group of poorly-defined, but possibly sub-oval cropmarkings has been recorded by aerial photography about 270m south-south-east of Balbrogie. Their character is uncertain. Aerial photography has recorded an arc of cropmark, possibly a segment of an enclosure ditch, in the corner of a field 400m south-east of Balbrogie steading (NO24SW 72).

Current State
There are no standing remains relating to this grange. The fields containing the cropmarks are currently under cultivation.

| *Grange* | Balgersho |
| *Abbey* | Coupar Angus |

Order	Cistercian
Parish	Coupar Angus
Council	Perth and Kinross
Location	Located due south of Coupar Angus at house of same name
NGR	NO 221 384
NMRS site	NO23NW 39
Site visits	N/A

History

This was not a grange but a ferm-toun belonging to Coupar Angus Abbey.

Grange	Balmyle
Abbey	Coupar Angus
Order	Cistercian
Parish	Kirkmichael
Council	Perth and Kinross
Location	Located in Strathardle to the north of Ballintuim
NGR	NO 100 555
NMRS site	NO15NW 21
Site visits	N/A

History

This was not a grange but a ferm-toun belonging to Coupar Angus Abbey.

Grange	Cambusmichael
Abbey	Scone
Order	Augustinian
Parish	St Martins
Council	Perth and Kinross
Location	In fields to the north-west of Cambusmichael farm and around Cambusmichael Church
NGR	NO 115 324
NMRS site	NO13SW 30
Site visits	16 August 2001

History

The lands of Cambusmichael were given to the abbey of Scone by King David I (1124-53). This grant was later confirmed by Malcolm IV (1163 x 1164) (Smythe 1843, 6). It is unclear if Scone Abbey ever possessed a grange or other administrative centre at Cambusmichael.

Archaeology

An area of c.1.5ha around Cambusmichael Church is enclosed by two widely spaced ditches which are only visible as cropmarks. The current occupants of the farm have discovered a silver short-cross penny of apparent twelfth-/thirteenth-century date on the farm (pers. comm. C. Smith).

Current State

The cropmarked field is under cultivation, Cambusmichael Church is overgrown with elder trees.

Grange	Campsie Linn
Abbey	Coupar Angus

Order	Cistercian
Parish	Cargill
Council	Perth and Kinross
Location	On a rocky promontory overlooking the River Tay
NGR	NO 1243 3394
NMRS site	NO13SW 10
Site visits	16 August 2001

History
The monks of Coupar Angus Abbey had a chapel and house at Campsie Linn. It has been claimed that this building was occupied by the abbey 'foresters' who supplied the abbey with timber and fuel by means of the 'Abbey Road' (NO13NE 24) through Strelitz Wood (Hunter 1883, 354). The Ordnance Survey investigator commented in 1969 that 'no well-defined road' is evident.

Archaeology
The *New Statistical Account* refers to the discovery of stones bearing the arms of the Hays of Errol, the principal benefactors of the monastery (NSA 1845). The site comprises the remains of five rectangular buildings ranged around a yard all reduced to their wall-footings. The two largest buildings probably represent the chapel dedicated to St Adamnan and the Abbots house.

Current State
The standing remains are heavily overgrown with deciduous trees and shrubs including invasive growth of rhododendron. The rerouting of the riverside access road has led to some damage of this site (2003).

Grange	Carsegrange
Abbey	Coupar Angus
Order	Cistercian
Parish	Errol
Council	Perth and Kinross
Location	In current settlement of Grange?
NGR	NO 27 25
NMRS site	NO22NE 18
Site visits	17 August 2001

History
In 1187 x 1195 William I confirmed the grant of the land of *Eddepolles* made by William de Haya to the monks of Coupar Angus Abbey (*RRS* ii, no 322). In 1225 or 1241 the monks of Coupar Angus Abbey are granted half a toft 'in the toun of Inchetore on the east side' for the causeway that the monks were making from Inchture to 'the grange of the monks in the territory of the Cars' (*Coupar charters*, I, no 37). In 1473/4 Dauid Gardnar is granted the tack of the 'orchardis of Kersgrange' (*Cupar Rental* I, 188-190). A notarial instrument of 1474 records an agreement between Coupar Angus Abbey and the Perth Charterhouse concerning the offerings of 'the Chapel of the Glorious Virgin Mary of Carsgrange' (*Coupar Charters* II, no 143).

Archaeology
There are no standing remains relating to this grange and no trace of a chapel.

Current State

The site of the orchards associated with this grange may still be visible. There are at least two areas of old and overgrown apple trees that may represent relict orchard. New houses are currently being built in the orchard adjacent to Carse Grange steading (pers. comm. C. Smith 2001).

Grange	Clene
Abbey	Scone
Order	Augustinian
Parish	Kinfauns
Council	Perth and Kinross
Location	Now occupied by Glencarse House (NO12SE 115)
NGR	NO 1955 2265
NMRS site	NO12SE 5
Site visits	11 August 2001

History

Glencarse House, an Adam style mansion house, (NO195 226) is probably located on the site of the former village of Clein (Clene). Clene is listed as a grange of Scone Abbey. The village may have been swept away when the current grand house was built (M. Stavert pers. comm.). 'Cleen' appears on Timothy Pont's map (Pont 26), as does 'Glendowak' (Glendoick), but not Glencarse. In the title deeds of the estate of Glendoick (to the north-east of Glencarse House), the estate is descibed as 'The Lands and Barony of Glencarse ... all and sundry the Lands and ancient barony of Clein and Mill Multures ... viz. – the lands and Mains of Clein ... crofts of Clein, all and whole the lands called *Abbotscroft of Clein*, together with the ruinous Mansion and Manor Place and the new Manor Place ... as also ... the lands called the Gardners lands, meadow park and wood of Clein, ground and place thereof woods and marsh of Clein and the bog of Clein and lands called the Hole of Clein ... the cornmill of Clein ....' (quoted in Melville (1939, 33-4) *The Fair Land of Gowrie*).

The manor and fortalice of Glendoick are on record in 1529, but it is not known whether the present house (built 1746-8) stands on the same site (RCAHMS, visited 1989). The lands and grange of Clene seems to have been located between the current grand houses of Glencarse and Glendoick.

Archaeology

There are no standing remains related to this grange.

Current State

The environs of the present Glencarse House was visited. There are modern farm buildings at Hole o' Clean, to the north-east of Glencarse House and north-west of Glendoick House. Adjoining fields are currently under cereal crop/stubble. A good contender for the location of the mill may be at Pepperknowes Farm, to the south-west of Glencarse House, where there are remains of recent stone-built mill buildings and a mill race associated with the Pow of Glencarse. In the cleft of Glencarse Hill, to the north of the grand houses, and at Hole o' Clean, are a series of waterfalls which could also have been used to power mills.

Grange	Coupar Grange
Abbey	Coupar Angus
Order	Cistercian
Parish	Bendochy
Council	Perth and Kinross
Location	Around Coupar Grange farm

NGR	NO 225 431
NMRS site	NO24SW 74
Site visits	16 August 2001

History
Malcolm IV granted this grange to Coupar Angus Abbey in 1159 x 1165 'with the church located within the grange' (Barrow 1960, 281).

Archaeology
An extensive series of cropmarks have been photographed in the fields surrounding Coupar Grange farm. The principal element is a large ditched enclosure which surround several rectangular features and numerous pits. This group of cropmarks is a Scheduled Monument (SAM no 7327). A steading at Easter Bendochy *c.*1km to the south of Coupar Grange contains worked stones which may have originated from the grange (NO24SW 67) although it may be more likely that they originate from Bendochy Church (see below). The current occupier of the Model Cottages, Coupar Grange has recovered a worked stone 'font' or 'bowl' from his garden and a fragment of worked, red sandstone from the cropmarked field (information August 2001, C. Smith).

Current State
The cropmarked fields are under cultivation. There are no visible standing remains.

Grange	Denhead
Abbey	Coupar Angus
Order	Cistercian
Parish	Coupar Angus
Council	Perth and Kinross
Location	North-east side of Coupar Angus settlements of Easter and Wester Denhead
NGR	NO 23 41
NMRS site	NO24SW 53
Site visits	N/A

History
Although Coupar Angus Abbey held lands at Denhead in the sixteenth century there is no evidence that there was ever a grange here.

Grange	Drummie or Drimmie
Abbey	Coupar Angus
Order	Cistercian
Parish	Blairgowrie
Council	Perth and Kinross
Location	Numerous settlements incorporating Drimmie name to north of River Ericht
NGR	NO 17 50
NMRS site	NO15SE 33
Site visits	21 August 2001

History
There are references to the settlement of Wester Drymie and its mill and mill lands in the Cupar Rental in 1557 (*Cupar Rental* II, 55). Land at Easter and Middle Drimmie is also referred to (*Cupar Rental* II, 129).

Archaeology
There are the ruins of a derelict mill complex at Old Milton of Drimmie, although the only datable material visible was roof slate and nineteenth-century ceramics (C. Smith 2001). No standing remains are visible at Easter, Wester or Middle Drimmie.

Current State
Site of Middle Drimmie now occupied by modern farmhouse. The site of Wester Drimmie may now be occupied by either Rannagulzion or Glenericht House. The buildings at Easter Drimmie are no longer part of a working farm.

Grange	Grange of Aberbothrie
Abbey	Coupar Angus
Order	Cistercian
Parish	Bendochy
Council	Perth and Kinross
Location	Farm of same name due north of junction of Rivers Isla and richt
NGR	NO 236 444
NMRS site	NO24SW 51
Site visits	17 August 2001

History
The lands of Aberbothrie were granted to the abbey of Coupar Angus by William I between 1166 and 1170. There are references to the tacks of this grange between 1443 and 1473, the mill of Abyrbothry in 1448 and two rentals of 1542 (*Cupar Rentals* I, 126-29, 134-135,141-142, 173-174; *Cupar Rentals* II, 190 and 218). The *Graingie de Abirbothre* is referred to in 1572 in the *Register of the Great Seal* (Thomson 1886, 537).

Archaeology
The cropmark of what is probably a circular enclosure (about 25m in diameter over all) has been recorded about 140m north-west of Grange of Aberbothrie farmsteading (NO24SW 42). There are no standing remains related to the grange.

Current State
The current farmer, Mr George Fleming, is very knowledgeable regarding the farm's association with Coupar Angus Abbey. The farm lies in an area which is very flat and low-lying and originally very marshy. A series of levees on the farm are reputedly associated with the monks of Coupar Angus although the more modern ones were built by the farmer's grandfather. The farmer is currently draining the fields (August 2001).

Grange	Grange of Airlie
Abbey	Coupar Angus
Order	Cistercian
Parish	Airlie
Council	Perth and Kinross
Location	Farm of same name
NGR	NO 3150 5110
NMRS site	no entry for Grange
Site visits	not visited

History
In 1212 the *abthane* of Erolyn was let to the Abbey of Coupar Angus by William de Malvoisine, Bishop of St Andrews (*Coupar Charters* I, no 21). Leaseholds of the Grange of Eroly are

mentioned in the *Coupar Rentals* from 1464-1484 and 1542, 1550 and 1560 (*Coupar Rental* I, 144, 152, 168-169, 229-230; *Coupar Rental* II, 201, 220, 242 and 273).

Archaeology
There are no standing remains associated with this grange. The former site of the medieval church of St Medan is now occupied by the eighteenth-century parish church and graveyard (NO35SW 29). St Madden's well was formerly located due north-east of Grange of Airlie (NO35SW 27). There is a reference to the discovery of at least two cists close to the site of the well in 1862 (NO35SW 28).

Grange	Grange of Elcho
Abbey	Elcho Nunnery
Order	Cistercian
Parish	Rhynd
Council	Perth and Kinross
Location	Farm of same name on south side of River Tay
NGR	NO 1414 2176
NMRS site	No12SW 25 (site of nunnery)

History
The Cistercian nunnery of Elcho was founded by David Lindsay of Glenesk before 1241 (Cowan and Easson 1976, 146).

Archaeology
The site of the nunnery church was excavated by the Perthshire Society of Natural Science in the late 1960s and early 70s (Reid *et al.* 1988).

Current State
Grange of Elcho farm is an active farm. The former Tay Salmon Smokers Factory due north of the nunnery is no longer operational.

Grange	Tullyfergus
Abbey	Coupar Angus
Order	Cistercian
Parish	Alyth
Council	Perth and Kinross
Location	Area around modern farms of East, West and South Tullyfergus
NGR	NO 214 488 (West Tullyfergus) NO 219 492 (East Tullyfergus) NO 218 481 (South Tullyfergus)
NMRS site	No entry
Site visits	17 August 2001

History
The lands of Tulifergus, Twlifergus or Tulyfergus are mentioned in the *Cupar Rentals* from 1442 until 1542 (*Cupar Rental* I and II).

Archaeology
There are no standing remains relating to this grange.

Current State
West Tullyfergus is no longer farmed and the farmhouse is now in private ownership. The land is now owned and planted by the Forestry Commission. East Tullyfergus is still an operational

farm. The farmer claims that a pool in the Den of Alyth, to the east of the farm, is part of a former mill lade although another informant referred to this feature as the 'swimming pool'.

Grange	Keithick
Abbey	Coupar Angus
Order	Cistercian
Parish	Coupar Angus
Council	Perth and Kinross
Location	Unlocated but maybe in vicinity of Mains of Keithick or Mills of Keithick
NGR	NO 203 385
NMRS site	NO23NW 40
Site visits	21 August 2001

History
Keithside, an alternative name for Keithick, is listed as a grange of Coupar Abbey and the lands were granted to the abbey by William I between 1171 and 1178.

Archaeology
The National Monuments Record lists two sets of cropmarks in this area:

NO23NW 10 2073 3868.
(NO 207 387) Cropmarks – Keithick Mains near Coupar Angus.

The site of the circular feature (26.0m diameter) on St Joseph AP is at NO 2073 3868, on the rounded summit of gently sloping ground, newly ploughed. The only ground evidence is slight traces of its surrounding ditch – on the north-east and south-west sides only. Nothing was seen on the ground to correspond with the other cropmarks except for a slight ditch in the area of NO 2078 3869. Enquiries at Mains of Keithick proved negative. Surveyed from St Joseph AP WA 42 and ground control.

NO23NW 56 2019 3812.
Aerial reconnaissance has revealed the presence of a rectilinear ditched enclosure on a level site overlooking the Coupar Burn, about 130m south-west of Mills of Keithick. The south-western and south-eastern sides are visible as cropmarks, while on the north-west and north-east the ground falls steeply, giving an estimated maximum size for the enclosure of about 60m square.

Information from RCAHMS (JRS) 10 December 1992. There are no standing remains relating to this grange.

Current State
The area around Mains of Keithick and Mills of Kethick is now intensively cultivated. The sluice indicated on the Ordnance Survey map at NO 204 382 is now filled in and according to the current tenants the area occupied by the rectilinear cropmark described above has been quarried away and subsequently filled in by Perth and Kinross Council.

FIFE GRANGES (36)

M. Roy

NMRS NO	NMRS NAME	TYPE OF SITE	MONASTERY	SAM/LISTED
NO 3580 2465 NO32SE 2	Balmerino Abbey grange	Grange	Balmerino Abbey (OCist)	SAM 3232
NO41NE NO 484 150	Balone		St Andrews Priory (OSA)	
NT 168 861 (Chapel) NT 177 859 (Bouprie Banks) NT 183 855 (Nether Bouprie) No NMR	Bouprie	Grange and chapel	Inchcolm Abbey	
NS99SE NS 979 903	Brankstone Grange			
	Byregrange		Culross Abbey (OCist)	
NO41SE NO 413 128	Drumcarro		St Andrews Priory (OSA)	
NT18NW NT1030 8770	East Barns called Grange		Dunfermline Abbey (OSB)	
	East Grange (Burntisland)		Dunfermline Abbey (OSB)	
NT08NW NT 001 889	East Grange (Culross)		Culross Abbey (OCist)	
NO50SE NO 546 040	Easter Grangemuir		Pittenweem Priory (OSA)	
NO32SE 11	Grange (Balmerino) includes New Grange	Grange	Balmerino Abbey (OCist)	
NO40SE 19	Grange (Elie)	Grange	North Berwick Nunnery (OCist)	
NT28NE 41 NT 270 885	Grange (Kinghorn)	Deserted Medieval Village (Possible)	Barony of Kinghorn	

NT28NW 284 NT 224 867	Grange Farm (Burntisland)	Village		
NO51SW 48	Grange Farm (St Andrews)	Farming and Fishing	St Andrews Priory (OSA)	
NT28NW 148 NT 225 865	Grange House (Burntisland)			
NO50SW	Grange of Abercrombie		Culross Abbey (OCist)	
NO21SW	Grange of Auchtermuchty			
NT18SE	Grange of Barnhill		Inchcolm Abbey (OSA)	
NT08SE NT 08 84	Grange of Gellat [?= Hills called Nether Grange]		Dunfermline Abbey (OSB)	
NO21NE 65	Grange of Lindores	Grange; Village; farmsteading	Lindores Abbey (OTiron)	
NO21NE16	Grange of Lindores	Grange	Lindores Abbey (OTiron)	
NT28NE NT 259 866	Grangehill (Kinghorn)		Dunfermline Abbey (OSB)	
	Grangemyre (Aberdour)		Inchcolm Abbey (OSA)	
	Hills called Nether Grange [?= Grange of Gellat]		Dunfermline Abbey (OSB)	
NO32SE	Kilmany Grange			
NS 989 892	Middle Grange (Culross)		Culross Abbey (OCist)	
NO 436 264 NO 426 259	Naughton [Easter Friarton ? Wester Friarton ?]		St Andrews Priory (OSA)	
NT28NW 241 NT 242 866	Nether Grange of Kinghorn Wester (Burntisland)		Dunfermline Abbey (OSB)	
NO	New Grange Farm (St Andrews)			
NO40NW NO 441 452 NO40SW NO 445 048	Newburn	Wester Newburn Easter Newburn	Dunfermline Abbey (OSB)	
NT28NW	Over Grange of Kinghorn Wester		Dunfermline Abbey (OSB)	

NO41NE NO 471 158 NO 476 161	Strathkinness		St Andrews Priory (OSA)	
NO40SW NO 424 033	The Grange (Upper Largo)			
	Under or Wood Grange [=Nether Grange?]		Dunfermline Abbey (OSB)	
NS98NE NS 984 895	West Grange		Culross Abbey (OCist)	
NO50SE NO 537 041	Wester Grangemuir		Pittenweem Priory (OSA)	

FIFE COUNCIL

Grange	Balmerino Abbey
Abbey	Balmerino
Order	Cistercian
Parish	Balmerino
Council	Fife
Location	South bank of River Tay
NGR	NO 3580 2465
NMRS site	NO32SE 2

History

Campbell claims that a grange existed at Balmerino on the north side of the abbey cloister garth (Campbell 1899, 205).

Archaeology

The Cistercian abbey of Balmerino dates from c.1229 and, like its mother-house of Melrose, had its claustral ranges to the north of the church. In the mid-nineteenth century a farm steading was erected on the north side of the abbey, probably over some of its demolished buildings and incorporating at least one of the monastic buildings. It is the intention to convert the farm buildings into residential units. As the first stage of that development, service trenches for water and sewage pipes were machine excavated around the perimeter of the steading, the excavations being carried out under the supervision of Scotia Archaeology Ltd. A large number of structures and features of probable medieval date were uncovered, the most significant of which are described here.

At the south end of the farm buildings were several walls of probable monastic origin. Two were aligned with the east and west walls of the monastic east range and also with those of a farm building further north. What appeared to be a corner of a substantial structure – perhaps the north claustral range or a building associated with it – lay to the west of these excavated walls. Further east, a stretch of the great drain was uncovered, running slightly east of north from the east range of the abbey. Only the top of the drain (large, roughly-worked sandstone flags) was uncovered although it was possible to measure its internal width as about 0.65m; its height was estimated at 1m. Another, smaller drain led into the great drain from a building beyond the east range of the abbey. One wall of this building was exposed in the extreme south-eastern corner of the site.

At the north end of the farm was a well-constructed cobbled road, thought to be monastic and probably linking the abbey with a jetty on the shore of the Tay estuary some 200m to the north. The road had pronounced cambers and was 9m wide, more than sufficient to accommodate two-way traffic (Lewis 1996).

Current State
Balmerino Abbey is a Scheduled Monument (SAM no 827) and therefore enjoys the level of protection that this designation affords.

Grange	Balone
Abbey	St Andrews Priory
Order	Augustinian
Parish	St Andrews and St Leonards
Council	Fife
Location	Fairly flat arable farmland, west of St Andrews and south of a B road
NGR	NO 484 150
NMRS site	No entry
Site visits	15 August 2001

History
The earliest reference to this grange is in 1187 when Pope Gregory VIII confirms *Grange of Ballothen* as one of the possessions of St Andrews Priory (*St Andrews Liber*, 64). References to it continue until 1248 (*St Andrews Liber*, 104).

Archaeology
No monastic remains are visible.

Current State
The former farm consists of eighteenth- or nineteenth-century farm buildings constructed of sandstone blocks bonded with lime mortar. These buildings have been renovated and turned into private housing. The original farmhouse is a sandstone and ashlar building. The surrounding farmland is owned by Melville Estates and is under cereal cultivation. No signs of pre-improvement remains were found.

Grange	Bowprie
Abbey	Inchcolm Abbey
Order	Augustinian
Parish	Dalgety
Council	Fife
Location	Rolling countryside west of Aberdour
NGR	Bouprie Banks NT 176 859; Nether Bouprie NT 182 853
NMRS site	No entry
Site visits	14 September 2001 (Bouprie Farm and Chapel Farm, only quick visit as owner not present)

History
There are references to the *Grangie de Beupre* in 1320, there is also a reference to a chapel associated with the grange (Easson and MacDonald 1938, 31). Fasti notes that a chapel, dedicated to St Martin and belonging to Inchcolm Abbey, was situated near Bouprie (Bouprie Banks: NT 176 858). The Ordnance Survey *Name Book* (ONB) compiler, who could not find any remains or obtain any further information, was informed that a chapel had stood in the vicinity of Chapel Farm (NT 168 859) (*Name Book* 1854; H. Scott (Fasti Eccles) 1950).

Archaeology
There are no standing remains related to this grange.

Current State
Nether Bouprie (now called Bouprie Farm) consists of a mixture of buildings. There are several probable eighteenth- or nineteenth-century rubble-built farm buildings, some of which are now occupied as a farmhouse. There are also modern (twentieth century) brick and concrete structures. The surrounding land is presently under pasture. The owner of both Nether Bouprie and Chapel Farm is Mr Stephen Kerr.

Bouprie Banks (now called Banks Farm) consists of many rubble-built sandstone farm buildings of eighteenth or nineteenth-century date. These have pantile, and occasionally corrugated-iron, roofing. The main farmhouse is apparently plastered and whitewashed, and has a slate roof. To the west of the farm are several modern barns of brick and corrugated metal. To the east of the farm stands an apparently modern (twentieth century), whitewashed, probable stone-built house. Surrounding the farm buildings are fields under cereal cultivation.

At Chapel Farm there is a mixture of buildings, with some eighteenth- or nineteenth-century rubble-built stone structures, commonly with brick or concrete renovation. There are also modern buildings wholly constructed of brick and concrete. The roofing on the older buildings is generally pantile, but there is also corrugated-iron roofing. The farmland to west and north, and also partly to the south, is under pasture. Elsewhere, to south and east, there are hilly, wooded areas.

Grange	Brankstone Grange
Abbey	?
Order	?
Parish	Culross
Council	Fife
Location	This house stands on a fairly steep sided hill, with ground sloping down steeply to north and south, beyond the house and gardens lies pasture. Woodland generally surrounds area. Brankstone lies north of the A907
NGR	NS 979 903
NMRS site	NS99SE 12 (farmsteads now removed); NS99SE 8.00, 8.01, 8.02 (Brankstone Grange, lodge and walled garden)
Site visits	30 August 2001

History
There is no surviving documentary evidence that suggests that the Grange element of this place name relates to its previous monastic function.

Archaeology
A Scottish baronial house called Brankstone Grange, or Haldane House lies on the site of two former farmsteads, visible on the first edition of the OS 6in map (Clackmannanshire 1866, sheet cxl). No monastic remains were visible.

Current State
A Scottish baronial style house stands on top of a fairly steep hill, on the site of the former farmsteads at Brankstone Grange. A date of 1867 was visible on a heraldic shield near the entrance on the north face of the building, a likely date for the erection of the house. A date of 1908 on guttering may relate to later additions or renovations. The house is built of sandstone and ashlar, with a slate roof. There are various nearby outbuildings of brick, with slate roofing. A lodge lies to the south-east, at the base of the hill, at the entrance to the estate. This is again a sandstone

building. To the south of the house, on sloping ground, lies a walled garden, constructed of rubble-build. The relatively poor state of the walls point to an early date for this structure, and it may be a relic of the former farm buildings. Beyond the house and its gardens lies pasture, both to north and west. There was no sign of any remains relating to monastic occupation.

Grange	Byregrange
Abbey	Culross Abbey
Order	Cistercian
Parish	Unknown, though possibly Culross
Council	Fife
Location	Not located

Grange	Drumcarro
Abbey	St Andrews Priory
Order	Augustinian
Parish	Cameron
Council	Fife
Location	Farm lies on hilly land, which rises gently from south to north, to the west of a B road and south of Drumcarrow Craig. The farmhouse lies on a slight hillock
NGR	NO 413 128
NMRS site	NO41SE 28.00
Site visits	15 August 2001

History
The *Grange of Drumcarin* is mentioned in a confirmation of Pope Gregory VIII dated to December 1187 (*St Andrews Liber*, 64). References to this grange continue until July 1248 (*St Andrews Liber*, 104).

Archaeology
No monastic remains were visible, though a well was visible to the north against the wall of a farm building. Drumcarrow Craig, to the immediate north-east of the farm, is the site of an unenclosed settlement of hut circles (NMRS No. NO41SE 2) and the remains of a broch (NMRS No. NO41SE 4).

Current State
The farm buildings are probably of eighteenth- or nineteenth-century date, and are generally of rubble-build. According to the owner several infilled arches visible in the wall of one farm building related to vaulted cellars running into raised ground to the east. An open well was visible to the north of the farm; another well was supposedly present to the south of the farm, near the farmhouse, though this has been infilled. The farmhouse is a sandstone building of apparently seventeenth- or eighteenth-century date. Rape and cereal are being cultivated, and some land is under pasture.

Grange	East Barns called Grange
Abbey	Dunfermline Abbey
Order	Benedictine
Parish	Dunfermline
Council	Fife
Location	Eastern outskirts of Dunfermline in the angle of Halbeath Road and Garvock Hill

NGR	NT 102 877
NMR	No entry

History
Henderson refers to this site in a 1567 resignation of abbey lands which details 'the seventh part of *Grange* or East Barns' and says that the Barns alluded to is probably the same as 'Low's Barns', half a mile east of Dunfermline (Henderson 1879, 214).

Archaeology
Low's Barns is marked as a sizeable building on the Ordnance Survey map of 1856. There have been no recorded excavations or stray finds on this site.

Current State
This site is now part of a substantial post-war housing estate.

Grange	East Grange (Burntisland)
Abbey	Dunfermline Abbey
Order	Benedictine
Parish	Probably Burntisland
Council	Fife
Location	Not located

Grange	East Grange
Abbey	Culross
Order	Cistercian
Parish	Culross
Council	Fife
Location	Farm lying both east and west of the B 9037. Hummocky ground slopes down slightly from north to south
NGR	NT 001 889
NMRS site	No entry
Site visits	30 August 2001, owner absent so quick survey only

History
There is a single sixteenth-century reference to *the lands of Eist Graing* in 1557 x 1585 (*Reg Dunfermelyn*, 489).

Archaeology
No monastic remains visible. A dovecot of probable eighteenth-century date (NMRS No. NT08NW 20) stands on the east side of the farm.

Current State
Eighteenth- or nineteenth-century rubble-built farm buildings stand on both sides of the road. There are also some twentieth-century brick and concrete buildings. To the east stands a harled farmhouse of probable sandstone construction, near a rubble-built dovecot. The farm consists of open pastures and fields with cereal cultivation.

Grange	Easter Grangemuir
Abbey	Pittenweem Priory
Order	Augustinian
Parish	Anstruther Wester

Council	Fife
Location	Lies to east of B road leading north from Pittenweem. Also to the east of Grangemuir House and Wester Grangemuir. Area consists of fairly flat farmland near the south coast of Fife
NGR	NO 546 040
NMRS site	No entry
Site visits	27 August 2001

History

A reference in the *Register of the Great Seal* dating to 1526 records the granting of the lands of Pittenweem Priory including *Grange-mure* (*RMS* iii, no 388).

Archaeology

No monastic remains visible.

Current State

Working farm consisting of a mixture of rubble-built and brick-built constructions. There is a rubble-built farmhouse of eighteenth- or nineteenth-century date to the south-east of the farm. One of the farm buildings has a north-south wall, which is of a coarse rubble-build with boulders of around 0.5m in size, bonded with coarse red-white lime mortar. The roughness of the build suggests that it may be a relatively early structure (sixteenth or seventeenth century). The farm is under cereal cultivation.

Grange	New Grange (Balmerino)
Abbey	Balmerino Abbey
Order	Cistercian
Parish	Balmerino
Council	Fife
Location	Farm stands on a riverbank to the north of a small waterway. Ground rises fairly gently from east to west
NGR	NO 360 228
NMRS site	NO32SE 11
Site visits	15 August 2001

History

The lands of this grange were divided into two estates after the Reformation, the west half was named New Grange and in a charter of 1572 mention is made of a principal 'house' or 'hall'. Campbell believed that this structure was built as the residence of the master of the grange and it continued in use as the mansion house of the Balfours until at least 1686 (Campbell 1899, 568-9).

Archaeology

Campbell also refers to an old granary which was demolished in 1859 which he suggests may have been part of the grange. This structure may be the long roofless building shown on the 6in map of 1855-6 (Campbell 1899, 568-9).

Current State

Property owned by Mr and Mrs Fox-Pitt. Many eighteenth or nineteenth-century rubble-built farm buildings are present; several of which are in a dilapidated state. One long building has required buttressing to remain upright. Farmhouse is sandstone with some ashlar decoration. Area around farm buildings is largely overgrown. Cereal cultivation is common in the area.

Grange	Grange (Elie)
Abbey	North Berwick Nunnery
Order	Cistercian
Parish	Elie
Council	Fife
Location	Site lies on ground sloping fairly sharply down from north to south. To the north and east the ground also slopes down, but less steeply. The site lies north-west of Elie
NGR	NO 4776 0017
NMRS site	NO40SE 19
Site visits	16 August 2001

History
It is claimed that the common pasture or links of Kincraig was granted to the convent of North Berwick in the late twelfth or early thirteenth century (Sibbald 1803). The same reference then states that the nuns built a grange or farmhouse which was burnt down (Ibid).

Archaeology
No monastic remains were visible, but to the west of the area lie the ruins of the eighteenth-century laird's house (NO40SE 19.01), which was formerly a farmhouse. It seems likely that is the same building that Sibbald is referring to.

Current State
There are various private residences occupying the site of the former grange, the oldest of which is a sandstone Georgian house. To the west stand the sandstone walls of a large farmhouse, of eighteenth-century date. This is in a dangerous condition and access has been blocked off. It was a three-storeyed structure. To the south lies well-kept pasture and housing, with a golf course at the bottom of the slope to the south. Cereals are being cultivated to north and east. To the west lies further pasture and open, hilly land.

Grange	Grange (Kinghorn)
Abbey	Dunfermline
Order	Benedictine
Parish	Kinghorn
Council	Fife
Location	Site lies on hummocky farmland to the west of the A 921 between Kinghorn and Kirkcaldy
NGR	NT 270 885
NMRS site	NT28NE 41
Site visits	28 August 2001

History
An entry of 1541 in the *Register of the Great Seal* confirms *the lands of Grange with tower, fortalice, manor, yards, orchards, dovecots, tofts, crofts and cotlands* to James Kirkaldy of Grange (*RMS*, iii no 2272).

Archaeology
There was formerly a hamlet of thatched cottages on the site, which had disappeared by 1849 (NMRS No. NT28NE 41). A vague cropmark is visible on top of a hill 500m south of Grange. This cropmark (NMRS No. NT28NE 9) represents an oval enclosure, much reduced by cultivation. The NMRS record states that it consists of a ditch roughly 2.5m wide and 0.2m deep, enclosing an area of 27m north–south by 20m east–west. There is a vague mound in the

southern part of the enclosure. There was no sign of these remains, due to cultivation of cereal crops. Monastic remains were not encountered. The owner of the farm mentioned a possible old chapel on the farm of Tyrie to the north. This is probably the 'Eglise Marie' (NMRS No. NT28NE 3), a gable end of which formerly stood around NT 2664 8904. When visited by the OS in 1959 no sign of this structure remained.

Current State
There are two main areas of building on this farm: Grange to the north, and Grange Cottages to the south. The cottages, probably formerly occupied by labourers, were rubble-built eighteenth or nineteenth-century constructions with some harled new build. Some have been renovated and are occupied as private residences, while others are in a more dilapidated state and are used for farm storage. The farmhouse is a probable nineteenth-century sandstone structure, partially built in Scottish baronial style, and partially harled. The surrounding farm buildings are of rubble-build, with corrugated-iron roofing and much brick repair and infilling. There are also buildings wholly constructed of brick. Both Grange and Grange Cottages lie on rising ground. There are two wooded natural mounds nearby, and the surrounding farmland is under pasture and cereal cultivation. There was no sign of earthworks or other remains of a former village.

Grange	Grange Farm (Burntisland)
Abbey	Unknown
Order	Unknown
Parish	Burntisland
Council	Fife
Location	The farm lies on sloping ground that rises from south to north. It lies on the A 909 on the north side of Burntisland. There is a little pasture to the south and woodland to the north but the area is largely built over. Grange House lies to the south, and according to the owner a farm called Grangemuir lies to the east. He also stated that the area of town to the south was also referred to as 'the Grange'
NGR	NT 224 867
NMRS site	NT 28 NW 2884
Site visits	29 August 2001

History
There is no surviving documentary evidence to confirm that this place name relates to its previous monastic function.

Archaeology
Supposedly a small village used to stand on the site presently occupied by the farm (NMRS No. NT28NW284), visible on the first edition OS 6in map (Fife and Kinross 1856, sheet 36). This 'village' may merely represent the farm buildings and associated enclosures. No monastic remains were visible.

Current State
The farm consists of generally rubble-built eighteenth or nineteenth-century farm buildings. Several have been renovated with brick or concrete, and there are also wholly brick buildings. There is pasture to the south, and woodland on the rising ground to the north. An overgrown field to the west is normally cultivated. An electricity sub-station also lies to the west.

Grange	Grange Farm (St Andrews)
Abbey	St Andrews Priory

Order	Augustinian
Parish	St Andrews and St Leonards
Council	Fife
Location	Site lies around 600m south of St Andrews and consists of fairly flat farmland
NGR	NO 515 148
NMRS site	NO51SW 48
Site visits	16 August 2001

History
On the 19 June 1248 Pope Innocent IV confirms the possessions of St Andrews Priory including *the grange which is called new* with all its pertinents (*St Andrews Liber*, 104). The *Register of the Great Seal* refers to St Andrews Cathedral Priory being in possession of *Grange* near St Andrews (*RMS*, v, no 2273).

Archaeology
A possible enclosure (NMRS No. NO51SW 37) visible as a cropmark at Grange Farm was evaluated in November 1999 prior to development of the area. This work did not find evidence relating to the supposed link between Grange Farm and the development of the ecclesiastical burgh of St Andrews. No prehistoric remains were encountered. No monastic remains were visible on visiting the site.

Current State
The site consists of a number of eighteenth- or nineteenth-century sandstone farm buildings, now converted into private housing, surrounded by an area of cereal cultivation. There are various modern buildings, of a recent housing development, especially to the south of the farm. There was no sign of monastic or other medieval remains.

Grange	Grange House (Burntisland)
Abbey	Unknown
Order	Unknown
Parish	Burntisland
Council	Fife
Location	Farmland to north of Burntisland. Ground slopes down fairly steeply from north to south. Grange Farm lies to the north
NGR	NT 225 865
NMRS site	NT28NW 148
Site visits	29 August 2001 (access denied by proprietor)

History
There is no surviving documentary evidence to prove that this place name has a monastic origin.

Archaeology
No monastic remains visible

Current State
Farm consists of eighteenth- or nineteenth-century harled buildings. Some rubble-build was visible. Pasture land lay on the rising ground to the north, while modern housing stood to the south.

Grange	Grange of Abercrombie
Abbey	Culross Abbey?

Order	Cistercian
Parish	St Monance
Council	Fife
Location	Farmland to north of St Monance
NGR	NO 518 029
NMRS site	NO50SW 1 (Abercrombie Church)
Site visits	16 August 2001

History
Grange of Abercrombie is listed as belonging to Culross Abbey in the *Register of the Great Seal*. This may be related to the chapel of Abercrombie, which was granted to Dunfermline Abbey by Malcolm IV in 1157 x 1160 (Barrow 1960, 209).

Archaeology
To the north-east of Abercrombie Farm stands the roofless stone Abercrombie Church, which is a scheduled monument (SAM no 818). There are several weathered, probably medieval sculptured stones in the walls of the church, which is now used as a family vault. The long walls of the church are oriented north-east to south-west, and the south-eastern wall has been restored, incorporating medieval stones. According to a stone plaque this restoration work was carried out in 1819 by Sir Robert Abercromby Bart of Birkenbog. No other remains related to the grange were encountered. The cropmark remains of a possible prehistoric mortuary enclosure (NMRS No. NO50SW 92) and various other possible prehistoric remains are located at No 524 029, to the east of the farm.

Current State
The farm consists of eighteenth- or nineteenth-century sandstone rubble-built buildings, some of which appear dilapidated, with missing pantiles. Bricks infill various openings. The surrounding land is under cereal cultivation, while to the south lies a small hamlet of nineteenth- or twentieth-century houses. To the north there was some potato cultivation. The remains of Abercrombie Church (described above) stand in a burial ground to the north-east.

Grange	Grange of Auchtermuchty
Abbey	Unknown
Order	Unknown
Parish	Auchtermuchty
Council	Fife
Location	Not located

History
There is a single entry in the *Register of the Great Seal* to 'the free tenandry of Grange of Auchtermuchtie' dated the 16 January 1623 (*RMS* viii, no 406).

Recommendations
Further documentary research is required to locate the site of this grange.

Grange	Grange of Barnhill
Abbey	Inchcolm Abbey
Order	Augustinian
Parish	Dalgety
Council	Fife

Location	Somewhere in the vicinity of Barnhill Bay?
NGR	NT 180 830 to NT 180 840
NMRS site	NT18SE 1 (Monk's Cave)
Site visits	No visit

History

There is a reference to the *grange of the Bernhill* in a charter dated 1 August 1559 (Easson and MacDonald 1938, 99). This document identifies Alexander Bell and Thomas Lovry as the occupiers of the land of the grange and also refers to the *stedingis of the grange*.

Archaeology

The Monk's Cave (NT18SE 1), on Charles Hill, is entirely artificial and is really the lower storey of a building, probably a ferry-house and warehouse connected with Inchcolm Abbey (NT18SE 7). The building stands on the edge of a low cliff which has been partly excavated; the doorway, of fifteenth-century date, opens into a vaulted cellar. The upper storey has been reduced to the level of the upper surface of the vault supporting it. (RCAHMS 1933).

Current State

This Grange site is not accurately located.

Grange	Grange of Gellet (East Barns? Hills?)
Abbey	Dunfermline Abbey
Order	Benedictine
Parish	Dunfermline
Council	Fife
Location	Farmland south of Dunfermline and east of the B 9156
NGR	NT 09 85
NMRS site	No entry
Site visits	29 August 2001 (access denied)

History

On the 24 October 1363 David II granted to Dunfermline Abbey the right to a port at *grange of Gellald* or at Westir Rossith with the consent of the lords of the same, for all goods and merchandise, both wool, hides and skins, and for the carriage, transport, export and delivery by their merchants to the said port; Saving the king's great custom from wool, hides and skins and other merchandise outside the bounds of the burghs of the monks and their regality (*RRS*, vi, no 311; *Reg Dunfermelyn*, no 391).

Archaeology

No monastic remains visible

Current State

The site consists of open, undulating farmland. The two farms of Easter Gellet and Wester Gellet lie on Lord Elgin's estate. Wester Gellet farm was not seen, but the surrounding farmland was under cereal cultivation. Easter Gellet farm contained a mixture of buildings including some dilapidated eighteenth- or nineteenth-century stone structures and some apparently concrete modern buildings. This was also under arable cultivation.

Grange	Grange of Lindores
Abbey	Lindores Abbey
Order	Tironensian
Parish	Abdie

Council	Fife
Location	Grange of Lindores is a village lying to the south-east of Newburgh and west of Lindores Loch
NGR	NO 254 165
NMRS site	NO21NE 16 and 65
Site visits	15 August 2001

History

In 1190 x 1195 King David I confirmed the possessions of Lindores Abbey including the church of *Lundors* with all its just pertinents and the land pertaining to the foresaid church (Abdie) by its right marches, in wood and plain, and the whole land on the west side of the burn descending from the big loch as far as the Tay, except the island called Redinche, and the mill of Lundors, namely the mill of that toun of Lundors, with all its suit and multure, provided that the earl's men shall doe all things pertaining to the mill as they were accustomed to do in the time when the earl held it in his own hand; and if the earl's mill cannot grind he shall cause his corn to be ground at the monks' mill without multure, and if the monks' mill cannot grind, they shall grind at the earl's mill their own corn, likewise without multure (*RRS*, ii, no 363). The grange is recorded in a rental of the abbey lands of *c.*1480 and again in a charter of feuferme of the abbey possessions by King James VI (Laing 1876). Laing records and illustrates a number of straw-thatched cottages with straw-bound chimneys around the farm steading which he considered offered 'to some degree the appearance of a grange of the olden times' (Laing 1876).

Archaeology

The ruins of Abdie Church are scheduled (SAM no 825) and are still visible in a graveyard beside Lindores Loch. No other standing remains that might relate to the grange are visible.

Current State

The village contains several rubble-built structures of eighteenth- or nineteenth-century date, but also includes many modern, twentieth-century houses.

Grange	Grangehill (Kinghorn)
Abbey	Dunfermline Abbey
Order	Benedictine
Parish	Kinghorn
Council	Fife
Location	Site lies on undulating farmland to west of Kinghorn, and above a steep slope over the coast to the south
NGR	NT 259 866
NMRS site	No entry
Site visits	28 August 2001

History

An entry in the *Register of the Great Seal* of the 7 Feb 1540/1 confirms to James Kirkcaldy of Grange *the lands of Grange with tower, fortalice, manor, yards, orchards, dovecots, tofts, crofts and cotlands* [and other lands], all incorporated into the free barony of Grange (*RMS*, iii, nos 2272).

Archaeology

No certain monastic remains were visible. To the south of the farmhouse, above the steep slope over the coast lay a wooded area. The owner of the farmhouse stated that rectilinear possible wall lines were visible in dry weather. One stone was visible above the ground in the east of this area, possibly part of a north–south running wall line. These may be the remains of a stone building of indeterminate date.

Current State
The farm has been split into two properties, consisting of the farmhouse and surrounding land to the south, and the farm buildings to the north. Associated with the latter is a new farmhouse to the north-east. The surrounding land is used for both pasture and cereal cultivation. The original farmhouse is a harled, slate-roofed structure of eighteenth- or nineteenth-century date. The farm buildings, to the north are mainly rubble-built, with some recent concrete build, and are in disrepair. They are also eighteenth- or nineteenth-century in origin.

Grange	Grangemyre (Aberdour)
Abbey	Inchcolm Abbey
Order	Augustinian
Parish	Aberdour
Council	Fife
Location	Not located

Grange	Hills called Nether Grange (Grange of Gellet?)
Abbey	Dunfermline Abbey
Order	Benedictine
Parish	Dunfermline
Council	Fife
Location	Probably another name for Grange of Gellet

Grange	Kilmany Grange
Abbey	Unknown
Order	Unknown
Parish	Kilmany
Council	Fife
Location	Current manse is located at place called Kilmany Grange
NGR	NO 32SE
NMRS site	NO32SE 43 (Listed manse)
Site visits	No visit

History
There is no documentary evidence to suggest that Kilmany Grange is of monastic origin.

Archaeology
A series of cropmarks at NO 384 214 (NMRS No. NO32SE 39) represents an enclosed settlement of prehistoric date.

Grange	Middle Grange (Culross)
Abbey	Culross Abbey
Order	Cistercian
Parish	Culross
Council	Fife
Location	Site lies to the west of the B 9037. The farm of East Grange lies to the east, while to the west stands West Grange. The farm buildings stand on a raised grassy knoll
NGR	NS 989 892
NMRS site	No entry
Site visits	30 August 2001

History
The lands of Middle Grange are referred to in an entry in the *Register of the Great Seal* dated to 1542/3 (RMS V, no 1675).

Archaeology
No monastic remains were visible. According to the owner a covered well (not visible) lies to the south of the farmhouse.

Current State
The main farmhouse contains elements of rubble-built sandstone structure, which probably date to the eighteenth or nineteenth century. According to the owner, the farmhouse was extended in the twentieth century. All other early farm buildings have been demolished, and the farm buildings that exist at present are of late twentieth-century date. The demolished buildings generally lay to the north of the farmhouse, in an area much disturbed by recent development. The surrounding area is under cereal cultivation.

Grange	Naughton (Easter Friarton and Wester Friarton?)
Abbey	St Andrews Priory
Order	Augustinian
Parish	Forgan
Council	Fife
Location	Easter Friarton lies to the east of the A92, while Wester Friarton lies to the west of this road. Both stand on land rising from south to north, to the south of the River Tay
NGR	Easter Friarton NO 436 264; Wester Friarton 426 259
NMRS site	No entry
Site visits	15 August 2001

History
A confirmation by Pope Gregory VIII dating to 1187 notes the possessions of the Abbey of St Andrews, including by gift of Robert sometime bishop of St Andrews *Grange of Adnachtin* with all its pertinents (*St Andrews Liber*, 64). In 1198 x 1202 there is a grant by Alan de Lasceles son of Alan de Lasceles and of Juliana de Sumeruile with the consent of Amabla his wife, to St Andrews, of *the mother church of his estate (fundus) of Adenacthen, viz the church of Forgrund with the chapel of Adhenacthen adjacent to that church, and with the carucate of land adjacent to the same church, and with all teinds and oblations and offerings and rights pertaining to the same church* in pure and perpetual alms. Witnesses Roger, Bishop of St Andrews, [elected 1189, consecrated 1198, died 1202], Duncan, Earl of Fife [1154-1204], Malcolm his son [Earl of Fife 1204-30] (*St Andrews Liber*, 260). On the 19 March 1269 Gamelin, Bishop of St Andrews grants to St Andrews, the *church of Forgrund in Fife with its chapel of Adnauthan and a carucate of land pertaining to the same church and all other things pertaining to the said church and chapel*, in which, by collation of Sir Alan de Lascel, they obtained the right of patronage for their own use for the fabric of the cathedral of St Andrews (*St Andrews Liber*, 174).

Archaeology
No monastic remains were visible.

Current State
Easter Friarton consists of a probable nineteenth-century harled stone farmhouse, with generally dilapidated rubble-built sandstone farm buildings with pantile roofing. These are of eighteenth- or nineteenth-century date. The surrounding fields are under cereal cultivation.

At Wester Friarton the main farmhouse stands on a slight hummock, with a walled garden to south and west. The farm buildings are mainly rubble-built sandstone structures, which are in good condition. The surrounding farmland is under pasture and cereal cultivation. According to the owner parts of this farm have already been protected by Historic Scotland.

Grange	Nether Grange of Kinghorn Wester (Burntisland)
Abbey	Dunfermline Abbey
Order	Benedictine
Parish	Burntisland
Council	Fife
Location	House standing in residential area on the east side of Burntisland. A wooded area lies to the north, where the ground slopes down from north to south
NGR	NT 242 866
NMRS site	NT28NW 241
Site visits	29 August 2001

History
On the 7 Feb 1543/4 George, Commendator of Dunfermline grants in feu ferme to Robert Dury of that ilk and Katharine Lundy his spouse *the lands of Nethir Grange of Kingorne Wester called lye Manis with keepership of the place or fortalice thereof*, for whose keepership the Commendator assigns the lands of Grefland and Cunnyngayrland, now called Brunteland lying within the shire of Kingorne; Rendering 6 chalders and 8 bolls of barley (*Reg Dunfermelyn*, no 554). On the 15 March 1605 Charter to Sir Robert Meluill of Brunteland and Lady Joan Hammiltoun, Lady Ross his spouse of *the lands of Neyer Grange of Kingorne Wester* (*Reg Dunfermelyn*, 498).

Archaeology
No sign of monastic remains.

Current State
The site has been extensively overbuilt and landscaped. A listed, harled sandstone house apparently in the Scottish baronial style stands in a landscaped garden, which falls in terraces to the south. A date on the east side of the building of '1904' suggests an early twentieth-century date, though it may well contain nineteenth-century elements. Twentieth-century buildings lie to the north, west and south of the house.

Grange	New Grange (Balmerino)
Abbey	Balmerino Abbey
Order	Cistercian
Parish	Balmerino
Council	Fife
Location	Not located
NMRS site	No entry
Site visits	None

History
Campbell suggests that New Grange was situated on the southern slope of the high ridge overlooking Balmerino but gives no precise location (Campbell 1899, 206). Further documentary research is necessary to try and locate the site of this grange.

Grange	New Grange Farm (St Andrews)
Abbey	St Andrews Priory
Order	Augustinian

Council	Fife
Location	Not located

Grange	Newburn
Abbey	Dunfermline Abbey
Order	Benedictine
Parish	Newburn
Council	Fife
Location	Both farms lie on farmland by the A915, to the north-east of Upper Largo
NGR	Wester Newburn NO 441 052; Easter Newburn NO 445 048
NMRS site	No entry
Site visits	28 August 2001 (Wester Newburn owner was not available)

History
In 1561 the rental of the teinds of *Newbirne* includes for *the terrouris aikeris* 1 boll of barley and 4 bolls of oats (*Reg Dunfermelyn*, p442).

Archaeology
No monastic remains were visible.

Current State
Wester Newburn farm contains eighteenth- or nineteenth-century rubble-built farm buildings, which are in poor condition with bowed and cracked walls. The farmhouse is harled and is apparently of twentieth-century date. Potato and cereal crops are being cultivated in the surrounding farmland.

The farm at Easter Newburm has been converted into two properties. To the south stands a harled, probably sandstone, farmhouse of eighteenth- or nineteenth-century date. The farm buildings, of similar date, to the north are rubble-built with pantiles and have been converted into private housing. The surrounding land is under cereal cultivation.

Grange	Over Grange of Kinghorn Wester
Abbey	Dunfermline Abbey
Order	Benedictine
Council	Fife
Location	Not located

Grange	Strathkinness
Abbey	St Andrews Priory
Order	Augustinian
Parish	St Andrews and St Leonards
Council	Fife
Location	Both Nether Strathkinness and Easter Strathkinness stand to the north of a B road, to the west of St Andrews. The farmland rises gently from south to north.
NGR	Nether Strathkinness NO471 158; Easter Strathkinness NO 476 161
NMRS site	No entry
Site visits	15/16 August 2001

History
There are twelfth-century references to the lands of Strathkinness being in the possession of St Andrews Priory but it is only in 1206/7 that a confirmation by Pope Innocent III to St Andrews Priory of its possessions mentions the possession as *Grange of Stradkines* (*St Andrews Liber*, 73).

Archaeology
No monastic remains visible. The owner of Nether Strathkinness stated that local tradition suggests that Easter Strathkinness was farmed by monks.

Current State
Both farms have rubble-built eighteenth- or nineteenth-century farm buildings, which are generally in good condition. Land under cereal cultivation surrounds both sets of farm buildings.

Some of the buildings on the north side of Nether Strathkinness are dilapidated, while others have been renovated. There are twentieth-century buildings, and the farmhouse itself may be an early twentieth-century structure. At Nether Strathkinness there was some land under pasture, and possibly a berry crop.

Easter Strathkinness also has many twentieth-century buildings.

Grange	The Grange (Upper Largo)
Abbey	Unknown
Order	Unknown
Parish	Largo
Council	Fife
Location	The house stands at 16 South Feus, Upper Largo, in a residential area to the south of the town
NGR	NO 424 033
NMRS site	NO40SW 147
Site visits	27 August 2001

History
There is no surviving documentary evidence to suggest that this place name is of monastic origin.

Current State
The site consists of a nineteenth-century (Georgian) sandstone house, with modern twentieth-century additions, apparently of concrete. Land to the south of the house is under cereal cultivation, but otherwise the house is surrounded by further housing.

Grange	Under or Wood Grange (Nether Grange?)
Abbey	Dunfermline Abbey
Order	Benedictine
Parish	Burntisland?
Council	Fife
Location	Not located, though may be same as Nether Grange of Kinghorn Wester

History
There is a reference in the Registrum Dunfermlyn to the teinds of *Wnder* (*Wude*) *Grange* in Kinghorn Wester (*Reg Dunfermlyn* 440).

Grange	West Grange
Abbey	Culross Abbey
Order	Cistercian
Parish	Culross
Council	Fife
Location	The site lies to the west of a B road, north of Culross and west of Middle Grange.
NGR	NS 984 895
NMRS site	NS 98NE 42 (West Grange House)
Site visits	30 August 2001 (owner not present)

History
There is a reference to *Grange Westir* in an entry in the *Register of the Great Seal* for 1542/3 (RMS V, no 1675). *West and Eist Grangis* are referred to in an entry for 1571-72 (Thomson 1886, 522).

Archaeology
No monastic remains visible.

Current State
The main farmhouse dates to around 1760 and the associated farm buildings are of eighteenth- or nineteenth-century date. These buildings are generally rubble-built sandstone structures, and there has been some renovation of the farmhouse. The farmhouse has a pantiled roof, while other buildings are roofed with corrugated iron. There are some twentieth-century metal buildings, and some sandstone buildings have openings infilled with brick. The farm buildings are surrounded by land under pasture. A modern harled house stands to the south-east.

Grange	Wester Grangemuir
Abbey	Pittenweem Priory
Order	Augustinian
Parish	Anstruther Wester
Council	Fife
Location	Site lies on fairly flat farmland to the north of Grangemuir House and approximately 2km north of Pittenweem
NGR	NO 537 041
NMRS site	No entry
Site visits	27 August 2001

History
There is a reference to *ville de Grangemure* in the *Register of the Great Seal* for 1572-72 (Thomson 1886, 755).

Archaeology
No monastic remains were visible.

Current State
The farm is owned by the Balcaskie Estate. The farm buildings appear to generally be eighteenth- or nineteenth-century rubble-built sandstone structures. Many buildings are harled or plastered. Several buildings have had openings infilled with rubble and mortar. There is cereal cultivation in the surrounding area as well as some wooded and overgrown land.

GRAMPIAN REGION (13)

J.C. Murray

NMRS NO	NMRS NAME	TYPE OF SITE	MONASTERY	SAM/LISTED
NJ93SE 24 NJ 9855 3010	Abbotshall	House	Kinloss Abbey (OCist)	
NJ82SW 140 NJ 8123 2079	Ashley Grange	Residential/ House		
NJ05NW 31.00	Dalvey House ALTERNATIVE(S): Grangehill; Dalvey House Policies	Farming and Fishing; Residential; Religion	Pluscarden Priory (Valliscaulian, later OSB)	L
NJ45SE 3	Davoch of Grange ALTERNATIVE(S): Tower of Strathisla	Defence; Religion; Farming and Fishing	Kinloss Abbey (OCist)	
NJ06SE NJ 094 616	East Grange		Kinloss Abbey (OCist)	
NO87SE NO 845 743	Grange of Kinneff			
NK14NW NK 11 46	Grange of Rawhill		Deer Abbey (OCist)	
NJ06SE NJ 063 607	Grange Farm		Kinloss Abbey (OCist)	
NJ06SE 11	Grange Hall	Grange	Kinloss Abbey (OCist)	
NO66NE NO77NW NO 700 657	Grangehall	Grangehall		
NJ81NW 24 NJ 8408 1653	Hatton of Fintray	'Abbey'; Buildings	Lindores Abbey (OTiron)	
NJ24NE19 NJ 2760 4924	Rothes Manse ALTERNATIVE(S): Mansfield House; The Grange	Manse; House		
	West Grange		Kinloss Abbey (OCist)	

ABERDEENSHIRE COUNCIL

Grange	Abbotshall
Abbey	Kinloss
Order	Cistercian
Parish	Ellon
Council	Aberdeenshire
Location	Between Mains of Waterston and River Ythan
NGR	NJ 9855 3010

NMRS site	NJ93SW 24
Site visits	30 October 2001

History
This structure has been identified as the hall erected by Abbot Thomas Crystall of Kinloss Abbey in 1532 (Simpson 1958).

Archaeology
The Ordnance Survey records the presence of visible wall fragments and loose stones and amorphous turf-covered banks on the flattish summit of a tree-grown promontory above the River Ythan. They also describe a walled garden 15m to the north-east of the site which is traditionally identified as the 'Abbot's Garden' (Ordnance Survey 1970). There is no record of any archaeological investigation on this site.

Current State
The flattish summit described in 1970, although very overgrown, still has the appearance of a summit with a number of depressions which may be structures. A *c.*5m diameter circular depression in the north-west corner of the site is visible overlooking the very steep fall to the Ythan river on the west and it is tempting to consider this as a possible trace of the circular tower? Only one stone is visible protruding through the grass on the east side of the depression. From this feature the ground slopes to the east and, although overgrown, seems to form a vaguely rectangular shape, *c.*5 x 11m. No trace of the 2m-long stretch of wall seen in the 1970 visit in the east of the promontory is now visible, and it appears that a number of trees that stood in the centre of the summit have fallen (or been felled?) and removed.

To the north of the promontory, the small 'garden' area enclosed by a dry stone wall is still intact and measures *c.*15 x 45m.

The site is screened from the arable field to the east by a narrow tree belt.

Grange	Ashley Grange
Abbey	?
Order	?
Parish	Keithall and Kinkell
Council	Aberdeenshire
Location	House named Ashlea Grange
NGR	NJ 8123 2079
NMRS site	NJ82SW 140
Site visits	Not visited

History
There are no documentary references to indicate that the name of this house has a monastic origin.

Grange	Dalvey House
Abbey	Pluscarden
Order	Valliscaulian later Benedictine
Parish	Dyce and Moy
Council	Moray
Location	House called Dalvey House
NGR	NJ 003 586
NMRS site	NJ05NW 31
Site visits	1 November 2001

History

Dalvey House was known as Grangehill until 1740. There are documentary references to *Grangegreen* and *Grangehill* belonging to Pluscarden Priory; there were two mills at *Grangegreen*, including one leased to Robert Dunbar of *Grangehill* (*RMS*, iv, no 2854; v, nos 667, 1664).

Archaeology

It is claimed that the well which lies immediately in front of the house was the original water supply for the grange. It is approached by a gently descending curving passage, *c.*14m long, with a vaulted roof. The Ordnance Survey investigator refers to two blocked doorways within this structure which he links with the grange.

Current State:

Dalvey House is the property of Major R.N.A. MacLeod.

There has been no change to the circumstances at Dalvey House since the 1971 visit. No traces of the earlier grange are visible in the front lawn, south of the house. This garden, however, is retained by a substantial wall with architectural features which give it the appearance of having been part of an earlier building. This is especially evident in the south-east corner, which seems to contain a vaulted chamber, much overgrown and in danger of collapse, which prevented a more detailed observation.

The passage to the well still exists although this is no longer the source of the water supply for the house.

The dovecot, north of the house, has recently been restored with an Historic Scotland grant, although there is now considerable spalling of the harling on its north face.

Grange	Davoch of Grange
Abbey	Kinloss Abbey
Order	Cistercian
Parish	Grange
Council	Moray
Location	Site currently occupied by parish church of Grange
NGR	NJ 480 515
NMRS site	NJ45SE 3
Site visits	30 October 2001

History

Thomas Crystall, Abbot of Kinloss, is said to have built a tower and fortalice on this site in 1525 (*Survey of the Province of Moray* 1798, 73).

Archaeology

There is no record of any archaeological investigation on this site.

Current State

No changes seem to have taken place since the site was last visited in 1967. The mound is a very impressive and prominent feature situated to the north of the River Isla. The moat is still visible on the west and north-west and, to a lesser extent, to the south. The entrance to the mound is located on the west side and crosses the line of the moat at the south-west corner at a point where it no longer survives. The mound is surrounded by mature trees, some of which appear to be close to falling down. The top of the mound is occupied by the Church of Scotland kirk of Keith, St Rufus, Botriphnie and Grange, which is located in the south-east sector. The church is still used for worship and the mound and its access is well kept.

Grange	East Grange
Abbey	Kinloss
Order	Cistercian
Parish	Kinloss
Council	Moray
Location	Farm of East Grange
NGR	NJ 094 616
NMRS site	NJ06SE
Site visits	1 November 2001

History
East Grange is on record as belonging to Kinloss Abbey (*RMS* vi, nos 1138, 2074).

Archaeology
There is no record of any archaeological investigations on this site.

Current State
There is nothing now visible that would indicate the location of earlier grange buildings. There are two possibilities for the siting of earlier buildings: the first is in the vicinity of a now derelict Edwardian villa at the entrance to the farm and the second, and more probable, is in the vicinity of an eighteenth-century cornmill. With the exception of these two buildings, the rest of the steadings are modern.

The owner, Mr Grigor Butler, said there was no local knowledge of any building earlier than the cornmill.

Grange	Grange of Kinneff
Abbey	?
Order	?
Parish	Kinneff
Council	Aberdeenshire
Location	current farm of Grange
NGR	NO 845 743
NMRS site	No entry
Site visits	Not visited

History
There is no documentary evidence to suggest that there is a monastic origin to this place name. Further documentary research would be useful to discover the reason for this place name.

Grange	Grange of Rawhill
Abbey	Deer
Order	Cistercian
Parish	Peterhead
Council	Aberdeenshire
Location	Western side of Peterhead in the vicinity of Middle Grange school or Grange Park
NGR	NK 11 46
NMRS site	No entry
Site visits	30 October 2001

History
Grange of Rawhill is mentioned in the *Register of the Great Seal* as being a possession of Deer Abbey (*RMS*, v, no 1309).

Archaeology
There is no record of any archaeological investigation on this site.

Current State
The location of a number of possible grange sites in this western area of Peterhead is problematic. With Grange of Rawhill, it is though to be in the vicinity of either Middle Grange School or Grange Park – a sheltered housing scheme to the west of the school. The only clear ground around Middle Grange School, lies west and south of the school and is a grassed play area with no surface indications of earlier buildings.

At Grange Park (Map ref: NK 1159 4611), the sheltered housing is surrounded by landscaped garden – again, with no visible signs of earlier structures.

Located slightly more to the west, is the area known as Upper Grange (Map ref: NK 1128 4610). Here, the house of Upper Grange is surrounded by garden and bordered to the north-east by a 12m band of mature trees which separates the house from a new housing development. An area, shown on the map as fields, is now partially built on with new houses. Only a small portion of land, immediately north-east of Upper Grange, is still free from development, but the indications are that this too will be built on. There are no visible signs of earlier buildings in this area.

Grange	Grange Farm/Grange Hall
Abbey	Kinloss
Order	Cistercian
Parish	Kinloss
Council	Moray
Location	Modern farm of Grange Farm and house called Grange Hall
NGR	NJ 063 607
NMRS site	NJ06SE 11
Site visits	1 November 2001

History
It has been suggested that the farm north of Grange Hall may be on the site of a grange of Kinloss Abbey mentioned in a Papal Bull of 1173 (Stuart 1872, 106).

Archaeology
There have been no recorded archaeological investigations on this site.

Current State:
The estate is now in the ownership of Major General Grant Peterkin.

Grange Hall is a large Victorian house dating to 1881, with open ground to the south, west and north of the building. No visible signs of earlier buildings can be seen and it is entirely possible that the Hall stands on the site of an earlier structure. The grid reference NJ 063 607, places the possible location of the abbey grange several hundred metres north of Grange Hall itself and more towards Grange Farm. Again, nothing is visible on the ground between the Hall and the farm steadings to the north.

A large, walled garden (semi-derelict) lies to the east of the Hall and is believed locally to be the Monks garden (information from farm manager). Nothing was visible in the wall structure that would indicate an early date but a thorough survey was not possible.

A hexagonal dovecot is located to the north of the farm steadings and was recently restored with a grant from Historic Scotland.

Grange	Grange Hall
Abbey	?
Order	?
Parish	?
Council	Aberdeenshire
Location	Farm called Grange Hall
NGR	NO 6996 6589
NMRS site	No entry
Site visits	2 November 2001

Current State
The current owner of Grange Hall is Mr Alastair Brownley (for about the last four years).

It is doubtful that a monastic grange ever existed on this site. Local belief is that the name 'Grange Hall' was only applied to the house and farm in the recent past as the then owner was given a nickname, which was a play on Balmaleedie, which he disliked. The current owner, Mr Brownley, would like to see it revert to its original name of 'Balmaleedie'. Certainly, nothing is visible to give any indication of the presence of earlier buildings on, or in the vicinity of, the present farmhouse and steading buildings.

Grange	Hatton of Fintray
Abbey	Lindores
Order	Cistercian
Parish	Fintray
Council	Aberdeenshire
Location	To the north of Hatton of Fintray
NGR	NJ 8408 1653
NMRS site	NJ81NW 24
Site visits	29 October 2001

History
The church of Fintray was dedicated to St Medan and belonged to the Abbey of Lindores (Scott 1926).

Archaeology
The *New Statistical Account* describes the minister of the church digging up the foundations of some buildings supposed to have belonged to the Abbacy of Lindores in Fife when he was improving his glebe. The buildings (denominated the Northern Abbey) are supposed to have been erected about the year 1386 from a stone bearing that date having been observed many years ago in the dyke of the burying ground, which had probably been composed of fragments of the demolished abbey of which no vestige now remains above the surface of the ground: but foundations of its walls occasionally intercept the digging of graves (NSA) 1845.

Easson states that this abbey is entirely imaginary. The lands of Fintray were granted to Lindores Abbey by its founder David, Earl of Huntingdon 1198-9 (Easson 1957).

Current State
The supposed location of this site lies *c.*15-20m south-east of an approximately eighteenth-/nineteenth-century cemetery and north of the Hatton of Fintray to Dyce road. It is planted with mature trees, with a small burn running through the south-west corner of the site. The site is bounded with a small dry stone wall. No upstanding building remains nor signs of wall foundations are visible anywhere within the supposed location of the 'enclosure'.

Grange	Rothes Manse/The Grange
Abbey	Not applicable
Order	Not applicable
Parish	Rothes
Council	Moray
Location	In town of Rothes
NGR	NJ 276 492
NMRS site	NJ24NE 19
Site visits	Not visited.

History

There is no evidence that this name has a monastic origin.

Grange	West Grange
Abbey	Kinloss
Order	Cistercian
Council	Moray
Location	Unknown

History

West Grange belonged to Kinloss Abbey (*RMS*, v, no 2323; vi, nos 1138, 2074). Further research is required to accurately locate this grange.

STRATHCLYDE REGION (15)

R. Cachart and D. Hall

NMRS NUMBER	NMRS NAME	TYPE OF SITE	MONASTERY	SAM/LISTED
NS35NE NS 37 57	Auchengrange		Paisley Abbey (OClun)	
NS46NE 20	Blackstoun	Grange	Paisley Abbey (OClun)	
NS40NE 8	Dalmellington	Grange	Vaudey Abbey, later Melrose Abbey (OCist)	
NS55NE 30 NS 580 556	Dripps	Building; Structures	Paisley Abbey (OClun)	
NS76SW 6	Drumpellier	Grange	Newbattle Abbey (OCist)	
NS45SW NS 43 51	Grange (Dunlop)			
NS43NW NS 41 37	Grange (Kilmarnock)	Grange	Kilwinning Abbey (OTiron)	
NS64NE NS 68 45	Grange (Strathaven)			
NS31SW NS 319 141	Grange of Maybole		Melrose Abbey (OCist)	

NS94SE 73 NS 967 426	Grangehall	Village; Farmsteads	Dryburgh Abbey (OPrem)	
NS35SE 2 NS 359 540	Grangehill	Farming And Fishing; Residential/ Tower-House (Possible); Farmstead	Kilwinning Abbey (OTiron)	
NS55SW 9 NS 532 545	Langrig	Tower (Possible)	Knights Templar, later Knights Hospitaller	
NS42NE 2 NS 4977 2726	Mauchline	Tower-House	Melrose Abbey (OCist)	SAM 325
NT14NW 31 NT1071 4652	The Grange (Dolphinton)	House		
NM 298 217 NM32SW 9 (cists at Fidden)	Slugan Dubh Isle of Mull	Fish trap, rigs and cists	Iona Abbey?	

Grange   Auchengrange
Abbey   Paisley Abbey
Order   Cluniac
Parish   Beith
Council   North Ayrshire
Location   East side of A737, 4km north-east of Beith
NGR   NS371 574
NMRS site   Not listed.
Site visits   30 August 2001

History

Auchengrange is mentioned in the Paisley Abbey rental books. According to records and letters in the possession of Mrs Davis, wife of the present owner, the house was built in 1780. The house was given the name Auchengrange sometime between 1857 and 1895. Previous to that it was called Wattiston or a variation of that name. Wattistone is shown on John Ainslie's map of 1796. Dr Andrew Crawford's 52-volume history of the area has some history of the families that lived in the house. Some rebuilding was carried out in the 1940s after a fire. The road up to Auchengrange is signed posted as Auchengrange Hill.

Archaeology

There is no known record of any archaeological investigation having taken place at Auchengrange.

Current State

Auchengrange estate comprises a large domestic nineteenth-century house which is listed. It is set in six acres of ground on a hillside overlooking Lochwinnoch and is no longer part of a working farm. To the rear of the house on the south-western side is a row of cottages and stables enclosing a cobbled courtyard which is now separately owned; these buildings could be eighteenth century in date. The stables have small, arched windows in the frontage and a larger one in the north gable end. The windows may have been designed to reflect buildings of an earlier date, perhaps grange structures situated on the site.

The owner of Auchngrange, Mrs Davis, knew of nothing in the vicinity that could relate to grange structures or features.

Grange	Grangehill
Abbey	Kilwinning
Order	Tironensian
Parish	Beith
Council	North Ayrshire
Location	East side of A737 north side of Beith
NGR	NS 3566 5470 (main residence)
NMRS site	None for main house of Grangehill which was visited. Other nearby associated sites are: ♦ Grangehill, Hill of Beith, Farming and Fishing; Residential/ Tower-House (possible); Farmstead NMRS Number: NS35SE 2 ♦ Court Hill, Beith, Mound NMRS Number: NS35SE 1
Site visits	30 August 2001

History

The barony of Beith was given to the (Tironensian) monks of Kilwinning Abbey (NS34SW 6) by the wife of Sir Richard de Moreville towards the end of the twelfth century. Their farm is clearly indicated by the name 'Grangehill' (NS 356 546) and 'The Maynes'. Blaeu's map indicates a castellated mansion or tower house on part of the Maynes, half a mile south-west of the Grange, where the abbot may have stayed when in the locality (this tower may have been the main building of the monks' grange: cf Mauchline Grange: NS42NE 2, secularised on the dissolution of the Abbey) (Love 1876).

Archaeology

NS 3597 5409. Traces of overgrown wall foundations of squared masonry 1.4m thick and 0.4m high where best preserved, are visible in a copse 200m north-west of Court Hill (NS35SE 1). Adjoining the foundations, a section 5.0m long and 0.6m thick of the present field wall consists of mortared masonry. Visited by OS (DS) 30 August 1956.

These remains are generally as described in the previous field report. The section of mortared masonry in the dyke is the remains of the south gable of a rectangular building. Surveyed at 1:2500. Visited by OS (EGC) 2 July 1964.

The significance of the remains described above is doubtful; the proportions of the building and vestiges of surrounding enclosure work are consistent with a deserted eighteenth-/ nineteenth-century farmstead, and there is no local tradition of this being a tower or mansion. Visited by OS (JRL) 18 January 1983.

There have been no known archaeological excavations at the site of the main house or within the adjacent grounds of Grangehill.

Current State

According to the present owner of Grange Hill the name appears in the Topographical Account of Cunninghame by Timothy Pont, *c.*1600s, which would probably place a residence on this site at that date. The owner also stated that Grangehill is mention in the *Black Book of Paisley* (1885). The present house appears to date from the eighteenth century and has undergone many renovations. The rear garden area was visited to look for older foundations where a wing had been recently removed but no early foundations were observed.

Close to the main house is a well-kept walled garden of one acre with high walls and a potting shed with pigeon loft. Renovations were carried out within the garden in the 1990s. The groundkeeper stated that recently the soil within the garden had been changed. A stone ornament set into the south wall is inscribed with the date 1872. Over the garden's east doorway is a triangular pediment inscribed 'Fear God Honour The King' below which is a plaque bearing the date 1929. The pediment appears to predate the plaque and may have been taken from elsewhere. There was nothing in the garden that could be seen to date from the time when there may have been grange buildings here in the medieval period but the present garden walls may well have been built on earlier foundations.

To the south-west of the walled garden is a former coachouse/stables which is now a residence. Outside the coachouse on the west side there is a large dump of architectural stone from some recent renovations. Most of this stonework looks nineteenth century but there are blocks which appear to be earlier. The earlier blocks may be from buildings that were incorporated into the coachouse when it was constructed.

Grange	Grange (Dunlop)
Abbey	Unknown
Order	Unknown
Parish	Dunlop
Council	East Ayrshire
Location	Approximately 5km to the north-east of Dunlop
NGR	NS438 524 (location of site visit at Mid Grange)
NMRS site	None
Site visit	30 August 2001

History

The 1:10,000 OS 1960s map shows five places with the Grange name: South Grange, Mid Grange Townend of Grange, Townhead of Grange and Grange View Cottage. The history of the various farms with the Grange name clustered in this vicinity is virtually unknown.

Archaeology

There are no known records of any archaeological investigations connected with these sites.

Current State

Townhead of Grange is uninhabited, Townend of Grange has been renovated and is occupied and Mid Grange, which was visited, is occupied and undergoing renovation. The present status of the other two sites is unknown.

The occupant of Mid Grange had some local knowledge and suggested that the local Grange sites here were close to a drove road. He also had knowledge of a nearby glebe field.

Grange	Blackstoun
Abbey	Paisley
Order	Clunic
Parish	Kilbrachan
Council	Renfrewshire
Location	Blackstoun farm is situated within the north-west angle of the M8 and A737 junction, to the west of Glasgow Airport
NGR	NS 457 660
NMRS site	NS46NE20
Site visit	13 September 2001

History

Blackston is noted in 1460 as a grange belonging to Paisley Abbey (Blackstown: NS 457 660), (D. Semple 1872, W.M. Metcalfe 1909).

Blackstown, the summer dwelling of the Abbots of Paisley, was built by George Shaw (abbot in the latter part of the fifteenth century); his arms can be seen on it. After the Reformation, the house was improved by James, Earl of Abercorn. It was in the possession of Alexander

Napier soon after 1730 when it was accidently burnt to the ground and a new mansion was built. This mansion has also been demolished (J.C. Hill 1953, W. Macfarlane 1907).

Archaeology
There are no known records of any archaeological investigation at Blackstoun Farm.

Current State
Blackstoun Farm is a working farm. The site of the former mansion is open and grassed. On the west side of the mansion site at NS 4585 6600 is a small, white building with bricked up door and windows. According to the present owner of the farm this building was part of the last mansion. It has a corrugated-iron roof and farm machinery is housed in a corrugated-iron open shelter attached to the building's east side. A garage-type door has been inserted in the south side. There is no indication on the ground of any other remains of the mansion.

The current owner of the farm stated that as far as he knew there were no upstanding building remains or field systems that could be attributed to the former grange. He did however believe that there was a burial ground somewhere in the vicinity. The present farmhouse was the former coach house of the later mansion.

Grange	Kilmarnock
Abbey	Kilwinning
Order	Tironensian
Parish	Kilmarnock
Council	East Ayrshire
Location	Kilmarnock
NGR	NS 41 37
NMRS site	None
Site visits	13 September 2001

History
A grange at Kilmarnock belonging to Kilwinning Abbey along with a site called Grangehill are mentioned in the *Register of the Great Seal* (*RMS*, v, no 2085). The exact location of these two sites is unknown.

Archaeology
There are no known archaeological records referring to a grange site at Kilmarnock

Current State
The name Grange appears on the OS 1:10,000 map at NS 417 378 on the west side of the town. That site comprises two schools and a large area of playing fields and a golf course to the west of the schools. In the town centre there is a major Grange Street and a lesser Grange Place. Grange Street may have originally led to the site of the grange which may well have been located to the west of the town within the school grounds or the golf course.

Grange	Grange of Maybole
Abbey	Melrose Abbey
Order	Cistercian
Parish	Maybole
Council	South Ayrshire
Location	Grange House is on the west side of the B7024, approximately 8km to the north of Maybole
NGR	NS319 141 (Grange House)

NMRS site   None
Site visit   13 September 2001

History
There is a reference in the *Book of Melrose* to Robert the Bruce confirming the lands of *Grange of Maybothyl* to the monks in 1301 (*Melrose Liber* no 351). Other sites in the vicinity with the grange name attachment are High Grange, Laigh Grange and Grange Mains which belongs to Grange House.

Archaeology
There are no known records of any archaeological investigation at Grange House.

Current State
Grange House is a listed eighteenth-century residence within extensive grounds. The owner knew of the grange connection and pointed out a high wall on the north-eastern side of the garden at the rear of the premises that she believed may date from the time of the grange. The wall was about 4m high and 0.75m thick, constructed mainly of large, rectangular, roughly-worked blocks of sandstone. The wall appeared to have been truncated at both ends. This fragment of wall appears to be the remains of a walled garden and may have been contemporary with grange buildings. Also pointed out was the course of a tunnel leading north-eastwards from the north-east side of the house. The entranceway in the garden was blocked. Apparently the tunnel had been partly truncated when oil tanks ware installed outside near the house and it was seen to be large enough to walk through in a crouched position. The function and date of the tunnel have not been ascertained but it is possible that it could be contemporary with grange buildings.

Grange	Langrig
Abbey	None known
Order	Templers, Hospitallers (land owned by these orders)
Parish	Mearns
Council	East Renfrewshire
Location	South side of Mearns, fields between Mearns Road and A77
NGR	NS 532 545
NMRS site	NS55SW9
Site visits	12 September 2001

History
It is not clear where the reference to this land belonging to the Templars and then the Hospitallers originates (see below). The only reference in the hospitallers rental of 1539-40 is to 'Neutount in lie mernis' and this is by no means an obvious reference to this site (Cowan et al. 1983, 21).

Archaeology Notes
NS 5329 5459 (information contained in letter from T.C. Welsh to OS, 22 September 1975). Possible Grange, Langrig: In a wood, 550ft OD, a natural, level rectangular mound up to 2m high, with its top measuring 27 x 16m, has remains of walls round its margin and an incomplete 12m square foundation over a 2m-thick wall at one end. On the higher side of the mound, exactly midway, is a small extension, 5 x 4m. The land here belonged to the Templars and later to the Hospitallers. E.R. Talbot (Glasgow University) who has seen the site thinks it may be a grange. He found the ditches acceptable and located, in a nearby dyke, a stone with two dressed faces and a chamfered edge which he suggested as part of a window jamb (Welsh 1975).

Site reassessed as remains of tower. Possibly the 'new manor' of Mearns mentioned *c.*1300 (Welsh 1983).

Archaeology
The site has been examined by T.C. Welsh on two occasions. In 1975 it was considered that the ruins could represent a grange, it was examined again in 1983 and reassessed as a possible castle site. It appears that no archaeological excavations took place at these times.

Current State
The state of the monument is virtually as described by T.C. Welsh. The site was somewhat overgrown at the time of visit and some aspects were difficult to distinguish. It appears as though the natural rock has been quarried in parts to conform with a rectangular pattern or layout. In general the build comprises walls of quarry stone upon moulded natural outcrops. The ruins have a cover of deciduous trees which may eventually cause damage.

Grange	Mauchline
Abbey	Melrose
Order	Cistercian
Parish	Mauchline
Council	East Ayrshire
Location	In private grounds in the centre of Mauchline
NGR	NS 497 272
NMRS site	NS42NE 2
Site visit	18 September 2001

History
Melrose Abbey held lands in Ayrshire, virtually represented by Mauchline parish, the first grant being made before 1177. At Mauchline, there was a grange, with offices, granaries, barns and a hospice (NS42NE 6) and chapel (the latter was to become the parish church). The nucleus of these buildings was this tower, probably built about 1450, when Andrew Hunter was Abbot of Melrose (his arms appear on a roof boss in the hall). It is rectangular inplan, with a basement area of two vaulted cellars, large ground floor room, hall on the first floor, and an attic in the roof; its ashlar walls are 5ft thick. Some repairs may have been carried out when it was secularised in the early seventeenth century, eg the square-headed windows may then have been inserted, and much more recently, the battlements have been restored. Buildings in the style of the eighteenth century have been erected to form a courtyard southwards from the tower. There is no evidence to suggest that a cell of the Abbey or a dependent priory developed here; this was simply the administrative headquarters of the barony (Childe and Simpson 1954).

Archaeology
An assessment was carried out in advance of environmental improvements adjacent to this tower, which displays the arms of Abbot Andrew Hunter (*c.*1444–71), probably as the focus for the buildings of a grange belonging to Melrose Abbey. The exact extent of the grange and the disposition of the buildings within is not known. The area surrounding the tower was only affected to a depth of 0.5m by the improvements. Very little was found at this depth, apart from an area of cobbles, possibly part of an eighteenth-century courtyard (Coleman 1993).

Trenching by mechanical digger alongside the east walls of the tower and the house of Gavin Hamilton was stopped as mortared wall stubs and associated deposits were revealed beneath modern demolition rubble. These features were then recorded and excavated by SUAT. The modern surface and bedding sealed a levelling layer of sandstone rubble, which was removed to reveal the foundation courses of two unconnected sandstone walls. On partial removal, these two walls and a slab drain were found to be built directly on bedrock, which had probably been levelled for the purpose. No features earlier than c.1700 were encountered above the bedrock. Given the close proximity of the site to the focus of an ecclesiastical settlement founded in the twelfth century, the absence of pre-eighteenth-century finds suggests that the levelling truncation down to bedrock south-east of Abbot Hunter's Tower removed all trace of prior activity (Falconer 1994).

Current State
The site visit confirmed that the exterior of Abbot Hunter's Tower is as previously described. Access to the interior was not gained. Two large architectural fragments were observed in the Mauchline Burn below the tower on the west side of the footbridge. They may have come from the wall edging the burn.

Grange	Dalmellington
Abbey	Vaudey Abbey, later Melrose Abbey
Order	Cistercian
Parish	Dalmellington
Council	East Ayrshire
Location	Unknown
NGR	NS 48 05 (Town of Dalmellington)
NMRS site	None
Site visit	18 September 2001 (Dalmellington town centre for photographic record)

History
Thomas de Colville granted a big hill-farm at Dalmellington (NS 48 05) to the Cistercians of Vaudey, but by 1223 the Lincolnshire monks were forced to transfer this estate to Melrose Abbey as it was 'useless and dangerous to them' because of attacks by the native population (Barrow 1980).

It is possible that Drumgrange (not visited) off the A713 to the north-west of Dalmellington may tentatively indicate a general location of the hill farm.

Archaeology
There are no known records of any archaeological investigation regarding Dalmellington Grange

Current State
The location and therefore the current state of the hill-farm or grange at Dalmellington are unknown.

Grange	Dripps
Abbey	Paisley?
Order	Cluniac
Parish	East Kilbride
Council	South Lanarkshire
Location	On the lands of Meikle Dripps Farm
NGR	NS 580 556
NMRS site	NS55NE 30
Site visits	12 September 2001

History
Apart from a reference to these lands being gifted to Paisley Abbey there is no other evidence to suggest that there is a grange on this site.

Archaeology
The NMRS record a U-shaped structure at Dripps and describe it as follows. A D-shaped promontory at a bend in Thorntonhall Burn, near the waterfall, features the grass-covered rubble remains of a rectangular building, 15 x 7m, probably an early longhouse. Partial defences are also evident. There may have been a monastic grange here, as the lands were gifted to Paisley Abbey. There has been no archaeological confirmation of this site (Welsh 1974, Welsh nd).

This site was recorded by GUARD during an assessment of a series of routes for a proposed southern orbital road to link the M77 with the A726 leading to East Kilbride. NS 580 556 Grass-covered building remains (Halliday 1997).

Current State
The occupants of Meikle Dripps Farm knew the general area but were uncertain about the ruins. A search of the given grid reference area revealed no evidence of a grass-covered structure or any other archaeological feature.

Grange	Grangehall (Northholm)
Abbey	Dryburgh
Order	Premonstratensian
Parish	Pettinain
Council	South Lanarkshire
Location	Grangehall Farm is located to the south-west of Lanark at the junction of a minor road off the east side of the A73 and to the south-east of Carstairs Junction
NGR	NS 968 4270
NMRS site	NS94SE 73
Site visit	19 September 2001

History
1173 x 1214 William I confirms to Dryburgh Abbey that land in Padenan perambulated by Robert son of Werenbert, his sheriff of Lanark, namely that land which the canons of Dryburgh held in the time of David I, Malcolm IV and himself (*Inglisberry Grange, now Grangehall*, in Pettinain parish); also grants the toft and croft at the chapel of Paduenan and as much common pasture of the same toun as pertains to the parson of that chapel (*RRS*, ii, no 262), see also *Dryburgh Liber*, no 47.

Archaeology
NS94SE 73 9685 4270
A village, comprising 19 roofed buildings, one partially-roofed building and one unroofed structure is depicted on the first edition of the OS 6-inch map (Lanarkshire 1864, sheet xxvi). Two courtyard farmsteads and some cottages comprising a total of 10 roofed buildings are shown on the current edition of the OS 1:10000 map (1978). Information from RCAHMS (AKK) 28 September 2000.

On the first edition OS map the village is named Grange.

Current State
The 'village' at the time of the site visit comprised a cluster of buildings representing one working farm homestead (Grangehall), an unoccupied large house (Northholm of Grange), various farm buildings, recent post-war cottages and for the former owner-occupier of Grangehall, a new bungalow. There were no signs of any remains earlier than the nineteenth-century. The track through the 'village' is called Grange Road and leads to Grange Cottage

The former owner of Grangehall and the present owner did not know of the historical background to the grange name. The former owner stated that Grangehall was formally called Midholm of Grange and that the house had been built *c*.1890.

Grange	The Grange
Abbey	None
Order	None
Parish	Dolphington
Council	South Lanarkshire
Location	On the east side of the A702 at Dolphington
NGR	NT 107 465
NMRS site	NT14NW 33
Site visit	19 September 2001 (visit aborted on approach to site when informed owner was not home and would not welcome visit for site photo, however owner's telephone number was supplied)

History

According to owner, the name (The Grange) is false. Apparently the house was formally a manse (first edition OS map verifies this). When the church sold the property around 1955 it was on the condition that the manse name was not used. The new owner gave the property its present name.

Grange	Drumpellier
Abbey	Newbattle Abbey
Order	Cistercian
Parish	Old Monklands (Monklands)
Council	North Lanarkshire
Location	Coatbridge, Drumpellier golf club car park
NGR	NS 7160 6495
NMRS site	NS76SW 6
Site visit	19 September 2001

History

In 1162 William I grants to the monks of Newbattle Abbey *Dumpeleder by its right marches, namely with Metherhauch [Medrox] and Maiueth [Myvot] and Glarnephin as far as Duniduffel [Dundyvan?] towards the east with all its just pertinents,* as Gillepatric Mac Kerin previously held it better and more fully, in wood and plain, in fields, meadows, pastures, moors and waters, as Baldwin his Sheriff of Lanark, Geoffrey his Sheriff of Edinburgh, Fergus son of Ferthet, Douenald son of Ewein, and Vctred his Sheriff of Linlithgow with certain others of his honest men seised them [the monks] on his orders in the same lands by its right marches between Lothian and Clydesdale, and by all other marches of *Dumpeleder* as the foresaid Gillepatric Mac Kerin previously held them, and perambulated it, showing the marches to them (*RRS*, i, no 198).

William I in 1165 x 1173 Confirms to Newbattle Abbey its possessions including, by gift of his brother Malcolm *Dunpeldre by its right marches, with Metherauch and all its just pertinents*, as Gylpatrik Mackeruy previously held it (*RRS*, ii, no 61).

Archaeology

There are no known records of any archaeological investigations at the site of Drumpellier House which could be the site of Drumpellier Grange buildings.

Current State
Drumpellier House has been demolished and the area now comprises rough ground with hard standing for car parking for the Drumpellier golf club.

Grange	Nethercraig
Abbey	Unknown
Order	Unknown, possibly Hospitallers
Parish	Eaglesham
Council	East Renfrewshire
Location	Approximately 2km south-east of Eaglesham
NGR	NS 596 509
NMRS site	NS55SE 12
Site visits	20 September 2001

History
There are no known historical references relating to a grange on the original site of the Nethercraig Farm. The steading was re-sited to its present location in the late nineteenth century.

Archaeology
The remains of Nethercraig Farm (re-sited late nineteenth century, to 50m west) are noted for rock-cut foundations and dun-like appearance (Welsh 1969, Bell 1976). The remains occupy a platform, built up on either side of a ridge, to form a subrectangular area about 32 x 32m. This is supported by a drystone wall on the north and east, and masonry on the south-west. The main building was originally L-plan, modified as a long-house 30 x 6m. The rock-cut portion is 22m long, on an elevated rock platform; the walls excavated from whinstone, up to 1.5m thick. West of this is a late rectangular building 13.5 x 6m, part masonry, part rock-cut, but here only 0.70m thick. A track runs between the buildings, but is post 1864. The Hospitallers' charters are in the Eglinton Muniments, Scottish Record Office (Bell 1976, Welsh 1969; 1983).

Current State
The site is within a field of rough pasture containing some natural rock outcrops. There is a quarry, used recently, located approximately 100m to the east of the site.

The building foundations, both rock cut and stonebuilt, are virtually as described by Welsh. It was noted during the site visit that the drystone wall on the north and east was three courses high and survived to a maximum height of 0.90m. Masonry on the south-west side of the platform was bonded with a very hard mortar. The corner of a building here (the south-west corner) was clearly visible, being two courses high (0.50m) along the south edge, and at the corner was 1.50m to the top of the platform.

Two complete red ceramic roof tiles were recovered form the fabric of the east drystone revetting wall. The present owner of Nethercraig commented that the tiles were probably used as weights on haystack covers. The style of the tiles is eighteenth/nineteenth century and they may have roofed the former Nethercraig steading.

ARGYLL AND BUTE COUNCIL

Grange	Slugan Dubh, Isle of Mull
Abbey	Iona?
Order	Benedictine
Parish	Kilfinichen and Kilvickeon

Council	Argyll and Bute
Location	On west coast of Mull north-west of Fidden
NGR	NM 298 217
NMRS site	NM32SW 9 (entry for cists at Fidden)
Site visits	July 2001

History

It has proved very difficult to trace any documentary evidence for granges belonging to the Benedictine abbey of Iona. There is therefore no definite proof that this site at Slugan Dubh relates directly to the abbey.

Archaeology

A shallow bay at Slugan Dubh is cut off by a large drystone wall that runs for at least 100m. This wall has a single course, stands *c.*0.50m high and is built of unshaped boulders. There are two gaps approximately 2m wide towards its south-western and south-eastern ends. This wall is of unknown date and appears to have functioned as a tidal fish trap. To the north-west of the fish trap is an extensive area of rig and furrow between Torr Gaineamhach and the beach. To the north-east of the fish trap are the remains of at least two stone cists. One of these has been broken into, presumably by sheep, and appears to be a long cist. There seems to be a strong chance that these are the same cists referred to in an NMRS entry of 1914 (NM32SW 9).

Current State

The stone wall of the fish trap is in very good condition and the rig and furrow also survives very well. At least one of the cists is eroding badly, mainly because it has been used as a sheep scrape.

BORDERS GRANGES (26)

Ray Cachart

NMRS NO	NMRS NAME	TYPE OF SITE	MONASTERY	SAM/LISTED
NY59NE 15 NY5758 9961	Abbey Knowe or Sike	Grange??	Jedburgh Abbey	
NT61SW NT 608 310	Abbotrule	Grange	Jedburgh Abbey (OSA)	
NT54SW 2	Blainslie	Grange	Melrose Abbey (OCist)	
NT43NE 29 NT 482 379	Buckholm (Buchelm)	Grange	Melrose Abbey (Ocist)	
NT62SW NT 601 225	Chesters Grange		Bishop of Glasgow	
NT53NW 7	Colmslie	'Chapel'; Grange (Possible)	Melrose Abbey (OCist)	
NT53SW 51	Darnick	Grange	Melrose Abbey (OCist)	

NT53NE 42	Drygrange	Grange	Melrose Abbey (OCist)	
NT53SE 50	Eildon	Grange	Melrose Abbey (OCist)	
NT82SW23 NT 812 221	Elliesheugh	Farmstead	Kelso Abbey (OTiron)	SAM 6002
NT43SE 22 NT53SW 39	Faldonside	Grange	Kelso Abbey (OTiron)	
NT53NW 17	Gattonside	Grange	Melrose Abbey (OCist)	
NT02SE NT 07 21	Grange Hill			
NT74NW 12 NT 71 46.	Greenlaw	Ecclesiastical Building		
NT53SW 53	Holydean	Grange	Kelso Abbey (OTiron)	
NT72SE 21	Hownam Grange	Grange	Melrose Abbey (OCist)	
NT54SE 19	Kedslie	Grange	Dryburgh Abbey (OPraem)	
NT15SE21 NT 19 52	Lamancha (Romanno Grange)	House; Sundial	Newbattle Abbey (OCist)	
NT73NE 15	Redden	Grange	Kelso Abbey (OTiron)	
NT40NW 20	Teviothead ALTERNATIVE: Ringwoodfield	Grange	Melrose Abbey (OCist)	
NT86NE NT 86 65	Three Burn Grange			
NT43NE 29	Whitelee (Melrose)	Grange	Melrose Abbey (OCist)	
NT53SW 54	Whitlaw	Grange	Kelso Abbey (OTiron)	
NT52NW 16	Whitmuir Hall	Grange	Kelso Abbey (OTiron)	
NT82NW 39 NT 845 268	Witchcleuch Burn	Farmsteads / Grange?	Kelso Abbey (OTiron)	SAM 4666, 4670
NT50NE 10	Wolfelee	Grange	Jedburgh Abbey (OSA)	

Grange   Abbey Knowe or Sike
Abbey   Jedburgh
Order   Augustinian
Parish   Castleton
Council   Scottish Borders

Location	West side B6357 approximately 3km north of Saughtree
NGR	NY 5758 9961
NMRS site	NY 59NE 15
Site visits	18 September 2002

History

Site of *Abbey* as marked on the OS first edition refers to the foundation remains of a building, possibly sheep folds called 'The Abbey' rather than indicating the site of an ecclesiastical Abbey (Watson). The building most likely acquired its name from Abbey Knowe.

The 'Abbey' place name is mentioned by Gordon in his *'Itinerarium Septentrionale'* 1726 as a specific location where he measured an ancient earthwork the called the Catrail. At this location Gordon found the earthwork measured its ordinary breadth of 26ft.

Archaeology

NY 59NE 15 *c.*5758 9961.

(AREA CENTRED NY 5758 9961) The round head of a cross, with a cross on each side was found in the Abbey Sike in May 1880, by John Chisholm, a shepherd. The fracture of the head from the shaft is recent and appears to have been done purposely. It has the character of a boundary cross.

J HARDY 1890

A finial cross described as 'Remains of Heap Cross', in Hawick Museum, corresponds with the description of that which was found in Abbey Sike. The equal-armed cross-hand is contained within a circle 16in in diameter.

RCAHMS 1956

As marked on the OS 1:10560 at NY 5740 9943 *Stone Cross-head found* AD *1850*. This cross-head fragment is sculpted with the handle of a sword, the remainder being lost with the cross shaft. This cross fragment is considered to be from a memorial cross dating from the mid-thirteenth or fourteenth century.

As marked on the OS first edition 1858-9, *Site of Abbey* at approximately NT 5729 9945 does not appear on the later maps.

Current State

At the time of the visit the area of interest was heavily overgrown with gorse and broom. It was noted that some quarrying had taken place on the south-eastern side of Abbey Knowe. At the base of Abbey Knowe, on the north side of the Dawston Burn, a track leading westwards to Saughtree Grain fords Abbey Sike. On the north side of the track about 0.60m to the west of the ford are parallel turf walls about 0.30m apart, extending approximately 130m and parallel to the track. There is possibly an entrance at the east end. The purpose and date of the walls are uncertain. These turf walls no doubt represent the feature known as the Catrail which was measured by Gordon at the beginning of the eighteenth century. At the 'site of Abbey' no building foundations were observed.

It is possible that the building once known as the 'Abbey' and the feature known as the Catrail could represent elements of a bercarie or monastic sheep grange.

Grange	Abbotrule
Abbey	Jedburgh
Order	Augustinian
Parish	Southdean
Council	Scottish Borders

Location	South-west of Jedburgh on west side of B6357
NGR	NT 608 130
NMRS site	NT61SW
Site visits	19 September 2002

History

A charter of 5 March 1642 grants the '*villam et terras de Abbottisreule…Grange cum molendino*' to William Count of Lothian (Thomson 1894, 410).

Archaeology

There is no record of any archaeological excavations at Abbotrule.

Current State

The present owners of Abbotrule kennels have no knowledge of any extant structures that could relate to grange buildings. The house called Grange appears to be nineteenth century. The overgrown remains of Abbotrule Church and graveyard were visited. It was noted that the grazed flat ground around church and on either side of the track leading south-west from the church would be ideal for a resisitivity survey. The ruins of old Abbotrule house, within a plantation of Scots pine to the south of the kennels, were visited. The remains of a large mansion building are completely overgrown by deciduous trees. There is a very high south-gable end standing to its original height and in a dangerous condition. Nothing was noted that could relate to medieval grange structures.

Grange	Blainslie
Abbey	Melrose
Order	Cistercian
Parish	Melrose
Council	Scottish Borders
Location	West side of A68 between Lauder and Earlston
NGR	NT 54 44
NMRS site	NT54SW 2
Site visit	17 September 2002

History

1175 x 1189 or 1190 Richard de Moreuille, Constable of the King of Scots, with the consent of William de Moreuille his son and heir, grants to Melrose the liberty and licence of sowing *the whole land of Blanesleye and the whole open land in circumference outside the wood as far as Ledre* and therein making their own use according to their own will and anywhere with their marches, except making an assart, as far as Windislaue and thence by the great street which descends by Windislaue towards laweder as far as the marches of Laweder. Witnesses include Jocelin, Bishop of Glasgow [1174-99] and Roland son of Uchtred [Lord of Galloway 1175-1200] (*Melrose Liber*, no 94).

1174 x 1189 or 1190 William de Moreville's grant in the same terms as no 94. Witnesses include Jocelin, Bishop of Glasgow [1174-99], Richard his father [died 1189 or 1190] and Avice of Lancaster his mother (*Melrose Liber*, no 95).

1189 or 1190 x 1196 William de Moreville, Constable of the King of Scots, grants to Melrose, in augmentation of the land of Milchesid, which they have from his father and himself, the whole land and pasture from the east head of the ditch which the monks made, which head extends as far as the great street which goes from Lawedr towards Birchinesid, and by the same great street, on the east side of the same street, southwards, whatever is contained within the named marches in his father's and his own charters which the monks have concerning Milchesid, and the foresaid street as far as Mereburn, which burn is the march between the *land of Bleinesley* and the land of Milchesid (*Melrose Liber*, no 99).

Archaeology

There was a grange, belonging to Melrose Abbey, at Blainslie. A charter of William the Lion, probably datable to about 1170 grants lands and permission to the monks to build. Further grants are made to them in a charter of Richard de Morville in 1180 (R.P. Hardie 1942; A. Jeffrey 1864). (Blainslie farm names appear on NT 54 43 and NT 54 44.)

Current State

Upper Blainslie was visited but there was no response from the farmhouse. In Nether Blainsly, local enquiries produced no knowledge of a grange connection. Nether Blainsly comprises the buildings of two farms dating from the eighteenth century most of which have now been converted into residential accommodation. Cursory inspection of the frontage buildings suggested that they date from eighteenth/nineteenth century.

Grange	Bucholm (Buchelm)
Abbey	Melrose
Order	Cistercian
Parish	Galashiels
Council	Scottish Borders
Location	East side of A7, 3km north of Galashiels
NGR	NT 482 379
NMRS site	NT43NE 29
Site visit	29 September 2002

History

1162 x 1189 or 1190 Richard de Moreville, Constable of the King of Scots grants to Melrose Abbey the liberty and licence to have at *Buchelm one vaccary for 60 cows and a house suitable for their work* within those same enclosures which were there before the grant of this licence (*Melrose Liber*, no 107).

The monks of Melrose were given permission by de Morville in 1180 or before, to build a house for 60 cows at Buchelm (Old Buckholm: NT 482 379). (R.P. Hardie 1942.)

Archaeology

There are no known records of any archaeological excavation on the site of Buckholm vaccary.

Current State

Enquiries at Buckholm farmhouse produced no further information regarding the Buckholm grange or vaccary. A visit was made to the ruined tower house at Old Buckholm (NT 4827 3790). The tower, built in 1582, is now in a very dangerous condition and has been fenced off. On the south side of the tower is a nineteenth-century farmhouse and derelict farm buildings, which were being renovated. A ruined cattle shed lies on the track to the north of the tower. There was no evidence of buildings predating the tower.

Grange	Chesters
Abbey	Bishop of Glasgow
Order	Augustinian
Parish	Ancrum
Council	Scottish Borders
Location	About 4km south-west of Ancrum on north side of River Teviot
NGR	NT 601 225
NMRS site	NT62SW
Site visits	19 September 2002

History
A charter of 17 February 1595-96 grants '*10 mercararum terrarum de Chesteris et Grange*' to Raguelli Bennet (Thomson 1890, no 406).

Archaeology
There are no known records of any archaeological investigation at the site of Chesters Grange.

Current State
The visit was made to Chesters Grange. The owner maintains that the present standing buildings date from mid-nineteenth century. To the west of the main house are redundant nineteenth-century farm buildings standing around a now grassed over courtyard. One barn has been converted into a high machine shed from a much earlier building with blocked windows and doorways. The owner stated that when builders were working on an adjacent conversion they found old 'foundation stones'.

Grange	Colmslie
Abbey	Melrose
Order	Cistercian
Parish	Melrose
Council	Scottish Borders
Location	About 4.5km to the north-east of Galashiels adjacent to Langshaw
NGR	NT 5132 3981
NMRS site	NT53NW 7
Site visit	17 September 2002

History
Between 1153 and 1165, Malcolm IV granted 'one stead in Cumbesley for building a cow-house for a hundred cows, and a fold' to the Cistercian Abbey at Melrose (NT 53 SW 30). (*Liber de Melros*, 6). The buildings of Cumbesley are mentioned in another charter of 1165 x 1214 (this would suggest that there was a grange, not a chapel, at Colmslie). (OPS1851.)

Archaeology
'At Colmsly (Colmslie: NT 512 396) there has been a chapel the ruins of which are yet to be seen. It has been dedicated to Columba, Abbot of Hi' (A. Milne 1743).

There appears to be no documentary evidence to support the idea that there was a chapel at Colmslie. Traditionally a chapel stood in a field between the farm of Cumbesley and the road on the north (A. Jeffrey 1864).

In Chapel Park two ash trees mark the site of a church dedicated to St Columba. Not a stone now stands, though the walls of an old mill close at hand contain incongruous stones. It has been said that the graveyard was ploughed up early last century (J. Freer 1892).

Centred NT 5132 3981. The field to the north of Colmslie, parcel number 1808 on OS 25in, was pointed out as Chapel Park by the occupiers of Colmslie. No trace of the chapel or the two ash trees was found. Visited by OS (WDJ) 25 January 1961.

Current State
In the area formally known as Chapel Park stands a new bungalow named Chapel Know. Higher up the slope, in the area where the chapel supposedly stood, a new sheep shed now stands. The owner, Mr Dunn, who is well-versed in contemporary local history does not know of any upstanding remains that could relate to a chapel or a grange.

Grange	Darnick
Abbey	Melrose

Order	Cistercian
Parish	Melrose
Council	Scottish Borders
Location	Unlocated
NGR	NT 53 34
NMRS site	NT53SE 50
Site visits	20 September 2002

History
Darnick is listed by the RCAHMS as a grange belonging to Melrose Abbey (RCAHMS 1956).

Archaeology
Darnick Tower, a sixteenth-century tower-house of the Heiton family, stands on the site of a predecessor destroyed in 1545. The tower is built on the T-plan with a three-storey oblong main block running east–west and a small stair wing projecting from near the middle of the south wall. A low, possibly original, outbuilding, containing a doorway, formerly projected from the west half of the south wall but this has been removed. The tower is of rubble with freestone dressings and was formerly harled.

The entrance is in the stair wing and bears the date 1595. The windows have been enlarged, the bartizan and garret have been rebuilt and an extension has been added to the eastern side, but otherwise the tower retains much of its original character. (D. MacGibbon and T. Ross 1892; RCAHMS 1956, visited 1933.)

Current State
Darnick Tower is now occupied as residential accommodation (2002).

Grange	Drygrange
Abbey	Melrose
Order	Cistercian
Parish	Melrose
Council	Scottish Borders
Location	Site now occupied by St Andrews College on east side of A68
NGR	NT 577 354
NMRS site	NT53NE 42, 53
Site visits	17 September 2002

History
According to Fordun, one of the granges belonging to Melrose Abbey was called Heldwii, or perhaps Hardwii. This stood at the present-day Drygrange (NT 577 354), and was the place where the monks had their principal store-house and granary (J.A. Wade 1861).

Archaeology
Architectural fragments, including Roman material, are incorporated into the summer-house on the lawn to the south of the house (RCAHMS 1956).

Current State
The summer-house has been recently renovated (2002) with HLF money, the architectural fragments are still as reported by RCAHMS. There are no visible structural remains that might relate to the grange.

Grange	Eildon
Abbey	Melrose
Order	Cistercian
Parish	Melrose
Council	Scottish Borders
Location	Norton Hall farm in settlement of Eildon due North of Newton St Boswells
NGR	NT 573 326
NMRS site	NT53SE 50
Site visits	20 September 2002

History
There was a grange, belonging to Melrose Abbey, at Eildon (Hardie 1942).

Current State
On a visit to Norton Hall Farm the owners showed me a stone water stoup which is now built into the south wall of the barn. This is the only visible element that might relate to the former grange.

Grange	Elliesheugh
Abbey	Kelso
Order	Tironensian
Parish	Morebattle
Council	Scottish Borders
Location	On the side of Ellisheugh Hill due North of Belford and Mowhaugh
NGR	NT 8120 2218
NMRS site	NT82SW 23
Scheduled Monument?	SAM 6002
Site visits	18 September 2002

History
The farmstead and field system at Elliesheugh probably originated as a grange belonging to Kelso Abbey (Shead 1975).

Archaeology
Situated on the north slopes of Ellisheugh Hill are the remains of probably the farm of Elliesheugh (see also NT82SW 44).

It consists of: (a) a large, turf-banked enclosure with traces of stone showing, measuring about 38 x 29m (north-east to south-west), with two small structures within the north-west angle; (b) the foundations of a rectangular building, about 18 x 5.4m, a slight turf bank runs from its south angle in a curve to the east angle of (a); (c) the foundations of a rectangular building, about 18 x 6.4m; (d) a roughly rectangular enclosure formed by a slight turf bank, measuring 25 x 16m (north-west to south-east); (e) just below the crest of the hill is a scooped-out structure divided into two compartments at different levels; it measures 19 x 11m overall, and would appear to be the remains of a large kiln. Visited by OS (WDJ) 19 August 1960.

Current State
Site as described above apart from some erosion damage in the south-western corner of the large enclosure. The site is normally grazed by sheep and cattle.

Grange	Faldonside
Abbey	Kelso

Order	Tironensian
Parish	Galashiels
Council	Scottish Borders
Location	Modern farm of Faldonside on south side of River Tweed or Faldonside House
NGR	NT 501 327
NMRS site	NT53SW 39 or NT43SE 22
Site visits	20 September 2002

History

A rent roll of 1300 shows that there was a grange, belonging to Kelso Abbey, at Foudon, which corresponds to the modern Faldonside (NT 501 327). There were 21 cottages, as well as the 'grangia' (granary or farm steading). (R.P. Hardie 1942.)

Current State

The current owners of both the farm and the house knew of nothing on their properties that might be connected with a monastic grange.

Grange	Gattonside
Abbey	Melrose
Order	Cistercian
Parish	Melrose
Council	Scottish Borders
Location	Unlocated
NGR	NT 5430 3506
NMRS site	NT53NW 17
Site visits	17 September 2002

History

Melrose had a grange, afterwards called Drygrange, at the east end of Gattonside (R.P. Hardie 1942).

Archaeology

Milne reports the finding of what he interprets as the remains of a pre-Reformation chapel 'near the vicar's house' (? vicinity of Vicar's Knowe: NT 5430 3506), Gattonside, and states that many of the stones, some of them curiously carved, were visible in 1743 built into that house. Cultivation in the vicinity had exposed vaults indicating 'that in time of Popery several good buildings stood here' (A. Milne 1743).

There is no documentary evidence for a chapel in this area. The ONB notes the finding of foundations which were interpreted as those of a castle at the south-east corner of Castle Field at the site now occupied by Springbank (NT 5435 3522), and also the existence in the middle of the village of Gattonside of 'a very ancient building' which was known as 'The Castle'. The west gable and parts of the side walls, obviously much older than the rest of the building, were 3ft thick.

Since Gattonside belonged to Melrose Abbey from the mid-twelfth century, it is most likely that there would be a castle there. Possibly all these buildings were part of the grange which the monks are known to have had there (*Name Book* 1859; A. Jeffrey 1864; J.A. Smith 1875).

The grange and lands of Drygrange were separate and distinct from those at Gattonside; both belong to Melrose Abbey (see also NT53NE 42) (J.A. Wade 1861).

Current State
Conversations with a knowledgeable local regarding this site indicated that nothing is known of any surviving structural evidence. There is nothing visible in Castle Field or in the vicinity of Springbank.

Grange	Grange Hill
Abbey	?
Order	?
Parish	Tweedsmuir
Council	Scottish Borders
Location	This hill lies above Hawkshaw Castle on the south side of the River Tweed
NGR	NT 07 21
NMRS sites	NT02SE 1 (Hawkshaw Castle) NT02SE 63 (unenclosed Prehistoric settlement)
Site visits	11 November 2002

Current State
The origin of this name for a massive hill on the south side of the River Tweed is not known. There is nothing in the vicinity to suggest any former connection to a monastic grange.

Grange	Greenlaw
Abbey	?
Order	?
Parish	Greenlaw
Council	Scottish Borders
Location	Modern settlement of Greenlaw
NGR	NT 71 46
NMRS site	NT74NW 12
Site visits	Not visited

Archaeology
An unimportant or unclassified site (grange, hermitage, large chantry, etc.) is plotted at Greenlaw (NT 71 46) (OS Monastic Britain (north sheet) 1950).

Further research is required to find out where the 1950 OS reference originates from and whether it is genuine.

Grange	Holydean
Abbey	Kelso
Order	Tironensian
Parish	Bowden
Council	Scottish Borders
Location	Modern settlement of Holydean
NGR	NT 537 302
NMRS site	NT53SW 53 (grange), NT53SW 2 (chapel and graveyard), NT53SW 23 (castle)
Site visits	19 September 2002

History
The house and lands of Holydean were included in the grant made by David I (1124–53) to the monks of Selkirk, and were confirmed to them, by renewed charters, after their translation

to Kelso. They had a grange at this place. (Holydean: NT 537 302). (*New Statistical Account* (NSA) 1845 (T. Jollie); N.F. Shead 1975.)

There is a reference in an Ordnance Survey *Name Book* of 1859 to 'The site of a chapel and graveyard, formerly in connection with Holydean Castle (NT53SW 24), as appears from a plan in the possession of Mr R. Blackie, farmer of Holydean.' (*Name Book* 1859.)

As this chapel is situated on the edge of a ravine called 'Ringan's Dean', its dedication would appear to have been to St Ninian. Information from OS Recorder (IF) 6 March 1979.

Holydean Castle: the greater part of this castle was demolished before 1793 to obtain material for building a farmhouse. The *Statistical Account* (OSA, 1793) states that the castle had a courtyard about 3-4 acre in extent, enclosed by a wall 16ft high and 4ft thick, protected by gun-loops about 30ft apart.

In the front wall there was an arched gateway with a strong iron gate. Inside the enclosure there were two strong towers, of three and five storeys respectively, besides porters' lodges, servants' hall, vaulted cellars, bakehouses etc. The present remains, now incorporated in the modern farm steading of Holydean, include the entrance gateway, dating from the late sixteenth or early seventeenth century, with an oval gun-loop on its east side.

Farther east there is an incomplete vaulted undercroft 17.5ft wide, with a present length of 26ft; that this was the bakehouse is shown by the large built-up fireplace, traceable in the surviving gable. The entrance lintel of one of the towers has been inserted above the entrance to the farmhouse. It bears a shield flanked by the initials V.K. for Walter Ker, and an inscription followed by a date, now illegible but given by the OSA as 1530. This date, however, seems to be too early as it was only in 1543 that Sir Walter Ker of Cessford married Isabel Ker of Ferniehurst, and not until 1571 that they received from the Commendator of Kelso Abbey a feu-charter for the lands of Halidene.

On the north of the steading there is a circular draw-well, 33ft 1in in diameter, housed in a niche. This well resembles the one inside the Earl's Palace at Kirkwall, which can be dated to 1606. Its traditional name, 'Hobby Ker's Well', may have come from Robert Ker, First Earl of Roxburghe, grandson of the laird of Cessford mentioned above (RCAHMS 1956).

The remains of Holydean Castle and Hobbie Ker's Well are as described above. The vaulted undercroft is now used as a tractor shed.

The RCAHM does not mention two short lengths of walling which are extant. The portion at NT 5374 3027 is 4.6m long, about 1.2m thick and 4.0m high, and houses Hobbie Ker's Well. The portion at NT 5375 3025 is 5m long, 1.2m thick and about 8m high, with a rectangular opening some 3.3m above ground level. Both fragments of wall are ivy-covered (Visited by OS (EGC) 8 February 1961).

Current State

There is an inscribed lintel above the main door of the house. Fragments of the castle buildings on the site are still visible. The current owner suggests that the former site of the chapel above Holydean at (NT 5366 3038) may be more likely to have been the location of buildings associated with the grange.

Grange	Hownam Grange
Abbey	Melrose
Order	Cistercian
Parish	Hownam
Council	Scottish Borders
Location	Modern farm of Hownam Grange
NGR	NT 784 226
NMRS site	NT72SE 21
Site visits	18 September 2002

History

1165 x 1174 John son of Orm grants to Melrose *the land of Hunedun* by those right boundaries which he perambulated between his land and the lands of Wittun, Grubheued, Cliftun and Molle and as the boundaries were perambulated between himself and the monks as far as that place where the small stream falls into Huneduneburne on the east side of Hulkiles Cross, and thence again by the same stream as far as its source, and then westwards as far as the small hill and thence across the slope between Brunecnolh and Helle and then descending by the boundaries which he made to them as far as Haufurlang done, and then as the burn descends into the Kalne; rendering annually 20s (*Melrose Liber*, no 127).

1166 x 1170 William I confirms to Melrose the grant by John, son of Orm of *the whole land … in the territory of Hunedun* (*RRS*, ii, no 72; *Melrose Liber*, no 128).

1185 Agreement between William, parson of Hunun, and Melrose Abbey, with the consent of John son of Orm, advocate of the church of Hunun and founder of the *Grange of Hunedune*, and with the consent of Jocelin, Bishop of Glasgow, whereby the monks will render each year to the church of Hunun 40d at Pentecost for teinds and all earthly exactions and all things from the *Grange of Hunedune* so that the grange will be quit by the boundaries contained in the charter of John son of Orm at the church of Hunum; and, if it should happen that the monks accept more land than they have in the foresaid parish, they will give from that land the garbal teinds or they will make a composition with the parson at the time (*Melrose Liber*, no 129).

1180 x 1199 Jocelin, Bishop of Glasgow confirms agreement between Hvctred de Grubesheued and Melrose, whereby Hvctred granted to Melrose the haugh beside the water of Kalne, by its right measures and boundaries, namely as the old course of the same water, and as the measures were placed between them and perambulated in [the fifth festival of Easter?] 1180; Moreover Hvctred grants to the monks a road across his land of Grubesheued to the land of the monks where their wagons can sufficiently go and return to their *grange of Hvnedun* (*Melrose Liber*, no 118).

1180 x 1199 William son of John son of Horm grants to Melrose, for the salvation of King William and David his brother, that donation which John his father gave to them of *the land of Hunedun* by those right marches which he himself perambulated to them between the land of Hunedun and the land of Wittun and between the land of Hunedun and the land of Grubeheued and between the land of Hunedun and the land of Cliftun and likewise between the land of Hunedun and the land Molle of [boundaries specified as in no 127] (*Melrose Liber*, no 130).

[undated, late twelfth-century, ?pre-1198] Anselm of Wichetune grants to Melrose the land with pertinents perambulated by himself and Glaj nephew/grandson (*nepos*) of Robert Avenel, with the cellerar and monks of Melrose, viz as the furrow (*sulca*) of the ploughland on the north side […it] from the road which lies from Hunedune towards Molle and goes as far as the rock, and from the rock as far as the well and as the same furrow goes from the well [missing] and then as far as Burnam, for the salvation of King William and David his brother; Furthermore he grants them his whole peatery which is between Molope and Berope and Herdstrete which divides the lands of Molle and Hunum; Moreover he grants them as much firewood in his wood of Molope as one horse can carry every year from Easter to the Nativity [missing]. Witnesses include John son of Horm, William his son (*Melrose Liber*, no 135).

1198 x 1214 Robert de Lincoln confirms to Melrose, for the salvation of King William, the Queen, Alexander his son and Earl David, that part of the land in the territory of Molle which Anselm de Wittun gave them with the adjacent meadows by all the marches and boundaries as contained in the foresaid Anselm's charter; Furthermore he grants them that whole peatery which is between Molope and Berope and Herdstrete which divides the lands of Molle and Hunum; Moreover he grants them as much firewood in his wood of Molope as one horse can carry as far as the *Grange of Hunedun*, every year from Easter to the Nativity of St Mary; To be held quit of forensic and all earthly service; and the monks shall have free and agreed entry and exit by his land for leading their firewood and peats and their other necessities without disturbance or molestation (*Melrose Liber*, no 136).

1174 x 1189 Patrick de Ridale grants to Melrose for the salvation of William of King of Scots, that part of land which they hold in the territory of Ywittune, viz towards the *Grange of Hunedune*, by the boundaries named and perambulated, namely as the old course of the water of Caalne divides the land of Ywittun and Grubbeheued, and thence up by the same water as that water divides the land of Ywittune and Hunum, and thence as far as the upper limit of the upper Halech and thence by the water across as far as Hoch of Heuiside, and thence descending by the same Hoch as far as Harehoudene, and thence up by Harehoudene as far as the place where the old wall begins at Harehoudene and so up by the wall as the wall goes westwards towards Ywittune from south of Harehoch as far as the place where the same wall turns northwards and thence from the wall westwards as far as the head of the stream and thence westwards a far as Elnecloch, and thence descending by Elnecloch as far as the boundaries of Merbothle, and thence descending by the stream which divides the land of Merbothle from Ywittune as far as Elstanes halech and so down between Elstannes halech and the land of Merbothle as far as the same stream falls into the Caalne. Witnesses include Jocelin, Bishop of Glasgow [1174-99], Ralph, Abbot of Cupar [1171-89] (*Melrose Liber*, no 166).

A grange, belonging to Melrose Abbey, at Howman is mentioned by Wade (Howman Grange: NT 784 226) (J.A. Wade 1861).

A charter of 28 August 1609 refers to '*Hownemgrange*' and '*Hownemgrange-mylne*' as being possessions of Melrose Abbey (Thomson 1892, 51).

Current State
On a visit to the farm the current owners showed me the site of a threshing mill with the iron mill wheel still *in situ*. None of the current farm buildings appear to be any older than the nineteenth century.

Grange	Kedslie
Abbey	Dryburgh
Order	Premonstratensian
Parish	Melrose
Council	Scottish Borders
Location	Modern settlement of Kedslie
NGR	NT 553 405
NMRS site	NT54SE 19 (grange), NT54SW 26 (farmstead)
Site visits	Not visited

History
There was a grange, belonging to Dryburgh Abbey, at Kedslie (NT 553 405). The monks acquired the lands about 1150; a description of them is given in a confirmatory charter of late twelfth-century date. Kedslie is noted among the 'spoyle' of Hertford's invasion of 1545 (R.P. Hardie 1942).

NT54SW 26 5492 4036
A farmstead comprising three unroofed buildings arranged around a courtyard, two roofed buildings and four enclosures, one of which is annotated, Sheepfold, is depicted on the first edition of the OS 6in map (Berwickshire 1862, sheet xxvi). One unroofed building is shown on the current edition of the OS 1:10560 map (1968).
(Information from RCAHMS (SAH) 22 September 2000).

Current State
The modern farm of Kedslie occupies this site.

Grange	Lamancha (Romanno Grange)
Abbey	Newbattle
Order	Cistercian
Parish	Newlands
Council	Scottish Borders
Location	Modern settlement of Lamancha on north side of A701
NGR	NT 19 52
NMRS site	NT15SE 21
Site visits	11 November 2002

History

The house of Lamancha incorporates work of several periods. The oldest part appears to be the vaulted basement which may have formed part of the 'little house' erected at Romanno Grange in 1663 (A. Pennecuik 1815). The building was lengthened considerably at some time before 1832, when further extensions were made. It was reduced and remodelled in 1927. In front of the house, there is a carved stone sundial, which probably dates to the turn of the seventeenth and eighteenth century (RCAHMS 1967, visited 1963; J.W. Buchan and H. Paton 1926-7; T. Ross 1890).

This building, and the sundial at NT 1995 5223 are as described and illustrated by the previous authorities. The present house, still known as Lamancha, is on the site of and incorporates the remains of Romanno Grange (Mrs R Munro, owner, Lamancha). Sundial surveyed at 1/2500. (Visited by OS (RD) 2 February 1970.)

A charter of 3 February 1620 refers to *'terras de Romano-grange'* as being one of the possessions of Newbattle Abbey (Thomson 1892, 771).

Current State

A visit to Lamancha House was attempted but rebuffed by the current owner who said that he has had 'problems' with Historic Scotland regarding certain renovations and did not want anyone involved in anything to do with them on his property!

Grange	Redden
Abbey	Kelso
Order	Tironensian
Parish	Sprouston
Council	Scottish Borders
Location	Modern farm of Redden on south side of River Tweed
NGR	NT 775 374
NMRS site	NT73NE 15
Site visits	12 November 2002

History

There was a grange, belonging to Kelso Abbey, at Redden (NT 775 374) (N.F. Shead 1975).

Current State

The current farm buildings and cottages date to the eighteenth and nineteenth centuries. The occupier of the cottage to the south-east of Redden Farm says that Edinburgh University carried out an excavation to the south-east of his cottage.

Grange	Teviothead or Ringwoodfield
Abbey	Melrose
Order	Cistercian
Parish	Teviothead
Council	Scottish Borders

Location	unlocated
NGR	unlocated
NMRS site	NT40NW 20
Site visits	Not visited

History

Between Bowan Hill (NT 4082 0542) and Priesthaugh (NT 4655 0471), probably lay the Grange of the monks of Melrose. The name is not known, and it fails to appear on Gordon's Map of Teviotdale about 1650, suggesting that it had lapsed by then (G. Watson 1950).

A charter of 28 August 1609 describes the '*terras de Ringwodfield*' and lists one of them as '*Grange*' (Thomson 1892, 51).

Grange	Three Burn Grange
Abbey	Coldingham Priory?
Order	?
Parish	Coldingham
Council	Scottish Borders
Location	Modern house called Three Burn Grange
NGR	NT 867 653
NMRS site	No entry for Three Burn Grange (NT86NE 46 Mid Grange)
Site visits	12 November 2002

History

The modern Ordnance Survey map shows a group of place names that all include the 'Grange' element, these are 'Three Burn Grange; Grange Cottage; Grange Plantation and Three Grange Burn, Mid Grange Burn and South Grange Burn'. Interestingly one of these place names, Three Burn Grange, is shown in a different location on the first edition Ordnance Survey map at NT 8635 6540. The modern Three Burn Grange was known as South Grange at the time of the first edition map.

Archaeology

There are no records of any archaeological finds or excavations on this site.

Current State

Three Burn Grange is said to have been a nineteenth-century hunting lodge. On a site visit some old stone wall foundations were seen and photographed, there is nothing upstanding that can definitely be associated with a former monastic grange.

Grange	Whitelee (Melrose)
Abbey	Melrose
Order	Cistercian
Parish	Melrose
Council	Scottish Borders
Location	Occupied by modern farm of Whitelee
NGR	NT 465 396
NMRS site	NT43NE 29
Site visits	20 September 2002

History

1 September 1310, agreement between William de Lamberton, Bishop of St Andrews for himself and his church on one part, and William de Foghow, Abbot of Melrose for himself and his convent on the other, after a long dispute between them and their predecessors concerning

the land of Carthaw adjacent to the *Grange of Witeley*, which the Bishop and his predecessors claimed to belong to them and their church with full right; the said abbot and convent and their predecessors asserting in opposition that the same land belonged to them and their monastery with full right. That for the good of peace the same foresaid land of Carthaw would be held in common during the life of the bishop as it was held on the day of the creation thereof, except the site of *Grange of Witley and the cowfold (vaccaria) and sheepfold (bercaria) and other buildings with enclosures anciently made* (*Melrose Liber*, no 414).

Probably about 1184, he gave them the further right to have at Witelei (Whitelee: NT 465 396) a house for 120 cows (or a sheep-fold), a house in which the monks might have a fire, and a hay-shed. They were not, however, to have any other lodges within the forest, but only wattled huts for temporary use (R.P. Hardie 1942).

Current State
This site is currently occupied by the working farm of Whitelee, there is nothing visible of any antiquity.

Grange	Whitlaw
Abbey	Kelso
Order	Tironensian
Parish	Galashiels
Council	Scottish Borders
Location	In the vicinity of Over Whitlaw Farm or White Law
NGR	unlocated
NMRS site	NT53SW 54
Site visits	19 September 2002

History
There was a grange, belonging to Kelso Abbey, at Whitlaw (White Law: NT 514 303; Over Whitlaw: NT 517 300; Nether Whitlaw: NT 513 295) (N.F. Shead 1975).

Current State
The farm buildings at Over Whitelaw Farm are no older than the nineteenth century. There is nothing else visible that might relate to a monastic grange.

Grange	Whitmuir Hall
Abbey	Kelso
Order	Tironensian
Parish	Selkirk
Council	Scottish Borders
Location	Modern house called Whitmuir Hall to south of A699
NGR	NT 503 273
NMRS site	NT52NW 16
Site visits	11 November 2002

History
There was a grange, belonging to Kelso Abbey, at Whitmuir (Whitmuir Hall: NT 503 273) (N.F. Shead 1975).

Current State
Whitmuir Hall is now a self-catering hotel. On a visit to Friarshawmuir conversations with several local inhabitants led to an examination of a former site of a tower house and an associated circular platform and scoops. The date and origin of these features is unclear.

Grange	Colpenhope Grange (Witchcleugh Burn)
Abbey	Kelso
Order	Tironensian
Parish	Yetholm
Council	Scottish Borders
Location	On the right bank of the Witchcleugh Burn at 200m OD
NGR	NT 845 268
NMRS site	NT82NW 39
Scheduled Monument?	SAM 4666
Site visits	18 September 2002

Archaeology

Farmsteads, Witchcleuch Burn. In rough pasture on the right bank of the Whitchcleuch Burn, a quarter of a mile east-south-east of Halterburn farm and at a height of 600ft OD, there is a complex of structures and enclosures a little over three acres in extent. The remains, which are best understood by reference to the plan (RCAHMS 1956, fig 595), are difficult to interpret in detail owing to damage resulting from stone-robbery and drainage, but two units, probably belonging to different periods, can be distinguished. The smaller unit, which is likely to be the later of the two, is represented by a three-roomed cottage (J), now reduced to its foundation-course of large boulders, with which are associated the garth (II) and a small outhouse (K). This unit is typical of the small crofts whose remains occur frequently on the lower slopes of the Cheviot foot-hills, and of which some appear from Stobie's map of Roxburghshire to have been occupied as late as 1770.

The larger unit consists of a trapezoidal enclosure, measuring overall 115yds from east to west by 103yds from north to south and surrounded by a bank which is accompanied on the north and east sides by an external ditch. On these latter sides the bank (I) formed of ditch-upcast, measures up to 15ft in thickness at the base by 2ft 2ins in height, while the ditch averages 14ft in width at the top, 8ft at the bottom, and 2ft 3ins in depth. In spite of their substantial size, the bank and ditch are clearly not defensive in the military sense; they were presumably designed, probably with the addition of a palisade or hedge on the crest of the bank, either to fence in stock or to protect crops grown within the enclosure from being ravaged by beasts grazing in the open ground outside. Both bank and ditch die out on the curve at the north-west corner and, if they ever existed on the west side, they must have been entirely obliterated. The limit of the enclosure on this side is indicated, however, by a slighter bank which first appears on the lip of the counterscarp of the ditch at the corner and, after a short break due to drainage-ditching, extends south to the north-east corner of the later garth (II).

On the south side the edge of the steep gully drained by the Witchcleuch Burn provides a natural boundary and no ditch was required here. A short segment of bank at the west end of the bluff may possibly be original, but elsewhere on this side the bank has been faced with drystone and may therefore be presumed to be secondary. One entrance to the enclosure, 15ft wide is situated in the centre of the north side, while there may have been a second at the south-east corner leading to the burn. Within the interior, which falls 70ft from east to west, the foundations of six buildings (C-H) can be traced; the largest of these (C) measures 33 x 25ft within a stony bank from 5-13ft thick, and may have been either a single-roomed cottage or a tower. Its entrance, in the east wall, opens into a small garth (L) which is bounded by a boulder-faced earthen bank with a ditch on its outer side. Two parallel ditches in the north-east quarter (M and N), with upcast banks on one or other of their lips, closely resemble the enclosure ditch, but their purpose is obscure. The only other internal features of interest are a large, rectangular, scooped floor (A) at the south-east corner, and a smaller circular scoop in the curve of the opposite corner (RCAHMS 1956, visited 29 May 1947).

Current State

The site is as described above. Some rabbit burrows were observed on the north and north-east boundary earthworks and one mole-hill.

Grange	Wolfelee
Abbey	Jedburgh
Order	Augustinian
Parish	Southdean
Council	Scottish Borders
Location	Wolfelee House
NGR	NT 5893 0922
NMRS site	NT50NE 10
Site visits	19 September 2002

History

Wolflee or Woole lies on the right bank of Wauchope Burn (sic). In early times it was the property of Jedburgh Abbey. The Turnbulls possessed part of the estate in 1621, and it eventually passed to the Elliots. (Wolfelee is situated at NT 5893 0922, on Catlee Burn.) (A. Jeffrey 1857.)

Current State

The main house at Wolfelee burnt down in 1975 and the area is now grassed over as a lawn.

DUMFRIES AND GALLOWAY GRANGES (27)

Martin Brann

NMRS NUMBER	NMRS NAME	TYPE OF SITE	MONASTERY	SAM/ LISTED
	Annan		Guisborough Priory (OSA)	
NX64NE NX 65 45	Balmangan or Grange of Senwick			
	Caerlaverock		Holm Cultram	
NX59SE NX56 93	Carsphairn		Vaudey Abbey (OCist)	
NX76NE 35 NX 798 667	Chapelton ALTERNATIVE(S): Old Grange Barn [part of Kings Grange?]	Farm-steading		
NX05NE NX 08 56	Culgrange			
NY17SW NY 112 749	Dormont Grange			
NS80NW NS 80 07	Eliock Grange			
NX64NE NX 680 470	Grange (Trail)		Trail Priory (OSA)	

NX98NW NX98SW	Grange (Dalswinton)			
NX98NW 7 NX 926 850	Grange (Friarcarse)	Religion/ 'Monastery'	Melrose Abbey (OCist)	
NY28SW NY 234 828	Grange (Tundergarth)			
NX76NE 36 NX 791 670	Grange Farm (Urr) [part of Kings Grange?]	Farmhouse; Farm-steading		
NX35NE NX 36 57	Grange of Bladnoch			
NX45NE NX 45 59	Grange of Cree			
NX98SE NX 95 80	Grange of Holywood		Holywood Abbey (OPrem)	
NX86NE	Grange of Kirkgunzeon		Holm Cultram Abbey (OCist)	
NX97NE	Grange of Lincluden		Lincluden Collegiate Church (formerly Lincluden Nunnery, OSB)	
NX88SE	Grangemylne (Dunscore) [part of Grange (Friarcarse)?]		Melrose Abbey (OCist)	
NX76NE 37 NX 785 671	Kings Grange	Country House		
NX46SW 8	Mains of Penninghame ALTERNATIVE(S): Penninghame Hall; Howe Ha'	Grange (Possible) Moat	Bishop of Galloway?	
NY07SE NY 053 734	Mouswald Grange ALTERNATIVE(S): Brocklehurst Farm			
NX96NE 33	Shambellie Grange ALTERNATIVE(S): Ahambellie Grange, Archway	Residential	Dumfries and Galloway	L
NY26NW NY 230 682	Stapleton Grange			
NX76SW NX 733 622	Threave Mains ALTERNATIVE(S): Threave-Grange			
NT10NW 11	Walls Frenchland	Moated Site	Knights Templar?	
NY29NE 12	Watcarrick Alternative(s): Chapel of Watcarrick	Funerary; Religion	Dumfries and Galloway	SAM 4720

Grange	Annan
Abbey	Guisborough Priory
Order	Augustinian
Parish	Annan
Council	Dumfries and Galloway
Location	Unknown
Scheduled	No
Site visit	Not visited

History

Guisborough Priory (Augustinian) Yorks had a *grange* at Annan (Stringer 1985, 204, ref *Cart ... de Gyseburne*, Brown (ed), ii, nos 1180-1, 1184-5, 1187-8). The exact location of this grange is not known. Further research is required to try and accurately locate it.

Grange	Balmangan or Grange of Senwick
Abbey	?
Order	?
Parish	Borgue
Council	Dumfries and Galloway
Location	Balmangan is situated 2km south-east of Borgue village.
Ownership	Mr N. Pickin, Balmangan
NGR	NX 650 457
NMRS site	NX64NE12
Scheduled	No
Site visit	September 2002

History

The history of Balmangan suggests that it has always been in secular ownership (Maxwell-Irving, 2000, 68). The nearby medieval church of Senwick was granted to Tongland Abbey by David II and confirmed by Michael, Bishop of Galloway (*c.*1355 x 59), its revenues having been held for some 40 years in 1410 when papal confirmation was sought. Parsonage remained with the abbey, while the vicarage appears to have been held by a canon of that house. The parish was united to Borgue 1670, held with Borgue from 1590.

Archaeology

No extant remains of a grange are known.

The decaying ruins of a sixteenth-century tower house (see *The Border Towers of Scotland: The West March*, Maxwell-Irving, 2000, 68 for details) adjoin the farmhouse which appears to be late eighteenth to early nineteenth century. The steading buildings on the other side of the road are all nineteenth and twentieth century in date.

The nearby ruins of Senwick Church and Manse (NX64NE16, NX64NE17) were visited in the course of the 1998 Dumfries and Galloway graveyards survey (database/archive in DGSMR) from which the following description is taken:

Senwick Church, remains of oblong building 16.7 x 7.6m over dilapidated walls 1.1m wide, varying from turf covered footings to 2m high, formerly divided into two almost equal compartments, possibly twelfth- or thirteenth-century walls survive up to 1.7m high in north-east corner only. The original mortar bonded walling is in poor condition and is at risk from the large tree growing on the wall. The rest of the building has collapsed to broad linear rubble spreads. Some medieval mouldings, presumably from the church are built into the adjacent walled burial enclosure of the Blairs. A drystone dyke has been built over most of the collapsed east wall of the church.

Senwick Manse, the ruins of the manse measuring approximately 17 x 6m stand approximately 20m to the east of the church. It has clay bonded walls, originally pointed or rendered. The east gable is largely intact with a surviving fireplace and window. Ground floor loop windows survive and a cupboard and cruck slot also remain in the south wall. There is much rubble from possible outbuildings and collapsed dykes to the north of the manse.

Grange	Caerlaverock
Abbey	Holm Cultram
Order	Cistercian
Parish	Caerlaverock
Council	Dumfries and Galloway
Location	Unknown
Ownership	Caerlaverock Old Castle is a property in care managed by Historic Scotland
NGR	NY 02 65
Scheduled	No
Site visit	Not visited

History

Radulph son of Dunegal, Lord of Strath Nith granted a lease to Holm Cultram Abbey of the lands of Conheath ('Colnehath') and Caerlaverock ('Karlaueroc'). This lease was confirmed by Malcolm IV (1153-1165) and subsequently by Pope Alexander III (1159-81). The exact date of the grant may have been 1157, for it was in that year the monks were given wayleaves through Annandale by Robert de Brus (*Holm Cultram Charters*, 52-3 and 122; Barrow, 1960, 278).

Sometime before 1174 a charter documented the rivalry between the Cistercian houses of Dundrennan, near Kirkcudbright, and Holm Cultram. It recorded an agreement between the two abbeys that on the eastern side of the Nith, in Radulph's territory, neither house was to acquire more land without the consent of the other. It would seem that the objection of Dundrennan, Abbey, an earlier foundation, led to Holm Cultram giving up Conheath and Caerlaverock, for there is no further mention of these lands in the abbey records (*Holm Cultram Charters*, 52-3) and the land appears to have passed to the Crown. About 1220 John De Maccuswell (*c.*1200-41), sheriff of Roxburgh and Teviotdale, was granted the barony of Caerlaverock by the king.

Archaeology

No extant remains of the twelfth-century grange have been found to date in Caerlaverock parish.

No specific mention of a grange sited in the lands of Conheath and Caerlaverock is made in the Holm Cultram charters, but one can be assumed. However, its location and that of an associated boat landing on the estate is unknown. Caerlaverock Old Castle and harbour, a site in the vicinity of Caerlaverock Parish Church, or Conheath (by Glencaple) could all be conjectured as the site of the twelfth-century monastic estate centre, but evidence remains to be found.

Recent excavations on the castle mound at Caerlaverock Old Castle, the earlier of the two thirteenth-century castles built by the Maxwells at Caerlaverock, 9 miles south of Dumfries on the Solway shore (NGR NY 027 654), revealed only evidence for the establishment of the moated castle in the late 1220s, its sequential development and abandonment in the 1270s in favour of the surviving triangular plan castle.

Grange	Carsphairn
Abbey	Vaudey Abbey (and Melrose Abbey)
Order	Cistercian
Parish	Carsphairn
Council	Dumfries and Galloway

Location	Unknown
NGR	NX 56 93
Scheduled	No
Site visit	Not visited

History

Vaudey Abbey (Cistercian), Lincs had a short-lived *grange* at Carsphairn (Stringer 1985, 321, n139, citing *CDS*, i, no 795).

Towards the end of the twelfth century, Thomas Colville leased to Melrose Abbey the lands of Kar, or Keresban, (Carsphairn), which formed part of the lands of Dalmellington. Alan, Lord of Galloway subsequently exchanged these lands for some lands in the Lammermuirs, and then let Kar to the abbey of Vaudey in Lincolnshire, who later gave the lands back to Melrose (Maxwell-Irving, 2000, *The Border Towers of Scotland; The West March*, 6).

Archaeology

No extant remains of a grange at Carsphairn are known.

Grange	Chapelton (Old Grange Barn)
Abbey	?
Order	?
Parish	Urr
Council	Dumfries and Galloway
Location	Chapelton farmsteading is *c.*1km west-north-west of Haugh of Urr village
Ownership	Mr D. Biggar, Chapelton Farm
NGR	NX 798 667
NMRS site	NX76NE 35 Farmsteading
Scheduled	No
Site visit	September 2002

History

The origin of the place name of Old Grange Barn is not known.

Archaeology

No extant remains of a monastic grange are known.

At Chapelton, to the south of the road there is a large house (NX76NE35.01) built in 1865 for James Biggar, who dealt in fertiliser, grain and seeds from the large steading to the north of the road. The house is accompanied by a walled garden (NX76NE35.02) of similar date. The steading buildings are rubble walled with sandstone dressings and late eighteenth and nineteenth century in date. The buildings include a former farmhouse and a long three-storey grain/seed store. It is possibly this building to which 'Old Grange Barn' refers. There has been some demolition and alteration to the steading to accommodate modern cattle sheds.

The site of a pre-Reformation chapel (NX76NE13) and a quarry are shown on the OS first edition map *c.*550m north of Chapelton farmsteading. At this location there is a slight hollow visible at the crest of the rise in the ploughed field. There are also much larger stones incorporated in the adjacent drystone dyke at this point than occur in the rest of the length of the dyke. Features and finds dating to the eight to ninth century AD have been found in excavations nearby (NX76NE38).

Grange	Culgrange
Abbey	?

Order	?
Parish	Inch
Council	Dumfries and Galloway
Location	Culgrange farm is sited *c.*2km south-east of Lochans, near Stranraer.
Ownership	Mr Hearn, Culgrange Farm
NGR	NX 082 567
NMRS site	NX05NE
Site visit	September 2002

History

The origin of the place name of Culgrange is unclear.

Archaeology

No extant remains of a monastic grange are known. The farmhouse and steading buildings appear lateeighteenth to nineteenth century in date with no earlier elements.

Known archaeological sites near to Culgrange farmsteading are all undated or interpreted as being prehistoric. Cropmarks reveal what may be the south end of a rectilinear enclosure (NX05NE 8) 450m north-west of Culgrange farmhouse and measuring 24 x 20m at least, within a narrow ditch (RCAHMS, 1985). Nothing of this site is visible on the ground. Two other enclosures identified from cropmarks (NX05NE 6 and 27) are sited 320m and 350m south-east of Culgrange farmhouse (RCAHMS, 1985). These are interpreted as palisaded settlements of the first millenium BC and have been scheduled together as SAM 7367 (HS scheduling description, 1999). A later prehistoric fort (NX05NE 2; SAM 7366) is sited on the opposite bank of the Piltanton Burn.

The place name Culgrange could perhaps be derived from 'kil-grange', which would point to an ecclesiastical connection. If the farm was ever a monastic grange, then the nearby Soulseat Abbey (NX100587) may have been the owner. The Premonstratensian abbey at Soulseat was ruinous by 1386.

Grange	Dormont Grange
Abbey	?
Order	?
Parish	Dalton
Council	Dumfries and Galloway
Location	Dormont Grange is located 900m north-north-east of Dalton village
Ownership	Mr Carruthers, Dormont, Dalton, Dumfries
NGR	NY 112 749
Site visit	September 2002

Archaeology

No extant remains of a monastic grange are known.

The house at Dormont (formerly Dormont Grange on the OS first edition map) appears to be late eighteenth/early nineteenth century and the extensive range of steading buildings, stables, walled garden and greenhouses are Victorian with no earlier elements apparent.

The Victorian mansion of Dormont, which was demolished in the 1950s, was sited 500m to the north of Dormont Grange. Its associated eighteenth- to nineteenth-century steading/stable/pheasantry buildings survive as ivy-clad ruins in woodland with dense undergrowth.

Grange Wood and Grange Quarry shown on modern OS maps are not featured on the OS first edition map. In the mid-nineteenth century, a house called Sandy Knowe stood where the quarry now is and the modern Grange Wood conifer plantation is shown as part of the deciduous Flosh Wood on the mid-nineteenth-century survey.

On current evidence it would seem that Dormont Grange was the home farm of the Dormont House estate and there appears to be no earlier monastic connection.

Grange	Eliock Grange
Abbey	?
Order	?
Parish	Sanquhar
Council	Dumfries and Galloway
Location	Eliock Grange is located 400m west of Mennock village, approximately 2 miles south-east of Sanquhar
Ownership	Mr Greenshiels, Eliock House, Mennock
NGR	NS 8041 0800
NMRS site	NS80NW 9
Scheduled	No
Site visit	September 2002

Archaeology

No extant remains of a monastic grange are known.

The farmhouse and steading buildings are late eighteenth/nineteenth century in date with no earlier elements. The mill dam shown on the OS first edition map has been planted with conifers.

On current evidence it would seem that Eliock Grange was the home farm of the Eliock House Estate and there appears to be no earlier monastic connection.

Grange	Grange (Trail)
Abbey	Trail Priory (St Mary's Isle, Kirkcudbright)
Order	Augustinian
Parish	Kirkcudbright
Council	Dumfries and Galloway
Location	The farmsteading of Grange is located at the foot of the western slopes of Grange Hill, 3km south of Kirkcudbright
Ownership	The farmsteading of Grange is owned by Sir David Hope-Dunbar, Banks Farm, Kirkcudbright. The house of Grange is owned by the resident Mr Donald Henry
NGR	NX 688 477
NMRS site	NX64NE
Scheduled	No
Site visit	September 2002

History

The two and a half merk land of St Mary's Isle, with the manor, wood and fish yare of the same; *the ten merk land of Grange*, the ten merk land of Torrs, and the seven and a half merk land of Little Galtway ... together with mills attaching to the land were listed as the possessions of the Priory of St Mary of Trail when these were granted to Thomas Lidderdale in 1572. (McKerlie, 1870-9, *History of the Lands and their Owners in Galloway*, vol.4, 178.)

Archaeology

No extant remains of a monastic grange are known.

The steading buildings at Grange are late eighteenth to nineteenth century in date, with much modern alteration. There are no earlier structural elements apparent. The mill dam to the east is now silted up and largely overgrown.

The house at Grange to the south of the steading is a late Victorian replacement of the building shown on the OS first edition map.

Grange	Grange (Dalswinton)
Abbey	?
Order	?
Parish	Kirkmahoe
Council	Dumfries and Galloway
Location	Unknown
Ownership	Sir David Langdale, Dalswinton Estate, Dalswinton.
NGR	NX 93 85
NMRS site	–
Scheduled	No
Site visit	Not visited

History
Reference in 1654 to 'grange and barony of Dalswinton' (*RMS*, vol.10).

Archaeology
No extant remains of a monastic grange are known.

The historical reference probably refers to a secular estate centre. The only medieval ecclesiastical site known at Dalswinton is that of St Bride's Chapel shown on the OS first edition map as 'Chapel (site of)'(NMRS site: NX98NW10; NGR: NX 9380 8526). The church of Dalswinton is referred to in 1319 and the Chapel of St Bride referred to in 1547 (A.C. Smith, TDGNHAS, 24, 1945-6, 160).

Due to the absence of the owner and reluctance of his employees to give permission, it was not possible to visit the site of St Bride's chapel in the course of the survey.

Grange	Friars Carse
Abbey	Melrose Abbey
Order	Cistercian
Parish	Dunscore
Council	Dumfries and Galloway
Location	Friars Carse is 6 miles north-north-west of Dumfries, on the west bank of the River Nith
Ownership	Friars Carse Hotel
NGR	NX 926 850
NMRS site	NX98NW7 Religion/'Monastery'
Scheduled	No
Site visit	September 2002

History
The lands of Carse were given by Affrica, daughter of Edgar, to the Melrose Abbey about the year 1215, and the administration of such an outlying estate would require some sort of grange (*TDGNHAS*, 25, 1948, 182-6).

In the early sixteenth century it was decided to feu out various of the abbey's lands to increase its revenue. Accordingly, in 1536 Abbot Andrew granted the £4 land of 'Freirkers', with the mill called the Grange Mill and the restricted multures of the £36 lands of Dalgonar and other lands, to John Kirkpatrick of Ellisland (Maxwell-Irving, 2000, *The Border Towers of Scotland; The West March*, 145-6).

Archaeology

No extant remains of a monastic grange survive, although the above documentary evidence suggests the probable existence of one.

A tower house was built by the Kirkpatricks in the second half of the sixteenth century and the tower at 'Freercarss' is shown on Pont's map of Nithsdale *c*.1595. However, no buildings of the medieval period survive. Grose reported that when the old ruinous buildings at Friars Carse were demolished in 1773 to make way for a new mansion it was found that the walls of the monks' old refectory were 8ft thick and the fireplace 12ft wide. Engravings of the tower and adjacent buildings prior to demolition were published by Cardonnel (1788) and Grose (1789) (Maxwell-Irving, 2000, *The Border Towers of Scotland; The West March*, 145-6).

A ninth- or tenth-century cross (NX98NW 12; NX 9252 8507) 1.9m high, standing on a modern base in the grounds of Friars Carse, is the sole survivor of many such crosses and carved stones brought to the site by Capt Riddell, who built a new house on the site in the late eighteenth century (*TDGNHAS*, 25, 1948, 182-6).

Current State

The late eighteenth-century residence was replaced by the present Scottish baronial style house of 1873, which now functions as a country house hotel. Level platforms overlooking the Nith are probably the result of eighteenth- and nineteenth-century garden landscaping. Extensive rhododendron growth in the gardens masks much of the landscape. In addition to the house/hotel there is an early nineteenh-century quadrangular stable block with dovecot. An entrance tower range, incorporating an armorial panel of 1598, was added in 1909. Elsewhere in the grounds is the late eighteenth-century Hermitage where Robert Burns and Capt. Riddell also enjoyed drinking bouts.

There are no obviously early structural elements in any of the surviving buildings.

Grange	Grange of Tundergarth
Abbey	?
Order	?
Parish	Tundergarth
Council	Dumfries and Galloway
Location	Grange farmsteading is at the foot of the eastern slopes of Grange Fell, approximately 7 miles east of Lockerbie
Ownership	The farmhouse and older steading buildings are owned by the residents, Mr and Mrs MacIvor
	The surrounding fields and the modern cattle sheds at the farm are in the tenancy of Mr Halliday of Crawthwaite Farm, Tundergarth
	The fields and forestry are owned by Liebfarm Ltd and managed by Scottish Woodlands (01556 502754)
NGR	NY 234 828
NMRS site	NY28SW 14
Scheduled	No
Site visit	September 2002

Archaeology

No firm evidence of the former presence of a monastic grange here is known.

The present farmhouse and steading buildings of Grange (NY28SW 14) are all late eighteenth/nineteenth century in appearance with more recent additions and alterations; although the farmhouse has clearly seen much addition and may possibly have earlier elements.

A lintel bearing the initials W.B. followed by A.B. and the date 1695 is incorporated above a doorway at the north end of the west range of the farmyard.

Enclosures and field systems (NY28SW 49, 54, 88, 89) recorded on Grange Fell by RCAHMS in the mid-1990s have since disappeared due the afforestation of most of the farm.

Current State
Most of the rough grazing land of Grange farm is now under conifers.

Grange	Grange Farm (Urr)
Abbey	?
Order	?
Parish	Urr
Council	Dumfries and Galloway
Location	Grange farmsteading is located *c.*2km west-north-west of Haugh of Urr village
Ownership	Mr Biggar, Grange Farm
NGR	NX 791 670
NMRS site	NX76NE 36
Scheduled	No
Site visit	September 2002

Archaeology
No extant remains of a monastic grange are known.

The present house and steading is *c.*1860s-70s with modern additions and alterations to the steading. A harled cottage by the entrance to the steading is probably the only surviving element of the earlier buildings of 'Nethertown of Grange' shown on the OS first edition map.

Grange	Grange of Bladnoch
Abbey	?
Order	?
Parish	Penninghame
Council	Dumfries and Galloway
Location	Grange of Bladnoch farm is sited *c.*7km east-north-east of Wigtown
Ownership	Mr and Mrs Ribbens, Mochrum Park
NGR	NX 365 575
NMRS site	NX35NE
Scheduled	No
Site visit	September 2002

Archaeology
No extant remains of a monastic grange are known.

The present farmhouse and steading of Grange of Bladnoch at NX 365 575 post-date the OS first edition survey. The house now called Mochrum Park (NX35NE 31; NX 3633 5718) was formerly called Grange of Bladenoch.

Grange of Bladnoch was in the possession of the Gordon family in 1619. An old house there of considerable size was mentioned by Symson in 1684. It has been added to and renamed Mochrum Park (McKerlie, 1870-9, *History of the Lands and their Owners in Galloway*).

The house of Mochrum Park appears a much altered eighteenth- and nineteenth-century house, but external cement rendering obscures a possible earlier core. There was, however, no opportunity in the course of the survey to examine the house or outbuildings closely. See listing description for details.

Grange	Grange of Cree
Abbey	–
Order	–
Parish	Penninghame
Council	Dumfries and Galloway
Location	Grange of Cree farmsteading is sited c.4km north-east of Wigtown on the west bank of the River Cree estuary
Ownership	Mr John Cousar, Grange of Cree, Wigtown
NGR	NX 454 595
NMRS site	NX45NE
Scheduled	No
Site visit	September 2002

History

The earliest reference to the property found by P.H. McKerlie (*History of the Lands and their Owners in Galloway*, 1870-9) was in 1666 when it was in possession of the Gordon family.

Archaeology

No extant remains of a monastic grange are known.

The farmhouse and steading buildings appear nineteenth century in date with twentieth-century additions and alterations.

The track heading north-east from the farmsteading formerly led to the Knockdoon Ferry. This was on the route of pilgrims to Whithorn. Spittal farm on the opposite bank of the Cree is the probable site of the hospital of 'Crithe' in the possession of Dundrennan Abbey in 1305 (Cowan and Easson 1976, 173).

Grange	Grange of Holywood
Abbey	Holywood Abbey (Dercongal)
Order	Premonstratensian
Parish	Holywood
Council	Dumfries and Galloway
Location	Unknown; but presumed to be close to Holywood Parish Church, c.2 miles north of Dumfries
Ownership	The parish church is owned by the Church of Scotland. The churchyard is managed by Dumfries and Galloway Council. The adjacent pasture fields belong to Kilncroft Farm
NGR	NX 95 79
NMRS site	NX97NE 1, NX97NE 87, NX97NE 171 (all aerial photographs)
Scheduled	No
Site visit	September 2002

History

There is a reference to '*lie Grange de Halywode*' in the *Register of the Great Seal* dated to 1598 (Thomson 1888, 234 no 717).

Archaeology

No extant remains of a monastic grange are known. The site of Kilncroft farm immediately to the west of Holywood churchyard is a potential site for a grange belonging to the monastery but only buildings of late eighteenth-/nineteenth-century appearance survive here.

Aerial photography (RCAHMSAP 1995) has revealed the cropmarks of a series of intersecting linear cropmarks in the field immediately to the south-east of Holywood Parish

Church (NX97NE 171). Similar cropmarks have been recorded 160m to the north-west (NX97NE 1) and in adjacent fields to the south (NX97NE 87). All these photographs are in the process of being rectified (RCAHMS 2002).

The present eighteenth and nineteenth-century Holywood Parish Church and its surrounding graveyard are presumed to be on the site of Holywood Abbey, although nothing of the monastery is now visible. The curving line of the road running around the outside of the south-western boundary wall of the graveyard possibly respects the line of a former roughly circular or oval monastic enclosure, extending further to the east than the present churchyard. Two large old tree stumps on the road verge attest to the antiquity of the curving road line and a track depicted on the first edition OS map, leading to the north-east corner of the churchyard, completes the conjectured circle or oval.

If the above conjecture is accepted then elements of the Premonstratensian house, possibly including buildings of the home farm or grange, might have been sited in the pasture immediately east of the present churchyard, although nothing is now visible there.

The circular/oval enclosure also suggests the possibility of an earlier ecclesiastical foundation which has long been suspected at Holywood. A recent article by Chris Crowe (*TDGNHAS*, 76, 2002, 113-118) sets out the case for a monastic foundation pre-dating the Premonstratensian abbey, evidence for which includes a curving earth bank to the west and north-west of the churchyard which can be traced for 900m. This may have formed part of the boundary of a 700m-diameter outer precinct similar to that at Hoddom (Lowe, *TDGNHAS*, 66, 1991, 13). A grange would probably have one element of such an enclosure.

Current State

The western half of the smaller of the two conjectured monastic enclosures is occupied by the active parish church and graveyard. The graveyard has been enlarged on the north-west side in recent years. The eastern half is improved pasture.

Grange	Grange of Kirkgunzeon
Abbey	Holm Cultram Abbey
Order	Cistercian
Parish	Kirkgunzeon
Council	Dumfries and Galloway
Location	Kirkgunzeon village and church are located *c.*6km north-east of Dalbeattie
Ownership	The parish church is owned by the Church of Scotland and then churchyard is managed by Dumfries and Galloway Council
NGR	NX 86 66 (Kirkgunzeon village)
NMRS site	-
Scheduled	No
Site visit	September 2002

History

Holm Cultram Abbey (Cistercian) Cumberland quickly established a *grange* at Kirkgunzeon, which it retained until the 1360s (Stringer 1985, 204, 207, citing *Reg of Holm Cultram*, (eds) Grainger and Collingwood, no 95g, and pp47ff; R.C. Reid, *Trans Dumfriesshire Galloway Natur Hist Antiq Soc*, 3rd Ser, 14 (1926-8), 201-15; *Melrose Liber*, ii, pp671-3).

1165 x 1174 Confirms to Holm Cultram Abbey *the land called Kirkewinin with all its just pertinents and right marches*, which land they hold of Huctred son of Fergus (*RRS*, ii, no 88).

1165 x 1173 Commands Uhtred son of Fergus and Roger of Minto to convene the older men of the district to make a sworn perambulation of the marches of *Kirkgunzeon* on behalf of Holm Cultram Abbey and Christian, Bishop of Galloway (*RRS*, ii, no 540).

1173 x 1193 Confirms to Holm Cultram Abbey that land in Galloway which Walter de Berkelay, King's Chamberlain, gave to them and confirmed in his charter (*RRS*, ii, no 256).

5 May 1360 Confirms to Sweetheart Abbey the grant by Dervorgilla of the lands of Loch Kinder [with defined boundaries, including] one ditch which is the division between the land of *the grange of Kirkwynny* and Loch Kinder, and the lands of Kirkpatrick Durham, 2 April 1273] (*RRS*, vi, no 235).

Archaeology

References to Holm Cultram's grange of Kirkgunzeon show that it was an extensive, holding, which would have made a valuable addition to its acres of sheep pasture. In addition to this grange, Uchtred also granted Holm Cultram abbey a saltworks nearby, on the Solway coast at Southwick (*Reg Holm Cultram,* nos 120 and 133a).

The original Holm Cultram charters make no mention of a church associated with the grange, but Jocelin, Bishop of Glasgow (1774-99) referred to 'the place and chapel in Galwiea called Kirkewinnin' (*Reg Holm Cultram,* no 136). No extant remains of the medieval church or other remains to be identified with the monastic grange are now in evidence at Kirkgunzeon village. However, continuity of worship and burial on the same site is probable and the present late eighteenth-century parish church set in a churchyard on the banks of the Kirkguzeon Lane burn is the most likely focus for the grange. A corn mill operated in the village until the early twentieth century. The surviving mill buildings appear to be eighteenth/nineteenth century in date, although as with New Abbey Corn Mill, they may have been on the site of a medieval mill forming an element of an estate centre.

With regard to a base for the monk's saltworkings, the farm of Fairgirth (NX 8781 5654; NX85NE 2), situated *c.*2km north-west of Sandyhills Bay, is one possibility that suggests itself. In its garden is the rubble of the medieval chapel of St Lawrence and the farmhouse itself, incorporates a sixteenth- or seventeenth-century building with a turret stair in the north-east corner. The nearby Saltpan Rocks on the west side of Sandyhills Bay (NX 893 548) may be monastic in origin. Holm Cultram Abbey lost all of its lands in Scotland in the fourteenth century following the Wars of Independence, but St Bees Priory and Kelso Abbey are also known to have had saltworkings along this part of the Solway coast. The determination of the exact ownership of these sites and at which period requires more detailed research.

Current State

The probable site of the grange is at Kirkgunzeon village and parish church. The church and churchyard are active and are immediately surrounded by pasture.

Grange	Grange of Lincluden
Abbey	Lincluden Collegiate Church from 1389 formerly Lincluden Nunnery)
Order	Benedictine nunnery until 1389; then college of secular canons
Parish	Terregles
Council	Dumfries and Galloway
Location	Unknown
Ownership	The ruins of Lincluden College itself are in the care of Historic Scotland
NGR	NX 966 779 (site of Lincluden College)
NMRS site	NX97NE
Scheduled	No
Site visit	Not visited

History

A priory of Benedictine nuns was founded at Lincluden c.1160, reputedly by Uchtred, son of Fergus, Lord of Galloway. It was suppressed in 1389 and the existing buildings taken over by a college of secular canons.

The cartulary of Lincluden, like those of all the other medieval religious houses in Dumfries and Galloway, does not survive and so there are no direct records of its landholdings. However, some information can be gleaned from post-Reformation transactions. In 1564 William Douglas, younger of Drumlanrig, obtained from his half-brother, the last provost of the college, a grant of the Mains of Lincluden (Gifford 1996 *The Buildings of Scotland: Dumfries and Galloway*, 236).

Archaeology

The farm of Lincluden Mains shown on the OS first edition survey just to the south-west of the site of the medieval nunnery would appear from the historical reference above to have been a grange. The area is now occupied by a housing estate, although the public house on Abbey Lane within the estate incorporates elements of the early/mid-nineteenth-century farmsteading buildings shown on the first edition map.

Grange	Grangemylne (Dunscore) (part of grange of Friars Carse?)
Abbey	Melrose Abbey
Order	Cistercian
Parish	Dunscore
Council	Dumfries and Galloway
Location	Possibly the site of Dalgoner Mill on the Cairn Water, c.800m south-west of Dunscore
Ownership	Mr Crawford, Dalgoner House, Dunscore, Dumfries
NGR	NX 8599 8393
NMRS site	NX 88SE 13 (Dalgoner Mill)
Scheduled	No
Site visit	October 2002

History

In 1536 Abbot Andrew of Melrose Abbey granted the £4 land of 'Freirkers', with the mill called the Grange Mill and the restricted multures of the £36 lands of Dalgonar and other lands, to John Kirkpatrick of Ellisland (Maxwell-Irving, 2000, *The Border Towers of Scotland; The West March*, 145-6).

Archaeology

From the above documentary reference a good candidate for the site of Grange Mill is Dalgoner Mill on the west bank of the Cairn Water. A corn mill and saw mill c.100m downstream are shown on the OS first edition map and a local resident (Mr Farish of 'The Linn') informed that both were in use until the mid-twentieth century. Both are roofless ruins of eighteenth-/nineteenth-century date.

A levelled area approximately 15m north of the corn mill, the west edge of which consists of overgrown rubble (corework?) could potentially be the site of an earlier structure.

Current State

The saw mill building has largely collapsed and has been substantially infilled by modern tipping. The walls of the corn mill and adjacent pigsties and swine-yard are largely intact. The water-wheels are absent at both the saw mill and corn mill but in the interior of the corn mill millstones and machinery are lying amongst the broken timber beams and rubble.

Grange	King's Grange (Urr)
Abbey	–
Order	–
Parish	Urr
Council	Dumfries and Galloway
Location	The country house called King's Grange is located *c.*2.5km west-north-west of Haugh of Urr village, and *c.*500m west of Grange farm
Ownership	Mr Farnham, King's Grange
NGR	NX 785 671
NMRS site	NX76NE 37 Country House
Scheduled	No
Site visit	September 2002

History

The earliest reference to the property found by P.H. McKerlie (*History of the Lands and their Owners in Galloway*, 1870-9) was the 25 May 1590 when Robert, second son of John Maxwell, Lord Herries, acquired Kings Grange (and Little Spottes). Unfortunately, McKerlie doesn't mention from whom they acquired it.

Archaeology

No extant remains of a monastic or a royal grange are known.

The present house of King's Grange appears to completely date to the second half of the nineteenth century and all of the other buildings shown on the first edition OS map have been demolished, with exception of part of Garden Cottage (NX76NE 37.01; NX7870 6703). Examination of the exterior of Garden Cottage shows that its west gable incorporates a wall of the north-west range of the quadrangular farmsteading shown on the OS 1854 map. However, the standard 0.6m thick random rubble construction of the walls of Garden Cottage do not suggest any medieval survival. The rest of the farmsteading was levelled to make way for a walled garden (NX76NE 37.02) which is enclosed by 0.3m thick stonewalls with brick quoins. The lodge house (NX76NE 37.03) was built in the 1870s

Current State

The site is occupied by the buildings and largely wooded grounds of a country house, as described above.

Grange	Mains of Penninghame
Abbey	Bishop of Galloway
Order	–
Parish	Penninghame
Council	Dumfries and Galloway
Location	The site is situated 400m south-east of Mains of Penninghame farm on the end of a slight natural spur flanked by two burns
Ownership	J. McConchie and Sons, Mains of Penningham, Newton Stewart
NGR	NX 4093 6052
NMRS site	NX46SW 8 Grange (possible); Moat
Scheduled	No
Site visit	September 2002

History

22 July 1566, precept for a charter of confirmation of the feu-ferme by Alexander, Bishop of Candida Casa and the Chapel Royal of Stirling, to Alexander Waus of Barnbarroch, [of lands in] the barony of Penninghame and sheriffdom of Wigtown, to be held of the bishop and his successors (*RSS*, v, no 2997).

23 May 1581, confirms feu by Alexander, Bishop of Candida Casa and the Chapel Royal of Stirling (with the consent of the chapter of Candida Casa to William Gordon of Awmurefade and Helen Stewart his wife, of £5 *lands of old extent of Bordland of Pennynghame with manor*, in his lordship of Pennynghame and the sheriffdom of Wigtoun, amounting in his rent to £10, 3 April 1566) (*RMS*, v, no 187).

14 Jul 1638, confirms feu-ferme by Thomas, Bishop of Candida Casa [to Alexander, Earl of Galloway, Lord Stewart of Garlies of, among others, *10 merklands of Grainge*, 5 merklands of Clarie with tower, 5 merklands of Over Bar, 5 merklands of Barlauchlane and 5 merklands of Barquhorrane of old extent in the parish of Penninghame and sheriffdom of Wigtown, resigned by Alexander Stewart of Clarie and Thomas Lidderdaill of Sanct-Marie-Ile and the same earl; together with the *corn mill of Penninghame called the bishops mill* with two crofts of Parkescroft (once possessed by John M'Laloquhen and Ronald M. his father) and Daviescroft (occupied by Gilbert M'Orde) in the said parish and sheriffdom; all incorporated by the said bishop into the free barony of Clairie. At Edinburgh ... 1637] (*RMS*, ix, no 833).

1684 'A large description of Galloway, the parishes in it' by Mr Andrew Symson, pp51-99: *Penninghame* was formerly 'the Residence of the Bishop of Galloway', but not listed among 'principal edifices' in that year [The Clary, Castle Stewart, Glasnick and The Grainge]. Patronage of the parish church belonged to the Earl of Galloway (Mitchell 1908, i, 75).

The following references were noted but not inspected:

NAS, GD10/187	31 March 1640 William Gordone of *Pennygham* mentioned.
NAS, GD10/370	29 Jan 1650 Legal action against William Gordoune of *Penninghame* by Alexander Lennox, son of John Lennox of Kallie, for payment of sums due to him under a marriage contract between said Alexander and deceased Margaret Gordoune, eldest daughter of the said daughter, dated 9 July 1639.
NAS, E219/17/1	Rental for collection of crops 1715-7 Galloway & Edinburgh.
NAS, E219/17/2	nd Annotated rental Galloway & Edinburgh.
NAS, E219/12/14	rentals of St Andrews, Galloway, Edinburgh, Brechin, Dunblane, Moray, Aberdeen & Caithness [post 1689].

Archaeology

Traditionally it is believed that Penninghame Hall was a residence of the bishops of Galloway, and, according to Chalmers (1824), the Bishops of Galloway owned the manor of Penninghame (before the Reformation), although their main residence was at Clary. A charter of 1564 (Reid 1960), granted by Bishop Alexander Gordon, records the names of 'Grange of Penninghame' and 'Clarie'. Symson (Macfarlane 1907) says that the bishop of Galloway did not then possess a house in his bishopric due to the dilapidation of church property during the Reformation.

The OS *Name Book* of 1845 records the remains of Penninghame Castle or Hall (known locally as 'Howe Ha') as surviving only as a small hollow on a knowe, perhaps marking its foundation, and an old road or avenue leading to it. The Hall is said to have belonged to the Gordons.

In 1966 the OS recorded that the site of Penninghame Hall was situated on a slight eminence surrounded by a dry moat and that surface remains and a scatter of building material suggests that there were three buildings flanking three sides of a courtyard.

This moated site is situated 400m south-east of Mains of Penninghame Farm on the end of a natural rise flanked by two burns. The shape of the topography has dictated its roughly triangular shape, and the 1957 OS 6in map shows the north, south-west and east sides of the ditched enclosure to be approximately 100m, 90m, and 90m long respectively, with the south angle cut off to form a short fourth side approximately 20m long. Ploughing of the site has now disguised the internal arrangements, although a slight hollow on the highest, central area of the enclosure probably represents the interior of a ruined building. The best-preserved section of the 6m-wide ditch is along the north side, surviving up to 1.5m deep. A drystone dyke field boundary runs along its inner edge, separating it from the rest of the site. The ditch can be also traced as a linear level terrace or slight linear depression 6m wide along the south-west and south-east sides. Only the inner scarp of the ditch is visible along the east side of the site. The now level ground to the east of the site is $c.2.5$m below the high point of the enclosure. A low 5m-wide outer bank can be traced along part of the north and south-west sides.

Current State
The site is improved pasture grazed by cattle and sheep and much of the site appears to be periodically ploughed. When visited the site was under pasture, with the turf cover in generally in good condition. However, there are problems, the main part of the site, to the south-east of the drystone dyke is gradually being levelled/eroded by ploughing. The edge of the ploughed area adjacent to the dyke shows the surface of the enclosure to have been reduced by $c.0.2$m.

Some churning of the surface of the site due to the location of animal feeders. Stone derived from ploughing is being tipped into the ditch along the north edge of the site. The inner bank of the north ditch has large areas of erosion (including linear sheep scrapes) caused by grazing stock. Hawthorn bushes (possibly a relict hedge) are established along part of the inner bank of the north ditch.

Grange	Mouswald Grange (formerly Brockhillhirst Farm)
Abbey	-
Order	-
Parish	Mouswald
Council	Dumfries and Galloway
Location	Unknown
Ownership	J. Kirkwood and Son, Mouswald Grange
NGR	NY 053 734
NMRS site	NY07SE 23
Scheduled	No
Site visit	September 2002

Archaeology
No extant remains of a monastic grange are known.

The name Mouswald Grange has been adopted since the mid-nineteenth century. On the 1854 OS map the farm is called Brockhillhirst. Examination of a copy of an 1816 Brocklehirst Estate map in the possession of the owners revealed no further evidence of a monastic connection. Only nineteenth-century cottages survive at the site of Old Brockhillhirst on the 1854 OS map.

Current State
The eighteenth- and nineteenth-century farmsteading, with more modern additions, incorporates a late eighteenth-century windmill tower, which at 13.3m is the tallest in Scotland. An adjoining building originally housed a corn-drying kiln.

Grange	Shambellie Grange
Abbey	Sweetheart Abbey
Order	Cistercian
Parish	New Abbey
Council	Dumfries and Galloway
Location	The farmsteading of Shambellie Grange is located *c.*600m north of Sweetheart Abbey Church at New Abbey
Ownership	Owned by: the Trustees of Shambellie Estate Resident tenant farmer: Mr Grierson, Shambellie Grange
NGR	NX 964 668
NMRS site	NX 96 NE 33
Scheduled	No
Site visit	September 2002

History

Presumed to be a grange of the nearby Cistercian abbey of Sweetheart, which was founded in 1273.

As the Reformation approached in the sixteenth century the last abbots of Sweetheart granted feus of all the farms surrounding New Abbey to their kinsmen, the Brouns. The rule of the abbots was finally ended in 1587 but the last abbot, Gilbert Broun, was not finally ejected from Sweetheart until in 1608. The raid and ejection of Gilbert Broun from New Abbey was led by a bishop, John Spottiswoode, who was created Archbishop of Glasgow in 1610. It would appear that shortly after he bought the superiority of the lands at New Abbey from the Crown and presented them to his son Robert. Robert Spottiswoode was executed for treason in 1646, during the Civil War, and the family forfeited their lands until the Restoration in 1660 (Stewart, 1989, 'Sweetheart Abbey and its owners over the centuries', *TDGNHAS*, 64, 1989, 58-70).

Archaeology

A painting of Shambellie Grange by Christine Ferguson dating to the 1860s or 1870s shows one of the steading buildings with a steep pitched roof of medieval character. No such buildings survive at the steading today. The steading consists of granite-rubble buildings of nineteenth-century date with modern additions.

However, an isolated fragment of a building or enclosure wall containing a door or gate arch survives in the stackyard. The wall fragment is *c.*4.1m long, *c.*3.4m high by 1.05m thick. The wall is built of granite rubble and pierced by a round-headed sandstone arch 1.85m wide and approximately 2.3m high. Sockets for internal hinges are visible on the north side of the jambs. Above the arch is a panel divided into two parts. The panel is now very eroded and detail is not very distinct. The 1911 RCAHMS description states: 'the upper part is dated 1649, while the lower division shows two bishop's croziers and either two hearts or stars, now very indefinite'. The tenant, Mr Grierson says that the date when legible was 1609. Either date reflects a recent change of ownership according to the history outlined above. A granite finial in the form of a miniature obelisk surmounts the apex of the gable.

The thick walling footed on massive granite boulders which survives up to the springing of the arch suggests that this is an authentic seventeenth-century remnant of the monastic grange or it could be earlier, with the date panel inserted to commemorate new ownership or refurbishment. A date of 1909 in the cement capping of the wall indicates when consolidation took place. The west end of the wall fragment was squared off in the course of the consolidation work, but the uneven boulder footings at the east end confirm that the walling originally extended further east.

Current State
The cement capping/surface corework at the east end of the wall has partially fallen away exposing loose corework to the weather. Elsewhere the masonry is generally in sound condition, although it would benefit from spot pointing throughout.

The ground surface around the archway has been eroded by *c.*0.2m. Contemporary archaeological deposits in the stackyard probably do not survive.

Grange	Stapleton Grange
Abbey	-
Order	-
Parish	Dornock
Council	Dumfries and Galloway
Location	Stapleton farmsteading is sited *c.*1.5 miles east-north-east of Annan
Ownership	Mr Logan, Stapleton Grange
NGR	NY 230 682
NMRS site	NY 26NW 33 Farmhouse; Farmsteading
Scheduled	No
Site visit	September 2002

Archaeology
No remains of a monastic grange are known.

The eighteenth- to nineteenth-century red sandstone farmhouse and steading buildings and more modern sheds have no earlier elements.

The farmsteading was labelled simply as 'Stapleton' on the OS first edition map and was presumably on the estate of the sixteenth-century Stapleton Tower (NY26NW 5) sited approximately 700m to the north-east.

A secular medieval moated site, Woodhall/Round Bush Cottages/Dornoch Wood (NY26NW6; NY 237 676) was located approximately 700m to the south-east, see 1999 *Moated Sites Survey Gazetteer*.

Grange	Threave Mains or Threave Grange
Abbey	-
Order	-
Parish	Balmaghie
Council	Dumfries and Galloway
Location	Threave Mains steading is *c.*600m west of Threave Castle near Castle Douglas
Ownership	Mr M. Ross, Netherhall
NGR	NX 733 622
NMRS site	-
Scheduled	No
Site visit	October 2002

History
There is an entry in the *Exchequer Rolls of Scotland* dating to 1456 that records '*xi li. Terrarum grangie de Treve*' (Burnett 1883, 192). A later entry of 1621 in the *Register of the Great Seal* records '*20 librat. Terrarum de Treve-grange ex unoquoque latere aque de Die, cum molendino et piscationibus*' (Thomson 1888, 73 no 228).

Archaeology
No extant remains of a monastic grange are known. The farmsteading now consists of

a derelict eighteenth-century farmhouse with a renaissance door surround and a single surviving nineteenth-century barn.

Note – the 'site of Glenlochar Abbey' shown on the OS first edition survey c.2km north of Threave Mains was a misnomer. This is the site of a Roman fort.

Current State
The farmhouse and steading are now abandoned. The farmhouse is a roofless shell and the steading buildings have been levelled apart from one intact barn range. The land surrounding the steading consists of regularly ploughed arable and pasture fields.

Grange	Walls Frenchland or Rogermoor
Abbey	–
Order	Knights Templar?
Parish	Moffat
Council	Dumfries and Galloway
Location	The site is located on a west-facing slope c.700m east-north-east of the motte and bailey castle of Auldton and some 600m north of the ruined Frenchland Tower. It is near the east corner of a field of improved pasture.
Ownership	Mr Brian Walker, Rogermoor Farm, Moffat
NGR	NT 1010 0602
NMRS site	NT10NW 11 Moated site
Scheduled	No
Site visit	September 2002

History
The *Name Book* (1857) records the site as the foundations of a number of houses, and that 'Walls' was a Chapelry belonging to the Knights Templars. No documentary evidence has been found to support this, although it may have derived from links with the remains of the possible hospital of St Cuthbert at Chapel Farm (NT 00 NE 11) to the west of the Annan Water.

Archaeology
The site is located on a west-facing slope c.700m east-north-east of the motte and bailey castle of Auldton and some 600m north of the ruined Frenchland Tower.

This probable moated site comprises two substantial two-compartment buildings, reduced to their grass-grown stone wall-footings, set on opposite sides of a yard and protected on the north-north-west and east-north-east by a ditch. The building on the south-south-east measures 22.7 x 7.2m overall; that on the north-north-west measures 23.7 x 6.7m overall, and at its east-north-east end there is a rectangular platform measuring 5.4 x 3.8m. The subdivided yard is closed on the east-north-east by the turf-covered footings of a stone wall and on the west-south-west by a severely wasted bank, whilst the entrance is in the south corner. The flat-bottomed ditch appears formerly to have been water-filled and is best preserved on the north-north-east, where it is 7.5m broad and 1.5m deep and accompanied by an internal bank 4.1m thick and 0.6m high; on the east-north-east it has been largely infilled.

There are traces of a possible dam at the west-north-west terminal of the ditch, where a rectangular platform measuring 8.7 x 4.2m overall may indicate the site of a mill. Although the ditch can only be seen on two sides and may have been a pond for a mill, it almost certainly indicates the presence of a moated site. (RCAHMS visit 1990).

The courtyard arrangement of buildings at Rogermoor is reminiscent of some monastic grange sites, Moorfoot (NT 25 SE 1) in Midlothian for example, a grange of Melrose Abbey. More likely builders, though, are the family of French, who held lands in the vill of Moffat in the thirteenth century (RCAHMS, 1997, 208).

Current State
When visited in September 2002 the site was covered in long grass masking much of the detail. It is located near the east corner of a field of improved pasture. The field around the monument is periodically ploughed, and when visited was under a silage crop.

This very well-preserved site is in generally good condition with sound turf cover. Most of the erosion to the banks of the ditch caused by grazing stock seen when visited in 1999 (in the course of the Moated Sites survey) is now grassed over. Shallow vehicle ruts visible across the courtyard in 1999 were invisible in the long grass when visited in September 2002.

Grange	Watcarrick
Abbey	Melrose Abbey
Order	Cistercian
Parish	Eskdalemuir
Council	Dumfries and Galloway
Location	The site occupies a small promontory on the west bank the White Esk, adjacent to the road between Eskdalemuir and Castle O'er
Ownership	Burial ground is (in theory) maintained by Dumfries and Galloway Council
	Open woodland/rough ground on north owned by the Tibetan Centre, Johnstone House, Eskdalemuir (013873 73232)
	Field to south-west owned by Tanlawhill Estates, Tanlawhill, Eskdalemuir
NGR	NY 2526 9634
NMRS site	NY 29 NE 12 Chapel; Burial-Ground; Earthwork; Grange
Scheduled	SAM 4720 'Watcarrick, earthwork 140 south of Bankhead'
Site visit	September 2002

History
Robert Avenel's grant of *Weidkerroc* to Melrose Abbey was confirmed by Malcolm IV in 1165 (Barrow 1960, 283).

c.1564 Rental of the Regality of Melrose: *Walteroccat* £6-13s-4d; *Walterocatgrange* £10 (Romanes 1917, 144).

Undated Rental of the Regality of Melrose: *Watcarrocoit* £6-13s4d; *Wattarikgrange* £10 (Romanes 1917, 241).

9 October 1582 Charter by the commendator of Melrose to William Douglas of Lochleven his father, of lands in the regality of Melrose, stewartry of Annandale and sheriffdom of Dumfries, including *Watcarrocoit* for £6 13s 4d and *Watcarrokgrange* for £10 (Romanes 1917, 308).

24 March 1613 Grants to William, Earl of Morton, Lord Dalkeith, lands including *Watcariot or Vaccariott*, previously incorporated in the tenandry of Dunfedling, regality of Melrose, stewartry of Annandale and sheriffdom of Dumfries; dissolved from the abbacy of Melrose by parliament June 1609 and incorporated into the free tenandry of Dunfedling, with feuars and tenants to hold of William; and tenandry to be taxed with temporal lords and barons, not as ecclesiastical lands (*RMS*, vii, no 826).

7 April 1613 Grants to Walter, Lord Scott of Buccleuch, lands as in no 826, resigned by William, Earl of Morton, Lord Dalkeith (*RMS*, vii, no 829).

15 & 20 April 1663 Marriage contract between James, Duke of Monmouth and Anna, Countess of Buccleuch listed the tenandry of Dumfadling, including *all and haill the lands of Wattcarrick ... all and haill the lands of Wattcarrickgrange*, granted by charter of James VI to Walter, Lord Scott of Buccleuch 7 April 1613 (Fraser 1878, ii, 468).

14 October 1664 Grants to James, Duke of Buccleuch and Monmouth, Earl of Dalkeith, Lord Scott of Whitchester and Eskdale and to Anne, Duchess of Buccleuch and Monmouth

[their estates including, in the tenandry of Dumfedling], *Watcariot … Watcarrickgrange* in the regality of Melrose and stewartry of Annandale, all incorporated in one tenandry of Dumfedling by charter under the Great Seal 7 April 1613; and all incorporated in one free earldom of Buccleuch in a charter under the Great Seal dated 26 August 1650 to the late Francis, Earl of Buccleuch (*RMS*, xi, no 673).

Archaeology

The well-preserved earthwork at Watcarrick is probably to be associated with a grange of Melrose Abbey established on lands granted by Robert Avenel. It occupies a small promontory reaching out into the haughland of the White Esk and is some 29m square within double banks and a flat-bottomed medial ditch, 9m wide and up to 2m deep below the platform. The interior is occupied by a burial-ground within which the chapel of Watcarrick formerly stood. The chapel is on record in 1305 and went out of use in 1722 (RCAHMS, 1997, 206, 208). Vestiges of the chapel could still be seen until near the close of the eighteenth century (J. and R. Hyslop 1912), but there are now no visible remains. The burial ground contains stones dating to the beginning of the eighteenth century. The entrance into the burial ground is on the west side where the construction of the road has obliterated the ditch and outer rampart. A 3m-wide causeway across the ditch on the east side marks the original enclosure entrance.

As partially shown on the RCAHMS plan, there is a second enclosure to the north of the graveyard. This is bounded by a broad shallow ditch and a low bank, 0.5m high and 1-1.3m broad, which can be traced for *c*.35m amongst the tussocks of rushes. The northern limit of this enclosure is indistinct. It may just be a later field enclosure.

Current State

The interior of the site is a burial ground maintained by Dumfries and Galloway Council.

The ditch and outer rampart on the north side and on the east side to the north of the causeway is open mixed woodland with a cover of rough grass. This ungrazed land is open to the road. Beyond the ditch on the north side, the land is open and ungrazed and covered in tussocks of rushes.

The ditch and outer rampart on the south side and on the east side south of the causeway is open to the cultivated field to the south. When visited this was under grass and grazed by sheep.

The earthwork outwith the graveyard is in a good state of preservation with a stable turf cover under the trees. The graveyard appears in good order, but has a number of leaning and fallen gravestones requiring attention and its boundary dyke is in need of urgent maintenance. It has collapsed into the ditch in several places.

HIGHLAND GRANGES (5)

Adrian Cox

NMRS NO	NMRS NAME	TYPE OF SITE	MONASTERY	SAM/LISTED
NH65SW NH 62 51	Allangrange		Bishop of Ross	
NH85SE	The Grange (Brackla)			
NH88NW NH 801 895	The Grange (Dornoch)			

NH33SE NH 37 30	Grange (Corrimony)			
NH64SE NH 67 40	Grange (Leys)			

Grange	Allangrange
Abbey	?
Order	-
Parish	Knockbain
Council	Highland
Location	Allangrange is located on the Black Isle, south-east of the village of Tore and south-west of Munlochy
Ownership	The owner was not present when the site was visited. However, permission to examine the surroundings and take photographs was obtained from the owner of Old Allangrange House by telephone, thanks to an employee
NGR	NH65SW, centred on NH 6244 5140 (Old Allangrange House). St John's Chapel is at NH 6252 5152.
NMRS site	NH65SW
Scheduled	Listed
Site visit	19 November 2002

History

ST JOHN'S CHAPEL (FROM RCAHMS RECORDS):
Of St John's Chapel, which is alleged to have belonged to the Knights Templar, only the east gable, with a triple lancet window, and portions of the side walls remain (D. MacDonald, A. Polson and J. Brown 1931).

The extant ruins of St John's Chapel consist of the north wall 2.6m high, the east wall, with the triple lancet window, at gable height, and the south wall, 3.3m high, containing two small windows. The west wall has been removed and replaced with an iron railing with a gate in its centre giving access to the central area of the chapel, which is used as a burial ground. Gravestones have been built into the inside face of both the north and south walls, and there are also several in the central area. The remaining walls are all 1.0m wide, and the area enclosed by these measures 10.0m east–west by 6.2m transversely. Revised at 1/2500. Visited by OS (RB) 17 March 1966.

Archaeology

Cropmarks have been observed in the field to the south of Allangrange Mains. No upstanding earthworks were noted. The overgrown trackway leading from Old Allangrange House to St John's Chapel may be of some antiquity and is now redundant and overgrown. A further track, shown on the OS map, leading roughly from the Old Allangrange House garden towards the chapel, has almost completely disappeared and a new bungalow now lies across its north-east end. The pond to the south-west of Allangrange Mains, along with its associated burn, is also of archaeological interest.

Current State

The area around Allangrange Old House is generally well-maintained, as is that around Allangrange Mains. The remains of St John's Chapel, while appearing structurally sound, should be periodically inspected and kept clear of bushes and undergrowth which could potentially weaken the surviving structure.

Grange	Corrimony
Abbey	?
Order	-
Parish	Urquhart and Glenmoriston
Council	Highland
Location	Corrimony lies approximately 8 miles west of Drumnadrochit and around 3 miles east-south-east of the village of Cannich
NGR	NH 3875 3055
NMRS site	NH33SE19
Scheduled	Listed
Site visit	18 November 2002

History
There is no documentary evidence to suggest that there was formerly a monastic grange on this site.

Archaeology
There is a chambered cairn less than half a mile to the east of these buildings, and another possible cairn is known to the south-west. A similar distance to the south of the Corrimony buildings is a small graveyard.

Current State
The buildings here are well-maintained, as are the gardens and associated ground around them. The bridge crossing the River Enrick also appears to be in reasonably good condition and is used by vehicular traffic.

Grange	Leys
Abbey	?
Order	-
Parish	Inverness and Bona
Council	Highland
Location	The Grange at Leys lies approximately 5km south-south-east of Inverness and can be accessed via a private road leading eastwards from the B861. The grange lies c.500m south of Leys Home Farm and Leys Castle
NGR	NH 6792 4041
NMRS site	NH64SE
Scheduled	Listed
Site visit	18 November 2002

History
Leys Castle, which lies approximately 500m to the north of The Grange, was designed by architect Samuel Beazley in 1833, with later additions by Alexander Ross.

Archaeology
The layout of the site is potentially of interest. The house, garden and outbuildings all lie within an enclosure bounded by stone walls, and further to the south-east there is a pond (now in an area of woodland). The embankment bordering the present garden lawn may possibly be a surviving earthwork relating to an earlier structure.

Current State
The house, garden and general environs are well-maintained and no threats were noted.

Grange	Brackla
Abbey	?
Order	-
Parish	Cawdor
Council	Highland
Location	This site is occupied largely by the various buildings of the Royal Brackla Distillery, with level and landscaped open ground in between them. The actual site of the specified grid reference is in/close to two very large, concrete distillery buildings
NGR	NH 8622 5160
NMRS site	NH85SE 33
Scheduled	No
Site visit	19 November 2002

History
There is no existing documentary evidence to suggest that this site was formerly occupied by a monastic grange.

Current State
The area around the distillery complex is well-maintained. Open areas are under grass. The grounds of Brackla House are less well maintained.

Grange	Dornoch (Grange Road)
Abbey	not known
Order	-
Parish	Dornoch
Council	Highland
Location	Grange Road lies on the eastern fringe of Dornoch
NGR	NH 8021 8965 (centred on)
NMRS site	-
Scheduled	No
Site visit	19 November 2002

History
There is no existing documentary evidence to suggest that this is the former site of a monastic grange.

LOTHIAN GRANGES (26)

Derek Hall

NGR AND NMRS NUMBER	NMRS NAME	TYPE OF SITE	MONASTERY	SAM/ LISTED	COUNCIL
NT 54 73 NT57SW 59	Bearford ALTERNATIVE(S): West Bearford	Grange; Mill	Newbattle Abbey (OCist)		East Lothian

NT 617 754 NT67NW	Beilgrange [=Grange of Edmondston?]	Grange	[Melrose Abbey (OCist)]		East Lothian
NT06SW 32 NT 013 624	Burngrange [part of Grange of Calder?]	?			West Lothian
NT36SW 16 NT 31 63	Dalhousie Grange	Residential		L	Midlothian
NT661 680 NT66NE 11	Friardykes	Grange (possible)	Melrose Abbey		East Lothian
NT 5925 7104 NT57SE 26	Garvald	Grange	Haddington Nunnery (OCist)		East Lothian
NT 29 68	Gilmerton-Grange	Grange	Newbattle Abbey (Ocist)		City of Edinburgh
NT 261 721	Grange (Edinburgh) [=St Giles Grange]	Grange	Harehope, Northumberland (Order of St Lazarus of Jerusalem)		City of Edinburgh
NT 221 613	Grange Dell	?			Midlothian
NT 000 787 NT07NW 64	Grange House	Country House	Culross Abbey (OCist)		West Lothian
NT 017 655	Grange of Breich	Grange	North Berwick Nunnery (OCist)		West Lothian
NT 528 765 NT57NW 27	Grange of Haddington, or Barns	Grange	Haddington Nunnery (OCist)	SAM no 764	East Lothian
NT 494 768 NT47NE 12	Grange of Haddington, or Byres	Grange	Haddington Nunnery (Ocist)		East Lothian
NT 607 751	Grangemuir	Grange	Melrose Abbey (OCist)		East Lothian
NT 652 720	Hartside	Grange	Melrose Abbey (OCist)		East Lothian
NT 293 701 NT27SE 4140	Kingston Grange	Residential			City of Edinburgh
NT 30 67	Melville Grange	?			Midlothian
NT 298 524 NT25SE 1	Moorfoot ALTERNATIVE(S): Chapel of Moorfoot	Grange	Newbattle Abbey (Ocist)	SAM 5976	Midlothian
NT 569 664 NT56NE 24	Newlands ALTERNATIVE(S): Grange of Nunland	Grange	Haddington Nunnery (OCist)		East Lothian

NT36SW	Newtongrange	Grange	Newbattle Abbey (OCist)		Midlothian
NT 641 631 NT66SW 11	Penshiel Grange ALTERNATIVE(S): Penshiel Tower	Grange	Melrose Abbey (OCist)	SAM 6028	East Lothian
NT 37 73	Prestongrange	Grange	Newbattle Abbey (OCist)		East Lothian
NT36SE 16	Southside Castle ALTERNATIVE(S): Southsyde House	Residential	Newbattle Abbey? (Ocist)	L	Midlothian
NT 653 655 NT66NE 7	Spartleton	Grange	Kelso Abbey (OTiron)		East Lothian
NT 375 627	Vogrie Grange	?			Midlothian
NT 557 627 NT56SE 11	West Hopes, Nunhope	Grange	Haddington Nunnery (OCist)		East Lothian

Grange	Bearford
Abbey	Newbattle Abbey
Order	Cistercian
Parish	Haddington
Council	East Lothian
Location	Modern farm of West Bearford to south-west of Haddington
NGR	NT 54 73
NMRS site	NT57SW 59
Site visits	29 August 2002

History

1153 x 1159 confirms to Newbattle Abbey the gift by his mother Ada, Countess of Northumberland of that *land which belonged to Robert son of Geoffrey in Haddingtonshire, namely Bereford* (*RRS*, i, no 136).

1189 x 1195 confirms to Newbattle Abbey the gift by Hugh Gyffard and William his son of the land of Kressewelle [now Monkrigg, near Bearford] (*RRS*, ii, no 296).

Archaeology

There are no records of any archaeological excavations on this site.

Current State

This site is now occupied by a working farm called West Bearford. There are no signs of anything upstanding that is any earlier than the eighteenth or nineteenth centuries.

Grange	Bielgrange (Grange of Edmondston)
Abbey	Melrose Abbey
Order	Cistercian
Parish	Whittinghame
Council	East Lothian
Location	On the south side of the road to Luggate due north-west of Stenton
NGR	NT 617 754

NMRS site   None
Site visits   29 August 2002

History

1165 x 1168 confirms the grant by Walter son of Alan to Melrose of *the land of Edmundestun* (*RRS*, ii, no 81).

[Late thirteenth century] Sir Alexander de Setun, son of Sir Seyr de Setun, grants to Melrose … the land of the *Grange of Eddemundistun* he grants without any retention; And for the good of having peace between the foresaid monks, lay brothers and servants of *Grange of Eddemundistun* and himself, his heirs and his men of Ruchelau, he grants that by reason of payment for infringement of park rights (*parcagii*) by either [party] one obol be taken for any flock and herd on each occasion outside the fields and meadows (*Melrose Liber*, no 223).

1289 x 1308 Patrick, Earl of March confirms to Melrose Abbey its possessions within his earldom [including] first the land of Hertesheuyd and of Spotte by the right marches contained in the charters of Earl Cospatric [1138-66] and of Earl Walleue his son [1166-82]; one toft with saltpan in the port of Beel by gift of the foresaid Earl Walleue; one carucate of land beside their *grange of Edmunddyston* by gift of Earl Patrick; 2.5 acres of land at Harcarres, and the whole arable land of Sorulesfelde, and the whole land of Moresschele within the ditch, without ploughing, by gift of his predecessors; common pasture on Lambremore by gift of Earl Walleue; the amicable composition made between his predecessors and the monks on the dispute which arose between them concerning the pasture towards the west of Ledre as the writs made thereon testify; the confirmation and warrandice by his predecessors on the land of Pittillishouch which Master William de Grenlau conveyed to them; the land which William de Alwenton conveyed to them in the territory of Halsington; the land which Patrick Corbeth gave them in the territory of Foghou with the easements of the toun thereof; the land of Pansscheles which they have by the gifts of John de Methkil and Henry de Belton; the land which Sir Adam de Gordon conveyed to them in the territory of Eastergordon together with the common pasture of the said town; W. John son of the Earl, William de Ramsay, Adam de Gordon, Henry de Haleburton, Edward de Letham knights (*Melrose Liber*, no 365).

18 December 1342 at the *Grange of Edmundistone* an agreement was made whereby Gilbert de Maxwell, lord of the half of the barony of Wyltone gave to Melrose, all his lands of the half of the barony of Wyltone with the right of patronage or advocation of the church of the said town; Rendering one silver penny at the Feast of the Nativity of St John the Baptist, at Melrose if sought; Provided that if Gilbert or the heirs of his body lawfully procreated pay to the abbey £40 of good and lawful sterling in cash in one day between sunrise and sunset at the monastery of Melrose, the said lands will revert to Gilbert and his heirs (*Melrose Liber*, no 475).

11 January 1342/3 Patrick de Dunbar, Earl of March confirms the confirmation of Melrose of his father Patrick de Dunbar, Earl of March, of their possessions: the land of Hertesheuyd and Spott by the right boundaries contained in the charters of Earl Cospatric [died 1166] and Earl Walleue his son [1166-82]; one toft with saltpan in the port of Beel by gift of Earl Walleue; one carrucate of land beside *the Grange of Edmundiston* by gift of Earl Patrick; 2.5 acres of land at Harcarres; the whole arable land of Sorulesfeld and the whole land of Moresschelle within the ditch without [ploughing? (*aracione*?)] by gifts of his predecessors; common pasture on Lambremore by gift of Earl Walleue; the amicable composition made between his predecessors and the monks concerning the pasture westwards of Ledre; the confirmation and warranty of his predecessors on the land Pittillishouch conveyed to them by Master William de Grenlau; the land which William de Alwentone conveyed to them in the territory of Halsyntone; the land which Patrick Corbeth gave them in the territory of Foghou with the easements of the toun thereof; the land of Pansscheles which they have by gifts of John de Methkil and Henry de Beeltone; the land which Sir Adam de Gordone conveyed to them in the territory of Estergordon together with the common pasture of the same toun (*Melrose Liber*, no 431).

March 1342[/3?] William, Bishop of St Andrews confirms an instrument of his predecessor William de Lambertone [concerning the teinds of the possessions of the *two granges of Edmonstone and Hertysheuid*, by composition anciently made between the monastery of Melrose and the church of Dunbar (in 1173, in the Synod in the church of St Cuthbert of Edinburgh, concerning the teinds of the possessions of the *two granges called Edmundestune and Hertisheuid*, whereby the monastery will pay every year 30s to the church of Dunbar, and the church of Dunbar can demand no more above these 30s from the monastery, which shillings are to be given at Martinmas); Item, certain letters of confirmation by Richard, Bishop of St Andrews [1165-78] (confirming the composition between the monastery of Melrose and the church of Dunbar concerning the teinds of the *two granges of Edmundestune and of Hertisheuid Spot* and of everything pertaining to the same granges); Item, certain letters testimonial of Andrew, Archdeacon and universal Clerk of Lothian (confirming the composition made in the presence of Richard, Bishop of St Andrews, between the monastery of Melrose and the Church of Dunbar, concerning the teinds of *the granges of Edmundestune and Hertisheuid*); On the vigil [14 Aug] of the Assumption of the Blessed Virgin Mary 1326, at the church of Dunbar] (*Melrose Liber*, no 443).

1371 x 1390 John, first-born son of the king, Earl of Carrick and Steward of Scotland confirms to Melrose Abbey the grants of his predecessors and ancestors, Earls of Carrick and Stewards of Scotland of all lands and tenements with their pertinents ... within the earldom of Carrick and lordship of Kyle with the Barmore within the sheriffdom of Ayr, together with the *grange of Edmondston* and land and tenement of Hertisheuide with their pertinents in Lothian (*Melrose Liber*, no 483).

Sunday 27 August 1452 Instrument that Dom John Medilmaste, Subprior of Melrose, procurator in name of the abbot and convent thereof, within the collegiate church of Dunbar made due diligence to have and obtain the presence of honourable men the dean, archpresbyter and other lords of the chapter of the said collegiate church, to intimate, insinuate, show, publish and notify them under public instruments transumpted by the underwritten public notary [Robert de Lythcw] of certain true copies of certain privileges of diverse supreme pontiffs concerning *the grange of Edmondestoune* with the same privileges or apostolic letters with sealed silken strings, duly heard and collated, of which apostolic letters [one is from Alexander, dated 9 December *Anno Pontificatus* 1; another is of Alexander dated 26 February *Anno Pontificatus* 1; a third is of Innocent, dated 30 October *Anno Pontificatus* 3; a fourth is of Innocent, dated 16 Feb *Anno Pontificatus* 1; a fifth is of Lucius III [1181-5], dated 18 April etc]; and although the said procurator, to validate the lawsuit between them on the teinds of the said *grange*, offered the foresaid copies to the above-mentioned lord archpresbyter, apprehended there personally for the time, and wished to intimate them to him, the same Archpresbyter refused to hear the copies in any way on behalf of the same procurator, but suddenly withdrew and absented himself; But at length the often mentioned procurator caused the aforementioned copies to be affixed to the doors of the said collegiate church and permitted them to stand there affixed in time of high mass when a multitude of people were gathered there to hear divine office, and in the presence of all and each there for the time, intimated, insinuated, published and notified them in so far as he was able (*Melrose Liber*, no 552).

19 September 1452 Instrument in the name of the abbot and convent of Melrose warning and inhibiting the dean and canons of the collegiate church of Dunbar, not to intromit in any way with the haywards/harvests(?) (*messibus*) or garbal teinds of the lands and possessions of their *Grange of Edmondestone*, in the diocese of St Andrews, collected for the first time in the yard of the same *grange* by the servants and administrators of the same abbot and convent, and going out thence for the occasion, owed by right to themselves and to no other; and not to vex, molest, despoil or disturb Lord Robert [de Logstone, Sacrist of Melrose] or anyone else deputed by the foresaid abbot and convent to administer and govern the same teinds, nor to offer any violence to them by themselves or another or others, nor to infringe or violate in any way their said privileges by any recquisitions, warnings, inhibitions or threats of any kind

made to them of their privileges (for the first time? *p'mitus*), notwithstanding the foresaid dean, archpresbyter and canons of the said collegiate church, with certain of their accomplices, rushed into a certain mass of grain collected there, and boldly throwing it to the ground, dragged away the garbal teinds from the same, and carried them off afterwards in certain carts ordered for this purpose, with force and a strong hand and cruelly despoiled diverse monks of the same monastery, deputed by the forsaid lords abbot and convent to protect and defend therein in any way the garbal teinds, the said monks according to their powers resisting diligently as far as possible and striving to impede the same despoilers by raising a great tumult between themselves in the people on that account (*Melrose Liber*, no 553).

16 May 1453 Indenture between the Melrose Abbey and the collegiate church of Dunbar concernings the disputes concerning the teinds of *the granges commonly called Edmonston grange and Hertishede*, which otherwise in the foundation of the said collegiate church were deputed for the repair and maintenance of the choir of the foresaid collegiate church and of its other ornaments, which have arisen or may arise in the future, whereby since the abbot and convent by their own labours and expenses and for their own use and by their own goods have cultivated or caused to be cultivated the foresaid *granges of Edmonston grange and Hertishede*, they shall pay to the foresaid dean and canons of the foresaid collegiate church really and with effect for the reparation of the choir and foresaid ornaments, annually in future in one of the said *granges*, in equal portions at Martinmas and Pentecost 12.5 merks usual money of the kingdom of Scotland, viz for the teinds of *Edmondston grange* with all its pertinents and appendages pertaining to the foresaid common fruits, since they have occupied them as previously mentioned, 6 merks, 3s 4d and the other 6 merks, 3s 4d likewise for the teinds, appendages and pertinents of *the Grange of Hertishede*. And if it should happen that the said abbot and convent at any time in the future occupy one of the said granges as previously mentioned, the other having been leased, for that which they occupy, they shall pay to the foresaid dean and canons without obstacle, annually 6 merks, 3s 4d money foresaid. And the foresaid dean and canons shall receive wholly and without impediment the teinds of the other which they do not occupy, and freely dispose of the same. And if it should happen that the same abbot and convent occupy in their own use, a half, quarter or less of the said places, for the size of the portion occupied by the same monks, they shall pay to the foresaid dean and chapter precisely according to the aforementioned form and at the times designated above (*Melrose Liber*, no 554).

9 October 1453, instrument that John Medilmaste, Subprior of Melrose and Brothers John Burnate and Thomas Stanehouse professed monks of Melrose, procurators for the abbey personally went to *the yard of the barn or granary of the abbey – commonly called Edmondestoune grange* and there in the presence of [a notary public Robert de Lythcw and other witnesses] published, intimated and caused to be read out openly and publicly certain privileges graciously granted to them and their monastery by diverse supreme pontiffs, together with a certain letter of agreement and composition written in parchment, between the abbey and the dean and canons of the collegiate church of Dunbar, on account of the good of peace, union and charity between them … concerning all the teinds of *Edmondestone grange* and Hertiseheuid (*Melrose Liber*, no 555).

6 March 1490/1 Robert Lawdir of Edrington binds and obliges himself to Melrose Abbey for 8 chalders of victual yearly to be paid to them for the ferme of their *lands of Edmondston grange* in Lothian, of which 5 chalders are to be of good and sufficient wheat, and 3 of meal good and 'markat lyk', to be delivered at his own cost to the abbey with same mete and measure as before for the time of his lease (*Melrose Liber*, no 578).

12 August 1534, lease to Elene Lawsoun, relict of Thomas Wod in *Edmonston grange*, and to Thomas Wod her son, of all and haill the forty shilling land pertaining to the abbey's *walkmill of the said grange* with the *onset* of the said mill and the *gerss sowme* pertaining to them which are excepted in the laird of Bass's tack and lease, for 19 years next after Whitsunday 1534 which shall be their entry to the said lands, mill, *onset* and *gerssowme* with the pertinents, lying between the abbey's *land of Edmonstoun grange* and Rouchlaw within the sheriffdom of Edinburgh and

constabulary of Haddington, by all right marches … in houses, buildings, yards, fields, bounds, pastures, leisures, free ish and entry and with all other sundry easements, profits, commodities; for the yearly rent of 40s good and usual money of Scotland, in even portions at Whitsunday and Martinmas. And if the abbey builds or causes to be built a walkmill on the said stead within the said lands at its own expense [missing words] Elen and Thomas will immediately pay yearly to the abbey the sum of 9 merks from the next term (*Melrose Liber*, no 597).

Archaeology
There is no record of any archaeological excavations on this site.

Current State
This site is occupied by a large farmhouse and outbuildings called Bielgrange. There is nothing upstanding any earlier than the eighteenth or nineteenth centuries.

Grange	Burngrange (Grange of Calder)
Abbey	?
Order	?
Parish	West Calder
Council	West Lothian
Location	Western side of village of West Calder
NGR	NT 013 624
NMRS site	NT06SW 32
Site visits	18 September 2002

Current State
The place name of Burngrange now applies to a row of houses on the main street, heading west out of the village of West Calder and a farm on the southside of these houses. There is nothing visible of any antiquity.

Grange	Dalhousie Grange
Abbey	Newbattle
Order	Cistercian
Parish	Cockpen
Council	Midlothian
Location	In vicinity of modern house of Dalhousie Grange
NGR	NT 3170 6390
NMRS site	No entry
Site visits	No visit

History
A charter of 28 July 1587 lists '*terras dominicales de Dalhoussy (exceptis mansione et gleba ministro ecclesie reservatis)*' as one of the lands of Newbattle Abbey (Thomson 1888, 443).

Archaeology
There are no records of any archaeological finds or excavations on this site.

Current State
Currently occupied by house still called Dalhousie Grange.

Grange	Friardykes
Abbey	Melrose
Order	Cistercian

Parish	Spott
Council	East Lothian
Location	Modern settlement of Friardykes in Lammermuir Hills
NGR	NT 661 680
NMRS site	NT66NE 11
Site visits	Not visited

History

There was a religious house at Friardykes (NT 661 680) to which the refractory priests from Melrose were occasionally banished. It was also closely connected with the (supposed convent) at Papple (see NT57SE 10) NSA 1845 (J. Lumsden).

It is said that the monk from Melrose was exiled to Friardykes by the superior for disobedience and a wall or dyke was built to enclose the portion of land which was allowed him. No trace of the dyke can now be seen (*Name Book* 1853).

Grange	Garvald
Abbey	Haddington nunnery
Order	Cistercian
Parish	Garvald and Bara
Council	East Lothian
Location	On headland above Papana Water north north-east of parish church
NGR	NT 5925 7104
NMRS site	NT57SE 26
Site visits	29 August 2002

History

30 March 1622 Grants to John, Viscount Lauderdale, Lord Thirlestane the possessions of the abbey [sic] of Haddington, including *Est Grange* (*RMS*, viii, no 306).

Archaeology

The first edition Ordnance Survey map of 1852 marks this site as 'Grange, site of' and seems to indicate that there was a structure still visible at that date.

Current State

The headland above the Papana Water is very overgrown with thistles and nettles and there is no visible stonework. None of the locals encountered knew anything about a grange on this site.

Grange	Gilmerton Grange
Abbey	Newbattle
Order	Cistercian
Parish	Edinburgh
Council	City of Edinburgh
Location	Somewhere in modern settlement of Gilmerton
NGR	NT 29 68
NMRS site	No entry
Site visits	Not visited

History

A charter of 3 February 1620 lists '*Gilmertoun-grange*' as one of the possessions of Newbattle Abbey (Thomson 1892, 771). The exact location of the grange at Gilmerton is unknown. Further research is required to accurately locate it.

Grange	St Giles Grange
Abbey	Harehope
Order	St Lazarus of Jerusalem
Parish	Edinburgh
Council	City of Edinburgh
Location	In Newington area of Edinburgh in vicinity of Grange Road
NGR	NT 2595 7167
NMRS site	NT27SE79
Site visits	6 November 2002

History

David I granted the Order of St Lazarus of Jerusalem, Harehope, Northumberland the church of St Giles, Edinburgh with its lands in the twelfth century (Barrow 1999, no 256). The Grange of St Giles, Edinburghshire is then recorded as being forfeited by the Friars of Harehope in 1375-6 (Thomson 1912, no 582).

The first edition Ordnance Survey map of this part of Edinburgh shows that the area is largely undeveloped. Grange Road is marked as are St Giles Villa and Grange Cottage. The ruins of the Convent of St Catherine of Sienna are marked as still standing between Sciennes Road and Grange Road.

Archaeology

Grange House: (NT 2596 7167). Demolished in 1936. The only remains are the eighteenth-century gate-piers and two late seventeenth-century offices. They (offices) stand at what was the north-east corner of the site. The house was built by Walter Cant in 1592 and grew into a large and mainly modern structure. Grange House took its name from the grange or farm of St Giles' Church. It ceased to be Church property in 1335, and by the sixteenth century it was owned by the family of Cant, from whom it was purchased by Sir William Dick of Braid in 1631. The oldest portion of the house dates from 1592, but the greater part of the building is of nineteenth-century works. A door lintel bears the date '1592': while in a wall of the outbuildings are arms bearing the dates '1613' and '1674'. The gate pillars are of seventeenth-century date (D. MacGibbon and T. Ross 1887-92 (RCAHMS 1951).

Current State

This area of Edinburgh is now the suburb of Newington and is occupied by domestic houses and gardens.

Grange	Grange Dell
Abbey	none
Order	none
Parish	Penicuik
Council	Midlothian
Location	To north of Penicuik to south of A702
NGR	NT 221 613
NMRS site	no entry
Site visits	26 September 2002

Current State

This site is occupied by two nineteenth-/twentieth-century buildings and a tennis court. There is no sign of anything that would connect it to a monastic grange.

Grange	Grange House
Abbey	Culross Abbey?

Order	?
Parish	Linlithgow
Council	West Lothian
Location	To the north of Linlithgow overlooking Linlithgow Palace and Loch
NGR	NT 000 787
NMRS site	NT07NW 64
Site visits	26 September 2002

Current State

The country house on this site has a date stone indicating that it was built in 1907. According to the son of the owner this house was built on a green field site by the same family who occupied the various other 'Grange Houses' in Grangemouth. There is no evidence to suggest that this place name has any connection with a former monastic grange.

Grange	Grange of Breich
Abbey	North Berwick nunnery
Order	Cistercian
Parish	Livingston
Council	West Lothian
Location	Grange Riding Centre and saddlery
NGR	NT 017 655
NMRS site	No entry
Site visits	18 September 2002

History

28 January 1568 Margaret Hume, Prioress of North Berwick feus to Alexander Hume, son of Patrick Hume of Polwart, *the lands of Grange of Breich, with mansions, halls, chambers, barns, gardens, houses, buildings and lands both arable and otherwise, for 6 merks of old feu and 3s 4d of augmentation* (*RMS*, iv, no 1920).

Archaeology

There are no records of any archaeological excavations on this site.

Current State

This site is currently occupied by the Grange Riding Centre and saddlery. The former farm buildings are still standing but appear no older than the eighteenth or nineteenth centuries. The one structure which may be earlier is a barn which is currently used to store bales of hay. This structure has several blocked windows on its eastern side.

Grange	Grange of Haddington (Barnes)
Abbey	Haddington nunnery
Order	Cistercian
Parish	Haddington
Council	East Lothian
Location	North-north-east of farm of Barney Mains above Hanging Craig
NGR	NT 5287 7655
NMRS site	NT57NW 27
Scheduled Monument?	SAM no 764
Site visits	11 September 2002

History

Barnis and Biris, called of old Grange of Haddington (Haddington Nunnery) (*RMS*, ii, no 610).

26 March 1319, declares that, despite any past or future ordinance, his gift to Sir Alexander de Seton, for his service in Ireland and in Scotland, of *the lands of Bernes and pertinents near Haddington and the place of the mill between Haddington and [?], called the East Mill* shall remain valid (*RRS*, v, nos 148, 149; see also pp126, 130).

10 April 1321, grants to Sir Alexander Setone *the lands of Barnis* within the sheriffdom of Edinburgh in free barony, doing service of two archers in the king's army and three suits of the court of Haddington at the three chief pleas of Haddington each year (*RRS*, v, no 178).

Archaeology

MacGibbon and Ross state that this remarkable structure was started by Sir John Seaton in the sixteenth century but never completed (MacGibbon and Ross 1887, 333-335). There are no records of any archaeological work on this site.

Current State

This structure is now used as a store for agricultural equipment and bales of hay (2002). It is generally in quite good condition although the interior is heavily overgrown with nettles and small shrubs.

Grange	Grange of Haddington (Byres)
Abbey	Haddington nunnery
Order	Cistercian
Parish	Haddington
Council	East Lothian
Location	Site now occupied by modern farm of Byres
NGR	NT 494 768
NMRS site	NT47NE 12
Site visits	6 November 2002

History

Volume 2 of the *Register of the Great Seal* refers to 'Barnis and Biris, called of old Grange of Haddington'(*RMS*, ii, no 610).

Archaeology

There are no records of any archaeological excavations on this site. The remains of a substantial rectangular structure, referred to locally as a 'castle', measure 6.3 x 5.2m with walls 0.7m thick. The extant remains are of two storeys; the ground floor is vaulted with slit windows in the north-east and south-west walls, a doorway in the south-west side and a square window on the south-east side, while the unroofed upper floor has a fireplace. No historical or traditional information could be gained from local enquiries (by OS (RDL) 31 October 1962). It is described as a dovecot on the first edition Ordnance Survey map.

Current State

The building described in the National Monuments Record can still be seen to the north of one of the farm cottages at NT 4958 7702. Its southern wall contains at least six reused large flat stones that have semi-circular cut-outs in them. It may be the presence of these that explains the previous identification as a dovecot. From conversations with the farmer, Mr Roy Black, he thought that someone from Historic Scotland had once visited and suggested to him that the building was a 'small keep' that once had a wooden staircase leading up to its first floor, the ground floor functioned as a byre for animals.

Grange	Grangemuir
Abbey	Melrose Abbey
Order	Cistercian
Parish	Whittinghame
Council	East Lothian
Location	On the north side of the road between Luggate and Bielgrange north north-east of Stenton
NGR	NT 607 751
NMRS site	None
Site visits	29 August 2002

History
There is a reference to the Grange at Grangemure, Haddingtonshire (Melrose Abbey) in the *Register of the Great Seal* dating to 28 August 1609 (*RMS* vii, no 139).

Archaeology
There is no record of any archaeological excavations on this site.

Current State
This site is occupied by a private house called Grangemuir and there is nothing upstanding that is any earlier than the eighteenth or nineteenth centuries.

Grange	Hartside
Abbey	Melrose Abbey
Order	Cistercian
Parish	Haddington
Council	East Lothian
Location	At the foot of Lothian Edge due south of Halls Farm
NGR	NT 652 760
NMRS site	No entry
Site visits	18 September 2002

History
March 1342[/3?] William, Bishop of St Andrews confirms an instrument of his predecessor William de Lambertone [concerning the teinds of the possessions of the *two granges of Edmonstone and Hertysheuid*, by composition anciently made between the monastery of Melrose and the church of Dunbar (in 1173, in the Synod in the church of St Cuthbert of Edinburgh, concerning the teinds of the possessions of the *two granges called Edmundestune and Hertisheuid*, whereby the monastery will pay every year 30s to the church of Dunbar, and the church of Dunbar can demand no more above these 30s from the monastery, which shillings are to be given at Martinmas); Item, certain letters of confirmation by Richard, Bishop of St Andrews [1165-78] (confirming the composition between the monastery of Melrose and the church of Dunbar concerning the teinds of the *two granges of Edmundestune and of Hertisheuid Spot* and of everything pertaining to the same granges); Item, certain letters testimonial of Andrew, Archdeacon and universal Clerk of Lothian (confirming the composition made in the presence of Richard, Bishop of St Andrews, between the monastery of Melrose and the church of Dunbar, concerning the teinds of *the granges of Edmundestune and Hertisheuid*); On the vigil [14 August] of the Assumption of the Blessed Virgin Mary 1326, at the church of Dunbar] (*Melrose Liber*, no 443).

Archaeology
There are no records of any archaeological excavations on this site.

Current State
This site is occupied by a shepherds cottage and another associated structure. There are no visible upstanding remains of an earlier date.

Grange	Kingston Grange
Abbey	none
Order	not applicable
Parish	Edinburgh
Council	City of Edinburgh
Location	Modern house of Kingston Grange
NGR	NT 283 701
NMRS site	NT27SE 4140
Site visits	Not visited

History
This house was built by Robert Adam in the late eighteenth century. It was originally called Sunnyside House but its name was changed to Kingston Grange *c*.1850. There is no evidence of any connection between the place name and a former monastic grange.

Grange	Melville Grange
Abbey	?
Order	?
Parish	Edinburgh
Council	City of Edinburgh
Location	On south side of City bypass
NGR	NT 3042 6765
NMRS site	NT36NW 197
Site visits	No visit

History
There is no evidence to suggest that this place name relates to a former monastic grange.

Grange	Moorfoot
Abbey	Newbattle (grange of Morthweth)
Order	Cistercian
Parish	Temple
Council	Midlothian
Location	In arable fields due east of Moorfoot Farm to south of Gladshouse Reservoir
NGR	NT 298 524
NMRS site	NT25SE 16
Scheduled Monument?	SAM no 5976
Site visits	30 August 2002

History
There is a reference to the grant of the lands of *Morthruweit* to Newbattle Abbey in 1140 x 1141 by David I. This land grant refers to the 'plain, meadows, pastures and grasses, by these named divisions, namely as the Blancheburne [Black Burn] descends from the hills and falls into Gledehus [Gladhouse], and as the Pardauarneburne [Tweeddale Burn] comes from the hills and falls into the Esh [South Esk] and as the two burns descend from the moss behind Tocchesheued [Toxside] on this side and on that into Gledehus and Esh' (Barrow 1999, no 97).

Archaeology

Carrick suggested that Moorfoot farmhouse and outbuildings were largely a reconstruction of the monastic grange (Carrick 1907). However the Ordnance Survey investigator indicated that he thought that was erroneous and was probably based on robbed mouldings that were built into the farmhouse. His description of the earthworks and standing-wall fragments in the standing area match the current state of the site (see below). In 1993 Aliaga-Kelly described the extensive series of earthworks and identified a potential mill lead (Aliaga-Kelly 1993, 62).

Current State

This site is currently being grazed by a small herd of cattle (2002). It is generally in a good state of preservation although there is bad river erosion taking place across the face of the eastern end of the standing structure (see sketch plan). This was also mentioned by the Ordnance Survey investigator in 1970. It appears that there is a quadrangular group of structures possibly indicating a group of ranges on the northern side of the standing building. To the north of this group is a sizeable earthwork bank that may represent some form of river defence? At the south-western corner of the scheduled area is a further group of earthworks apparently associated with a capped drain or lade that runs the length of the site. Derek Hall agrees with the previous identification of this set of features as being associated with a mill.

Grange	Newlands
Abbey	Haddington nunnery
Order	Cistercian
Parish	Garvald and Bara
Council	East Lothian
Location	At modern farm of Newlands
NGR	NT 569 664
NMRS site	NT56NE 24
Site visits	18 September 2002

History

The grange of Nunland is referred to in a charter of 1327 in later charters the name is changed to 'Newlandis' (Harvey and MacLeod 1930).

Archaeology

There are no records of any archaeological work on this site.

Current State

The current farm of Newlands is comprised of buildings of eighteenth- or nineteenth-century date, there is no sign of anything earlier.

Grange	Newton Grange
Abbey	Newbattle Abbey
Order	Cistercian
Parish	Newbattle
Council	Midlothian
Location	unlocated
NGR	NT36SW
NMRS site	No entry
Site visits	Not visited

History
A charter of 3 February 1620 refers to the *'terras ac terras dominicales de Newtoungrange'* as being one of the former possessions of Newbattle Abbey (Thomson 1892, 770).

Archaeology
There are no records of archaeological finds or excavations relating to this grange site.

Current State
Area occupied by the modern settlement of Newtongrange.

Grange	Penshiel
Abbey	Melrose Abbey (formerly Isle of May)
Order	Cistercian
Parish	Whittinghame
Council	Midlothian
Location	Due south of Penshiel Cottage and south-west of Whiteadder Reservoir
NGR	NT 641 631
NMRS site	NT66SW 11
Site visits	29 August 2002

History
On the 11 January 1342/3 Patrick de Dunbar, Earl of March confirmed the confirmation of Melrose of his father Patrick de Dunbar, Earl of March, of their possessions: *the land of Pansscheles* which they have by gifts of John de Methkil and Henry de Beeltone; the land which Sir Adam de Gordone conveyed to them in the territory of Estergordon together with the common pasture of the same toun (*Melrose Liber*, no 431).

Archaeology
There is no record of any archaeological excavations at this site. A measured survey was carried out by RCAHMS in July/August 1982 but the resulting drawings have never been inked up. This survey data includes (1) A site plan at 1:500 (2) A ground floor plan of the main building at 1:100 and (3) A section running from north to south across the building and the courtyard area to the north. A sketch book dating to 1901 also exists in RCAHMS which includes nine views and details of the building at Penshiel. Of most interest in this group are two views of the eastern end which show the vaulted roof still standing (RCAHMS sketch book 8 April 18 1901, Willie Lee Ferguson).

Current State
This site was scheduled as an ancient monument in 1994. Part of the scheduled area is fenced off in the middle of an arable field that is currently being grazed by sheep and young cattle (2002). The upstanding building remains are being choked by nettles on their lower courses and in the interior of the standing building the nettles have grown up to the springers of the vault. The northern face of the northern wall of the standing building has gone leaving the rubble core visible. There is only one rabbit burrow visible on the south-eastern side of the building. The fencing off of the scheduled area seems to have reduced the number of rabbit burrows but as this fence is simply post and wire maybe some sort of rabbit control measures have been carried out. The standing building is being heavily choked by nettles and some of the stonework appears to be very loose and unbonded.

Grange	Preston Grange
Abbey	Newbattle Abbey

Order	Cistercian
Parish	Prestonpans
Council	East Lothian
Location	Unknown
NGR	NT 37 73
NMRS site	No entry
Site visits	6 November 2002

History

1179 x 1189 William I confirms the grant to Newbattle Abbey by Robert de Quency and Seyr de Quency his son of the *grange of Prestoun* (RRS, ii, no 241). [See *SHR*, 30 (*), 41-9 and *Newbattle Registrum* nos 64, 65; the grange of Preston [Prestongrange, East Lothian] had been leased to Newbattle by Robert de Quinci in 1170 for 20 years, in return for which the abbey was to pay off Robert's debt of £80 to a certain Jew named Abraham.]

'The history of Morrison's-Haven may be given in a few words. In April, 1526, James V empowered the monks of Newbotle, the discoverers of coal in the same vicinity to construct a port within their own lands of Prestongrange (Parl Rec 129). Near the west end of the town of Prestonpans, the monks erected a harbour which was called New-Haven, and this name was changed to Acheson's-Haven, and afterward obtained the name of Morrison's-Haven, from the proprietor, at the commencement of the seventeenth century. It is reckoned one of the safest harbours on this shore of the Forth, having 10ft of water at stream tides (OSA 1796). It is a customhouse port by the name of Prestonpans, extending along the southern shore of the Forth, four and twenty miles between the ports of Dunbar and Leith'. So erected in 1710 (MS Customhouse report) (G. Chalmers 1888).

A charter of 28 July 1587 refers to '*molendinariis prope Prestoun-grange, cum portu lie Achesonis-hevin*' as being a former possession of Newbattle Abbey (Thomson 1888, 443).

Prestongrange (now the club house of the Royal Musselburgh Golf Club) is a long baronial house, its entrance front – facing north – virtually all by W.H. Playfair. The western half of the south front is earlier. The earliest datable part is its late sixteenth-century centre, extended to the east in the seventeenth century. This house was recast internally about 1750. The first stage of Playfair's work, begun in 1830, consists of a three-storeyed block to the south, with an octagonal entrance tower, and some development to the east end. In 1850 he added a square tower to the east. During internal alterations in 1962, a large painted ceiling dated 1581 was discovered; the greater part of it has now been placed in Merchiston Tower (NT27SW 13). (C. McWilliam 1978; G. Murray, M.R Apted and I. Hodkinson 1966).

Archaeology

There are no records of any archaeological work in this area.

Current State

The Grange is now occupied by the Scottish Mining Museum and the site of Morrison's Haven is filled in. The building known as Preston Grange remains the clubhouse of the Royal Musselburgh golf club.

Grange	Southside Castle
Abbey	Newbattle Abbey
Order	Cistercian
Parish	Newbattle
Council	Midlothian
Location	Current farm of Southside
NGR	NT 3693 6385

NMRS site	NT36SE 16
Site visits	Not visited

History
A charter of 28 July 1587 refers to *'terras de Southsyde'* as a former possession of Newbattle Abbey (Thomson 1888, 443).

Archaeology
Southside or Southsyde Castle is an L-shaped house of the first half of the seventeenth century; it was semi-ruinous about 1850, but it has been altered and modernised and is now in use as a farmhouse. The building was originally four storeys in height, but the roof has been lowered to provide a storey less; the angle-turrets still rise to their original level. Mullioned dormer windows have been added, and a modern two-storeyed addition has been made in the re-entrant angle. The interior is much altered, the vaulting in the wing having been removed, though the basement of the main block is still vaulted.

Prior to the Reformation, Southsyde was a possession of (the Cistercian) Newbattle Abbey; this house is said to have been built by Patrick Ellis in 1640-4, though it looks to be earlier than this, and possibly Ellis only made alterations to an existing building.

N. Tranter 1962; D. MacGibbon and T. Ross 1892; RCAHMS 1929, visited 1915

Current State
This site is occupied by the working farm of Southside.

Grange	Spartleton
Abbey	Kelso Abbey
Order	Cistercian
Parish	Stenton
Council	East Lothian
Location	Spartleton Hill and Edge lie to the north of the Whiteadder Reservoir
NGR	NT 653 655
NMRS site	NT66NE 7
Site visits	29 August 2002

History
Lands at Spartleton are referred to in the Kelso Abbey rental book in 1300 (Shead 1996, 365).

Archaeology
There are no records of any archaeological excavations in this area.

Current State
There are no obvious structures or other features visible on either Spartleton Hill or Edge. However, Gamelshiel Castle (SAM no 5606) lies directly below the hill on its southern side and it is tempting to consider that this structure might relate to the grange? This building is represented by two upstanding north and south walls that stand to height of *c*.10m. It appears to have been a small tower house measuring *c*.10 x 7m with a vaulted basement.

Grange	Vogrie Grange
Abbey	?
Order	?
Parish	Borthwick

Council	Midlothian
Location	Not visited
NGR	NT 374 627
NMRS site	NT36SE74
Site visits	Not visited

History
There are no documentary references to a monastic grange at Vogrie.

Archaeology
The cropmarks of a possible settlement have been revealed by oblique aerial photography (RCAHMSAP 1995), at the edge of a field 50m west-north-west of Vogrie House West Lodge (NT36SE 44). It is defined by an arc of ditch and measures at least 65m in diameter. Information from RCAHMS (KJ) 8 July 1999.

Grange	West Hopes, Nunhope
Abbey	Haddington nunnery
Order	Cistercian
Parish	Garvald and Bara
Council	East Lothian
Location	At or in the vicinity of West Hopes
NGR	NT 557 627
NMRS site	NT56SE 11
Site visits	18 September 2002

History
The grange of Nunhope, belonging to the Cistercian nunnery of Haddington, is referred to in various charters, e.g. 1327 and 1526 (Waterston 1952, 28, 31, 37).

Archaeology
There have been no recorded archaeological excavations on this site.

Current State
The former farm of West Hopes is now a private residence and none of the buildings would appear to be any older than the late eighteenth/early nineteenth century. This farm was used as the film set for the Walt Disney film 'Greyfriars Bobby'. Following a conversation with the current owner Mr John O'Brien a set of earthworks on the north side of the Fall Burn were investigated. These appear to define the wall of a structure measuring 16 x 14.4m. There are sizeable stones visible in the earthwork, which would seem to represent a wall foundation. Mr O'Brien said that the local shepherd could not identify these remains as belonging to any structure connected with sheepfarming. The walled field in front of West Hopes contains a sizeable linear earthwork standing 2 or 3m high and 4-5m wide. This seems unlikely to be a natural feature and the author wonders if it may be an earlier dam across valley of the Hopes Water?

APPENDIX 1
LIST OF POTENTIAL SCOTTISH MONASTIC INDUSTRIAL GRANGE SITES

FORMAT OF GAZETTEER

Each site entry indicates, where possible, the abbey and order responsible for the industry. The other entries may have an original monastic connection, although it is not possible to prove this. Note that most of these sites are on privately owned land and you should, if possible, always ask permission to visit them.

DUMFRIES AND GALLOWAY (14 SITES)

NAME	ABBEY	ORDER	NGR	NMR	INDUSTRY
Salt Pans Bay, Galdenoch	None known	N/A	NW 9645 6160	NW96SE 11	Salt
Salt Pan Bay, Aries	None known	N/A	NW 964 974	NW96SE 18	Salt
Saltpans, Ardwell	None known	N/A	NX 070 472	NX04NE 30	Salt
Chapel Rossan	None known	N/A	NX 1090 4505	NX14NW 10	Salt
Saltpan Point, Port William	None known	N/A	NX 337 432	NX34SW 6	Salt
Saltpan rocks, Sandy Hills	None known	N/A	NX 892 548	No entry	Salt
Colvend	Holm Cultram Abbey	Cistercian	NX 8687 5280	NX85SE 9	Salt and copper
Saltcot Hills	None known	N/A	NY 0535 6516	NY06NE 16	Salt
Powfoot to Browwell	None known	N/A	NY 1465 to NY 0867	NY16NW 42	Salt
Wanlockhead	Newbattle Abbey	Cistercian	NS 87 13	NS81SE 2, 87, 13	Lead
Redkirk Point (Rainpatrick)	Melrose Abbey	Cistercian	NY 3010 6503	NY36NW 5	Salt

Preston	Melrose Abbey	Cistercian	NY 950 550	No entry	Salt
Salterness	Melrose Abbey	Cistercian	NY 9760 5430	No entry	Salt
Lochindello	Melrose Abbey	Cistercian	Unlocated	No entry	Salt

SOUTH LANARKSHIRE (5 SITES)

SITE	ABBEY	ORDER	NGR	NMR	INDUSTRY
Drake Law 1	Newbattle Abbey	Cistercian	NS 9078 2138	No entry	Lead mining
Drake Law 2	Newbattle Abbey	Cistercian	NS 9021 9775	No entry	Lead mining
Drake Law 3	Newbattle Abbey	Cistercian	NS 9021 9796	No entry	Lead mining
Kirkgill	Newbattle Abbey	Cistercian	NS 9130 2118	No entry	Church site
Glencaple	Newbattle Abbey?	Cistercian	NS 9180 2165	No entry	Gold extraction?

THE SCOTTISH BORDERS (3 SITES)

SITE	ABBEY	ORDER	NGR	NMR	INDUSTRY
Lead Law, Sillerholes	Newbattle Abbey?	Cistercian	NT 145 533	NT15SW 32	Lead mining
Darnick	Melrose Abbey	Cistercian	NT 5273 3260	NT53SW 44	Tiles
Bourjo	Melrose Abey	Cistercian	NT 548 327	NT53SW 33	Quarry

WEST LOTHIAN

Site Name   Hilderston
Industry   Silver Mines
Abbey   Torphichen Preceptory?
Order   Knights of St John
Parish   Linlithgow
Council   West Lothian
Location   Silver mines located at NS 989 716 (other sites in the Hilderston industiral landscape were also visited)
NGR   NS 989 716 (sunken shafts of silver mine)
NMRS site   NS97SE34
Site visits   13 July 2004

History

The earliest reference to silver at Hilderston is in an entry in the Rental of the Knights of St John of Torphichen dated to 1539-40 (Cowan, MacKay and MacQuarrie 1983, 1). This states a rental of '*Villa de Hilderstoun set to tennentis for xx merkis maile in the zeir and xijs' of weddir siluer pait mertimes with uther dewiteis and dew service vsit and wont*' (Ibid 1983, 1). It is not clear whether this reference implies that mining was taking place at this date although the fact that the metal is specifically referred must make this a very strong possibility.

    Silver is on record as being discovered at Hilderston in 1606 and there were at least seven shafts. In 1613 the mine was let to a private firm. The precise date of abandonment is unknown but it must have closed soon after 1614. The lease was renewed in 1870 but the project was abandoned in 1898 (Cadell 1925).

Archaeology

There are no known records of any archaeological excavation in the area of the silver mines. A theolodite survey and an assessment of the Hilderston industrial area was recently carried out by University of Glasgow (Photos Jones et al. 1999).

Current State

Generally a heavily eroded, post medieval/early modern industrial landscape littered by the remains of sites for silver mining, lead mining, coal mining, limestone quarrying and lime-making.

The silvermine site is located at the bottom of the south slope of Cairnpapple hill. At the site three depressions are clearly visible on the hillslope on the north side of the Miners Burn. These hollows represent the locations of backfilled mine shafts. The depressions have diameters of approximately 3 m and are arranged east–west over a distance of about 25m. The OS grid reference for the eastern most hollow is NS 9896 7154.

Blair's House, (Blair was probably an overseer for the mining operations) represents overgrown and turf covered footings 36m in length and 6m wide with compartments of differing length. Centred on NS 99007159 adjacent to the Linlithgow Road.

Miners cottages, 50m to the south-west of Blair's House are overgrown turf covered footings 57m in length and 5m wide, aligned east–west, also known as the long row. The row is divided into seven compartments with frontages on the south side. Centred on NS 9905 7155 facing a track on the north side of the Miners Burn.

Lime kilns are located on the east side of a flooded quarry at NS 9920 7158. They have been cut into a small hillock (the hillock is probably man made). The remains of the frontages of at least three kilns were observed. These were formed of mortared large ashlar blocks and in a deteriorating condition. The entrances were partly blocked but it was possible to photograph the vaulted interior of one of the kilns which was approximately 2m in height and at least 3m in length.

EAST LOTHIAN (5 SITES)

SITE	ABBEY	ORDER	NGR	NMR	INDUSTRY
North Berwick	North Berwick	Cistercian nuns	NT 5465 8505	NT58SW3.02	Tile manufacturing
Prestonpans	Newbattle Abbey	Cistercian	NT 38 74	NT37SE 15, 19	Salt and coal
Westpans	None known	N/A	NT 3644 7326	NT37SE 93	Salt
Birsley Brae	Newbattle Abbey	Cistercian	NT 392 728	NT37SE 66	Coal
Cockenzie	None known	N/A	NT 398 757	NT37NE 1	Salt

EDINBURGH, CITY OF (1 SITE)

Site Name	Edinburgh, Portobello, Joppa Salt Pans
Industry	Salt
Abbey	None
Order	N/A
Parish	Edinburgh
Council	Edinburgh, City of

Location	Portobello, B6415, north side
NGR	NT 3210 7340 (centred)
NMRS Site	NT37SW 214
Site Visit	12 July 04

History
A plaque on Rock Cottage reads 'Rock Cottage sixteenth century oldest house in Portobello, salt produced on this site at Joppa Salt Pans 1630-1953'. The roads sign next on the west side of the cottage reads 'Joppa Pans'.

Archaeology
None known.

Current State
Rock Cottage is residential and in good repair. The building does not appear to be listed or scheduled. On the seashore below the cottage, are the remains of three well-eroded wooden posts about 0.10m in diameter and 0.10m in height, aligned east–west. These may have acted as uprights for some sort of wooden framework for the retention or control of sea water during the time of salt panning.

FALKIRK COUNCIL (3 SITES)

SITE	ABBEY	ORDER	NGR	NMR	INDUSTRY
Kerse House, Grangemouth	Arbroath Abbey, Newbattle Abbey, Holyrood Abbey, Torphichen Preceptory	Tironensian; Cistercian; Augustinian; Order of St John	NS 9155 8166	NS98SW 80	Salt
Grangepans, Boness	None known	N/A	NT 00 18	NT08SW 93	Salt
High Airth	Holyrood Abbey	Cistercian	NS 897 873	NS88NE 17	Salt

MORAY (3 SITES)

SITE	ABBEY	ORDER	NGR	NMR	INDUSTRY
Croy	Pluscarden Abbey	Valliscaulian then Benedictine	NJ 167 527	NJ15NE 2	Ironmaking and glassworks
Quarrywood	None known	N/A	NJ1845 6375	NJ16SE 22	Quarry
Salterhill	Spynie Palace?	Bishops of Moray	NJ 2075 6682	NJ26NW 8	Salt

NORTH AYRSHIRE (1 SITE)

Site Name	Saltcoats
Industry	Salt
Abbey	None known

Order   N/A
Parish   Ardrossan
Council   North Ayrshire
Location   Saltcoats harbour pier
NGR   NS 2453 4094
NMRS Site   NS24SW 44
Site Visit   27 October 2004

History
NS 2453 4094. Old pier head probably includes part of the harbour works of Robert Cunningham built in 1686 as part of a saltpan and colliery complex (Butt 1967).

Archaeology
None known.

Current State
A harled, nineteenth-century two-storey building measuring 5 x 11m is the only structure now on the pier head. It has gable end chimneys and a slate roof. The upper floor has three windows, the lower two, all now bricked up. There is an outside stairway on the south gable end. The doorway on the ground floor is open and the building inside is derelict. There was no physical indication as to the former function of this building.

PERTH AND KINROSS (4 SITES)

SITE	ABBEY	ORDER	NGR	NMR	INDUSTRY
Parkfield Farm, Scone	Scone Abbey	Augustinian	NO 1470 2505	No entry	Clay pits
Balcormoc (Quarrymill)	Scone Abbey	Augustinian	NO 1250 2530	No entry	Quarry
Kincarrathie	Scone Abbey	Augustinian	NO 1223 2480	No entry	Quarry
Nethergask	Inchaffray Abbey	Augustinian	NN 9862 1743 or NN 930 170 or NN 960 170	Entry for Gascon Hall	Quarry
Craigie	Bishop of Dunkeld		NO 120 440		Quarry

SOUTH AYRSHIRE (3 SITES)

SITE	ABBEY	ORDER	NGR	NMR	INDUSTRY
Greenan Castle	Melrose Abbey	Cistercian	NS 311 193	NS31NW 26	Salt
New Prestwick	None known	N/A	NS 341 249	NS32SW	Salt
Pan knows, Turnberry	Melrose Abbey	Cistercian	NS 2065 0785	NS20NW 13	Salt

APPENDIX 2
LIST OF SCOTTISH MEDIEVAL HOSPITALS

SCOTTISH MEDIEVAL HOSPITALS BY TYPE (178)

Almshouses (26)

HOSPITAL NAME	COUNCIL AREA	DATE	TYPE	NGR/NMRS
St Leonard, Lauder	Scottish Borders	1175x1189	Almshouse	NT 5551 4574 NT54NE 14
Arbroath Almonry	Angus	1178	Almshouse	NO 642 412 NO64SW 9
St Leonard, Ednam	Scottish Borders	1178	Almshouse	NT 7343 3578 NT73NW 11
St Leonard, Horndean	Scottish Borders	1240	Almshouse	NT 9049 4962 NT94NW 15
St Leonard, Lanark	South Lanarkshire	1249	Almshouse	NS 889 439 NS84SE 18
Monkshome, Newburgh	Aberdeenshire	1261	Almshouse	NK 000 254 NK02NW 9
St Mary and St Congan, Turriff	Aberdeenshire	1272/3	Almshouse	NJ 72 49 NJ74NW 1
St Mary, Segden	Scottish Borders	1296	Almshouse	Unlocated No entry
St Catherine, Dunfermline	Fife	1327	Almshouse	NT 089 873 NT08NE 8
St Mary, Edinburgh	City of Edinburgh	1438	Almshouse for poor women	NT 261 735 NT27SE 47
Linlithgow	West Lothian	1448	Almshouse	NT 001 772 NT07NW 28
Peebles	Scottish Borders	1462	Almshouse	NT 252 405 NT24SE 71
Peebles	Scottish Borders	1464	Almshouse	NT 250 403 NT24SE 70
St Nicholas, Glasgow	City of Glasgow	1464	Almshouse	NS 600 654 NS66NW 10

APPENDIX 2

St Mary and St Paul, Edinburgh	City of Edinburgh	1469	Almshouse	NT 260 739 NT27SE 28
Haddington	East Lothian	1478	Almshouse	NT 517 735 NT57SW 39
Over Hospital	Stirling	1482	Almshouse	NS 792 937 NS79SE 69
Dunfermline	Fife	1488	Almshouse	NT 092 874 NT08NE 95
East Port, Linlithgow	West Lothian	1496	Almshouse	NT 050 772 NT07NW 27
St Mary, Aberdeen	City of Aberdeen	1531-2	Almshouse	NJ 938 087 NJ90NW 9.02
St Mary Virgin, North Berwick	East Lothian	1541	Almshouse	NT 5545 8534 NT58NE 11
Spittal's (Nether Hospital), Stirling	Stirling	1546	Almshouse	NS 793 935 NS79SE 31
Jedburgh	Scottish Borders	1553	Almshouse	NT 64 20 or NT 65 20, no entry
Maisondieu, Edinburgh	City of Edinburgh	1582	Almshouse	NT 258 736 NT27SE 42
Cowane's, Stirling	Stirling	1637	Almshouse	NS 791 936 NS79SE 20
St Leonard, Dunfermline	Fife	Undated	Almshouse	NT 097 866 NT08NE 28

Bedehouses (almshouses for bedesmen or women) (4)

HOSPITAL NAME	COUNCIL AREA	DATE	TYPE	NGR/NMRS
St John Baptist, Corstorphine	City of Edinburgh	1538	Bedehouse	NT 200 727 NT27SW 51
Buchanan's Hospital, Dumbarton	West Dunbartonshire	1636	Bedehouse	NS 3980 7520 NS37NE 16
Cullen	Moray	Undated	Bedehouse	NJ 5086 6608 NJ56NW 7
Oyne	Aberdeenshire	Undated	Bedehouse	NJ 6934 2358 NJ62SE 3

Hostels for travellers or pilgrims (8)

HOSPITAL NAME	COUNCIL AREA	DATE	TYPE	NGR/NMRS
St Leonard, St Andrews	Fife	1144	Pilgrims and Travellers and then old women and poor men	NO 512 166 NO51NW 9

Ardross, Earlsferry	Fife	1154	Pilgrims and Travellers	NT 480 993 NT49NE 3
Holy Trinity, Soutra	Scottish Borders	1164	Travellers or Pilgrims	NT 452 584 NT45NE 1
Portincraig, Broughty Ferry	City of Dundee	1187/89	Travellers or Pilgrims	NO 46 30 NO43SE 23
Latheron	Highland	1290	Travellers or Pilgrims	ND 198 335 ND13SE 54
Kilpatrick	West Dunbartonshire	1418	Travellers	NS 463 730 NS47SE 7
Shean Spittal, Allt A'Gharbh-Choire	Aberdeenshire	Undated	Travellers or Pilgrims	NO 1491 1991 NO17NW 1
Maisondieu, Spittal	Dumfries and Galloway	Undated	Pilgrims	NX 357 579 NX35NE 26

Hospitals for the care of the sick (2)

HOSPITAL NAME	COUNCIL AREA	DATE	TYPE	NGR/NMRS
St Peter, Aberdeen	City of Aberdeen	1179	Care of the Sick	NJ 940 076 NJ90NW 16
St Leonard, Dalkeith	Midlothian	1528	Care of the Sick	NT 303 661 NT36NW 26

Poorhouses (39)

HOSPITAL NAME	COUNCIL AREA	DATE	TYPE	NGR/NMRS
North Berwick	East Lothian	1154	Poor and Travellers	NT 553 885 NT58NE 21
St Germains	East Lothian	1170	Poorhouse	NT 426 747 NT47SW 1
St Thomas, Portmoak	Perth and Kinross	1184	Poorhouse	NO 1825 0015 NO10SE 35
St Mary, Scotlandwell	Perth and Kinross	1214	Poorhouse	NO 1866 0154 NO10SE 5
St Mary, Kincardine O'Neil	Aberdeenshire	1224	Poorhouse	NO 592 998 NO59NE 6
St Nicholas, Boharm	Moray	1232	Poorhouse	NJ 318 516 NJ35SW 2
Maison Dieu, Elgin	Moray	1237	Poorhouse	NJ 223 626 NJ26SW 12
Kelso	Scottish Borders	1260	Poorhouse	NT 73 34 No entry
Maison Dieu, Brechin	Angus	1267	Poorhouse	NO 596 603 NO56SE 13

APPENDIX 2

St John and St Mary Magdalene, Polmadie	City of Glasgow	1285	Poorhouse	NS 601 626 NS66SW 23
Maison Dieu, Jedburgh	Scottish Borders	1296	Poorhouse	NT 6514 2087 NT62SE 28
St Leonard, Peebles	Scottish Borders	1305	Poorhouse	NT 2837 3943 NT23NE 17
St Mary Magdalene, Perth	Perth and Kinross	1327	Poorhouse	NO 11 21 NO12SW 29
St Magdalene's, Linlithgow	West Lothian	1335	Poorhouse	NO 0112 7714 NO07NW 20
Nethergate, Dundee	City of Dundee	1390	Poor and Sick	NO 3999 2989 NO32NE 2
Dalkeith	Midlothian	1396	Poorhouse	NT 332 674 NT36NW 45
St Mary Magdalene, Arrat	Angus	1412	Poorhouse	NO 645 590 NO65NW 8
St Anthony, Leith	City of Edinburgh	1418	Poor and the Sick	NT 269 760 NT27SE 6
Strathblane	Stirling	1429	Poorhouse	NS 56 79 NS57NE 46
St Paul's, Perth	Perth and Kinross	1434	Poorhouse	NO 1143 2365 NO12SW 18
Dunglass	East Lothian	1443	Poorhouse	NT 766 718 NT77SE 62
Covington	South Lanarkshire	1448	Poorhouse	NS 97 39 NS93NE 31
St James, Trailtrow	Dumfries and Galloway	1455	Poorhouse	NY 1550 7223 NY17SE 13 (this entry wrongly gives the location as Trailtrow farm) NY17SE 12 (site of Trailtrow Chapel)
St Thomas Martyr, Aberdeen	City of Aberdeen	1459	Poor and the Sick	NJ 941 062 NJ90NW 47
Mary of Gueldres, Stirling	Stirling	1462	Poorhouse	NS 79 93 NS79SE 70
St Martha, Aberdour	Fife	1474	Poorhouse	NT 193 856 NT18NE 14
St Catherine/St Mary, Kirk of Shotts	North Lanarkshire	1476	Poorhouse	NS 843 629 NS86SW 2
St Mary, Lasswade	Midlothian	1477	Poor, Sick and Travellers	NT 301 661 NT36NW 25

St James, Kinghorn	Fife	1478	Poorhouse	NT 2787 NT28NE 15
St Anne, Perth	Perth and Kinross	1488	Poorhouse	NO 1194 2350 NO12SW 19
St George's, Dunkeld	Perth and Kinross	1506	Poorhouse	NO 0256 4262 NO04SW 2
St Catherine's, Perth	Perth and Kinross	1523	Poorhouse	NO 1128 2377 NO12SW 15
Blacader's, Glasgow	City of Glasgow	1524-25	Poorhouse	NS 600 656 NS66NW 20
St Mary Magdalene, Edinburgh	City of Edinburgh	1537	Poorhouse	NT 256 734 NT27SE 23
Fail	South Ayrshire	1560	Poorhouse	NS 4212 2863 (monastery site) NS 424 277 (Spittalside Farm)
Ayr	South Ayrshire	1615	Poorhouse	NS 341 216 NS32SW 22
Culross	Fife	1637	Poorhouse	NS 992 860 NS98NE 15
Maison Dieu, Dunbar	East Lothian	Undated	Poorhouse	NT 6800 7862 NT67NE 4

Leper hospitals (23)

HOSPITAL NAME	COUNCIL AREA	DATE	TYPE	NGR/NMRS
Adniston, West Morriston	Scottish Borders	1177 or 1296	Leper	NT 58 43 NT64SW 9
St Nicholas, St Andrews	Fife	1178	Leper then Poorhouse	NO 518 159 NO51NW 28
Harlaw	Dumfries and Galloway	1195	Leper	NY 434 790 No entry
Old Cambus	Scottish Borders	1214x1216	Leper	Unlocated
St Peter, Rathven	Moray	1224-26	Leper then Almshouse	NJ 443 656 NJ46NW 1
St Mary, Montrose	Angus	1246x1265	Leper and then Poorhouse	NO 713 583 NO75NW 6
St John, Uthrogle	Fife	1293	Leper	NO 338 135 NO31SW 9
Aberdeen	City of Aberdeen	1333	Leper	NJ 941 072 NJ90NW 13
St Ninian, Glasgow	City of Glasgow	1359	Leper	NS 5910 6443 NS56SE 23
St Mary Magdalene, Musselburgh	East Lothian	1386	Lepers and the Poor	NT 34 72 NT37SW 48

Elgin	Moray	1391	Leper	NJ 226 626 NJ26SW 17
St Mary, Spittal-on-Rule	Scottish Borders	1425/26	Leper	NT 588 199 NT51NE 1
Ayr	South Ayrshire	1448	Leper houses	Unlocated
Stirling	Stirling	1464	Leper	NS 79 93 No entry
Dumbarton	West Dunbartonshire	1469	Leper	NS 407 767 No entry
St Laurence, Haddington	East Lothian	1470	Leper	NT 5015 7372 NT57SW 11
Edinburgh	City of Edinburgh	1477	Leper	Unlocated
Dundee	Dundee	1498	Leper	NO 11 21 NO43SW 38
Banff	Aberdeenshire	1544	Leper	NJ 684 632 NJ66SE 37
Perth Leper Hospital	Perth and Kinross	1577	Leper	NO 124 239 No entry
Greenside	City of Edinburgh	1591	Leper	NT 262 744 NT27SE 36
Rigg	Dumfries and Galloway	undated	Leper	NS 714 117 NS71SW 4

Unknown function (76)

HOSPITAL NAME	COUNCIL AREA	DATE	TYPE	NGR/NMRS
North Queensferry	Fife	1165	Unknown	NT 12 80 NT18SW 28
Levern Water, Crookston	City of Glasgow	1180	Unknown	NS 51 61 NS56SW 8
St Leonard, Perth	Perth and Kinross	1184	Unknown	NO 1124 2293 NO12SW
Inverkeithing	Fife	1196	Unknown	NT 128 826 NT18SW 27
St John the Apostle, Scone	Perth and Kinross	1206x1227	Unknown	NO 11 26 NO12NW 48
St James, Stirling	Stirling	1221x1225	Unknown	NS 795 944 NS79SE 71
St Leonard, Edinburgh	City of Edinburgh	1239	Unknown	NT 265 729 NT27SE 74
Annan	Dumfries and Galloway	1258	Unknown	NY 187 670 NY16NE 19 NY16NE 141
Fortune	East Lothian	1270	Unknown	NT 53 79 NT57NW 60

Duns	Scottish Borders	1274	Unknown	NT 78 53 NT75SE 28
St Mary the Virgin/ St Mary Magdalene, Rutherford	Scottish Borders	1276	Unknown	NT 6537 3124 NT63SE 11
St Thomas of Aconia, Spittalhill	South Ayrshire	1283 or 1298	Unknown	NS 403 334 NS43SW 12
St Peter, Roxburgh	Scottish Borders	1286	Unknown	NT 717 340 NT73SW 20.01
St Cuthbert, Red Spittal, Ballencrieff	East Lothian	1291	Unknown	NT 485 780 NT47NE 35
St John, Hutton	Scottish Borders	1296	Unknown	NT 921 530 NT95SW 7
Houston	East Lothian	1296	Unknown	NT 56 78 NT57NE 6
St Leonard, Torrance	South Lanarkshire	1296	Unknown	NS 635 534 NS65SE 2
Cree Spittal	Dumfries and Galloway	1305	Unknown	NX 468 606 or NX 465 604 NX46SE 3
Maison Dieu, Roxburgh	Scottish Borders	1305	Unknown	NT 717 340 No entry
St Mary Magdalene, Roxburgh	Scottish Borders	1319	Unknown	NT 717 340 NT73SW 20.02
St John, Roxburgh	Scottish Borders	1330	Unknown	NT 717 340 NT73SW 20.03
Bara	East Lothian	1340	Unknown	NT 55 70 NT57SE 14
Wheel	Scottish Borders	1347	Unknown	NT 6047 0008 NT60SW 5
St John the Baptist, Arboath	Angus	1352	Unknown	NO 625 404 NO64SW 9
St Magnus, Spittal	Highland	1358	Unknown	ND 158 548 ND15SE
Lazarite House, Elgin	Moray	1360	Unknown	NJ 21 62 NJ26SW 110
St John the Baptist, Helmsdale	Highland	1362	Unknown	ND 0246 1562 ND01NW 17
Obsdale	Highland	1384	Unknown	NH 66 69 NH66NE 40
St John the Baptist, Edinburgh	City of Edinburgh	1392	Unknown	NT 25 73 NT27SE 402
St Mary the Virgin, Eassie	Angus	1418	Unknown	NO 355 466 NO34NE 5
St Leonard, Ayr	South Ayrshire	1420	Unknown	NS 335 196 NS31NW 4

APPENDIX 2

Hadden	Scottish Borders	1432	Unknown	NT 789 361 No entry
St John the Baptist, Dundee	City of Dundee	1442	Unknown	NO 4182 3094 NO43SW 24
St Anthony, Dundee	City of Dundee	1443	Unknown	NO 4067 3064 NO43SW 27
St Mary, Hamilton	South Lanarkshire	1459	Unknown	NS 71 55 NS75NW 21
St Nicholas, Leith	City of Edinburgh	1488	Unknown	NT 267 766 NT27NE 9
Kilmarnock	East Ayrshire	1491	Unknown	NS 42 37 NS43NW 33
Smailholm	Scottish Borders	1492	Unknown	NT 645 363 NT63NW 8
St Thomas Martyr, Hamilton	South Lanarkshire	1496	Unknown	NS 727 599 NS75NW 13
Kirk O'Field, Edinburgh	City of Edinburgh	1510	Unknown	NT 259 733 NT27SE 20
Cockburnspath	Scottish Borders	1511	Unknown	NT 756 705 NT77SE 29
Fairnington	Scottish Borders	1511	Unknown	NT 647 281 NT62NW 4
Spittell Croft, Dunblane	Stirling	1516	Unknown	NN 7815 0110 No entry
St Giles, Edinburgh	City of Edinburgh	1541	Unknown	NT 257 735 NT27SE 122
Nenthorn	Scottish Borders	1542	Unknown	Unlocated NT63NE 12
Spittal of Drymen	Stirling	1548	Unknown	NS 54 89 NS58NW 17
Spittal of Arngibbon	Stirling	1550	Unknown	NS 607 941 NS69SW 14
Holy Trinity or Trinity House, Leith	City of Edinburgh	1555	Unknown	NT 269 760 NT27NE 31
Wigtown	Dumfries and Galloway	1557	Unknown	NX 43 55 No entry
Geilston	West Dunbartonshire	1560	Unknown	Uncertain No entry
Masonedew, Maybole	South Ayrshire	1574	Unknown	NS 29 09 NS20NE 14
King James, Edinburgh	City of Edinburgh	1614	Unknown	NT 270 760 NT27NE 26
Allan's Hospital, Stirling	Stirling	1725	Unknown	NS 795 937 NS79SE 32
Spittal of Glenmuick	Aberdeenshire	1732	Unknown	NO 307 850 NO38NW 2

Ancrum	Scottish Borders	Undated	Unknown	NT 6475 2470 NT62SW 6
Earlston	Scottish Borders	Undated	Unknown	NT 57 38 NT53NE 17
Newstead	Scottish Borders	Undated	Unknown	NT 56 34 NT53SE 37
Selkirk	Scottish Borders	Undated	Unknown	NT 47 28 NT42NE 22
Longbedholm	Dumfries and Galloway	Undated	Unknown	NT 054 061 NT00NE 75
King's Scar, Sanquhar	Dumfries and Galloway	Undated	Unknown	NS 790 088 NS70NE 12
St Cuthbert's, Moffat	Dumfries and Galloway	Undated	Unknown	NT 0739 0549 NT00NE 11
Meikle and Little Spittal	Dumfries and Galloway	Undated	Unknown	NX 02 53 NX05SW 15
Spittal, Auchterderran	Fife	Undated	Unknown	Land owned by hospital in Edinburgh (Trinity College) NT 210 943 NT29SW 23
Ousdale	Highland	Undated	Unknown	ND 070 200 ND02SE 31
Spittal Shore	Highland	Undated	Unknown	NH 56 49 NH54NE 11
Irvine	North Ayrshire	Undated	Unknown	NS 32 38 NS33NW 36
Lazarite House, Lanark	South Lanarkshire	Undated	Unknown	NS 88 43 NS84SE 64
St Leonard's Spittal	South Lanarkshire	Undated	Unknown	NS 67 58 NS65NE 24
Spittal, Carnwath	South Lanarkshire	Undated	Unknown	NS 988 449 NS94SE 7
Spittal House	South Lanarkshire	Undated	Unknown	NS 772 447 NS74SE 9
Causewayhead	Stirling	Undated	Unknown	Knights Hospitallers NS 8050 9580 No entry
Spittal Glen or Craigbrock Farm	Stirling	Undated	Unknown	NS 5451 8119 (Spittal Glen) NS 5421 8107 (Craigbrock Farm)
Gartmore Spittal	Stirling	Undated	Unknown	NS 5061 9718 No entry

Spittal of Arnbeg	Stirling	Undated	Unknown	NS 629 949 NS69SW 1
Spittalton	Stirling	Undated	Unknown	NS 685 992 NS69NE 9
Spittal, Balfron	Stirling	Undated	Unknown	NS 54 89 NS58NW 17

Hospital date and dedication

Dedication	12th	13th	14th	15th	16th	17th	18th	Undated	
St Leonard	4	4	1	1	1	0	0	0	11
St John	0	4	4	1	1	0	0	0	10
St Peter	1	2	0	0	0	0	0	0	3
St Germain	1	0	0	0	0	0	0	0	1
St Thomas	1	1	0	2	0	0	0	0	4
St Mary	0	6	0	7	2	0	0	0	15
St Mary Magdalene	0	2	2	1	1	0	0	0	6
St Catherine	0	0	1	1	0	0	0	0	2
St Nicholas	1	1	0	2	0	0	0	0	4
St Cuthbert	0	1	0	0	0	0	0	1	2
St George	0	0	0	0	1	0	0	0	1
	8	21	8	15	6	0	0	1	

Hospital by type

	Alms	Poor	Leper	Pil/Trav	Sick	Bede	Unknown
12th	3	2	3	2	1	0	3
13th	4	8	4	0	0	0	13
14th	1	4	4	0	0	0	12
15th	10	13	7	0	0	0	20
16th	5	5	3	0	1	1	12
17th	1	2	0	0	0	1	1
18th	0	0	0	0	0	0	2
Undated	1	1	1	2	0	2	12

BIBLIOGRAPHY

Agnew, A. 1893 *The Hereditary Sheriffs of Galloway.* Edinburgh, 2nd.
Armstrong, Captain and Son 1775 *A New Map of Ayrshire, Comprehending Kyle, Cunninghame, and Carrick.*

Bannatyne Club 1849 *Registrum de S. Marie de Neubotle.* Edinburgh.
Barrow, G.W.S. et al. (eds) 1960- *RRS Regesta Regum Scottorum.* 8 vols, Edinburgh.
Barrow, G.W.S. (ed.) 1999 *The Charters of King David I.* Woodbridge.
Beveridge, D. 1885 *Culross and Tulliallan.* Edinburgh and London. 2 vols.
Brann, M., Cachart, R., Cox, A. and Hall, D.W. 2002 *Gazetteer of monastic granges in Dumfries and Galloway, Highland, Lothian and Scottish Borders Councils.* Report prepared for Historic Scotland.
Brann, M., Cachart, R., Glendinning, B. and Hall, D.W. 2000 *Gazetteer of Medieval Hospital Sites in Argyll and Bute, Ayrshire, Edinburgh City, Dumfries and Galloway, Renfrew, Stirling and West Dunbartonshire Council Areas.* Report prepared for Historic Scotland.
Brown, J.M. (ed.) 1977 *Scottish Society in the Fifteenth Century.*
Brown, R 1927 'More about the mines and minerals of Wanlockhead and Leadhills', *Trans Dumfriesshire Galloway Natur Hist Antiq Soc*, 3rd, 13 (1925-6), 63.
Butt, J. 1967 *The industrial archaeology of Scotland. The Industrial Archaeology of the British Isles.* Newton Abbot.

Cachart, R., Hall, D.W. and Middleton, M. 1998 *Gazetteer of medieval hospital sites in Scottish Borders and Fife council areas.* Report prepared for Historic Scotland.
Cachart, R., Hall, D.W., Kaye, R., Roy, M. and Smith, C. 2001 *Gazetteer of monastic granges in Aberdeenshire, Angus, Argyll and Bute, North, South and East Ayrshire, Dundee, Falkirk, Fife, North and South Lanarkshire, Moray, Perth and Kinross, East Renfrewshire and Stirling Councils.* Report prepared for Historic Scotland.
Cachart, R., Murray, C. and Hall, D.W. 1999 *Gazetteer of medieval hospital sites in Aberdeenshire, Glasgow City, Highland, Lanarkshire and Moray council areas.* Report prepared for Historic Scotland.
Cadell, H.M. 1925 *The rocks of West Lothian.* Edinburgh.
Cambuskenneth Registrum 1872 *Registrum Monasterii S Marie de Cambuskenneth.* Grampian Club, Edinburgh.
Cameron, K. 1998 'West Pans Pottery, Musselburgh (Inveresk parish), evaluation', *Discovery Excav Scot*, 1998, 33. Edinburgh.
Cameron, K. and Glendinning, B. 2003 'West Pans Pottery, 64 Ravensheugh Road, Musselburgh (Inveresk parish), watching brief', *Discovery Excav Scot*, 2003, 60. Edinburgh.
Chalmers, G. 1887-94 *Caledonia: or a historical and topographical account of North Britain.* Paisley, 7 vols and index.

Cochran Patrick, R.W. 1878 *Early Records Relating to Mining in Scotland*. Lanark.
Coleman, R. and Perry, D. 1997 'Moated sites in Tayside and Fife', *Tayside and Fife Archaeol J*, Vol 3. Glenrothes.
Cowan, I. and Easson, D. 1976 *Medieval religious houses: Scotland*.
Cowan, I., MacKay, P.H.R. and MacQuarrie, A. 1983 *The knights of St John of Jerusalem in Scotland*. Edinburgh.
Crawford, J.C. and James, S. 1979 'Wanlockhead Miners library, 1756-1979', *Trans Dumfriesshire Galloway Natur Hist Antiq Soc*, 3rd, 54 (1979), 97-104.
Cullum, P.H. 1993 'St Leonard's Hospital, York: the spatial and social analysis of an Augustinian Hospital' in Gilchrist, R. and Mytum, H. (eds) *Advances in Monastic Archaeology* BAR British Series 227. Oxford.

Donnachie, I. 1971 *The industrial archaeology of Galloway, The Industrial Archaeology of the British Isles*. Newton Abbot.
Downs-Rose, G. 1984 'Draining the Wanlockhead Lead Mines: a note on the introduction and use of hydraulic pumping engines', *Trans Dumfriesshire Galloway Natur Hist Antiq Soc*, 3rd, 59 (1984), 70-81.
Downs-Rose, G. and Harvey, W.S. 1973 'Wanlockhead, Dumfries-shire', *Counc Brit Archaeol Calendar Excav*, 1973, Summaries, 22. York.
Downs-Rose, G. and Harvey, W.S. 1979 'Lead smelting sites at Wanlockhead: 1682-1934', *Trans Dumfriesshire Galloway Natur Hist Antiq Soc*, 3rd, 54 (1979), 75-84.
Dunfermline Registrum 1842 *Registrum de Dunfermelyn*. Bannatyne Club, Edinburgh.
Dunlop, A.I. (ed.) 1953 *The Royal Burgh of Ayr: seven hundred and fifty years of history*. Edinburgh, 88.

Eckford, R. 1928 'On certain terrace formations in the south of Scotland and on the English side of the Border', *Proc Soc Antiq Scot*, 62 (1927-8), 112.
English Heritage 1997 Monuments Protection Programme, Monument Class Description. *http://www.eng-h.gov.uk/mpp/mcd/mcdtop1.htm*
Ewart, G. 2003 'Dymock's Building, Bo'ness (Bo'ness and Carriden parish), post-medieval urban' *Discovery Excav Scot*, 2003, 75-76, Edinburgh.

Fawcett, R. 2003 *Scottish Abbeys and Priories*, Batsford.
Fawcett, R. and Oram, R. 2004 *Melrose Abbey*, Stroud.
Ferrier, W.M. 1980 *The North Berwick Story*. Edinburgh.
Fittis, R.S. 1885 *Ecclesiastical Annals of Perth*.

Gilchrist, R. 1995 *Contemplation and Action. The Other Monasticism*. Leicester.
Graham, A. 1939 'Cultivation terraces in south-eastern Scotland', *Proc Soc Antiq Scot*, 73 (1938-9), 291.
Grampian Club 1872 *Registrum de Cambuskenneth 1147-1535*. Edinburgh.

Haggarty, G. 1984 'Observations on the ceramic material from phase 1 pits BY and AQ' in Tabraham, C. 'Excavations at Kelso Abbey', *Proc Soc Antiq Scot*, 114 (1984), 395-7.
Hall, D.W. 1995 'Archaeological excavations at St Nicholas Farm, St Andrews 1986-87' *Tayside and Fife Archaeological Journal* 1, 48-75.
Hall, D.W. and Cachart, R. 1997 *Gazetteer of medieval hospital sites in Angus, Perth and Kinross and East, West and Midlothian council areas*. Report prepared for Historic Scotland.
Hamilton, J. and Toolis, R. 1999 'Further excavations at St Nicholas Farm, St Andrews' *Tayside and Fife Archaeological Journal* 5, 87-105.
Hannah, W.W.T. 1931 'The Romanno Terraces: their origin and purpose', *Proc Soc Antiq Scot*, 65 (1930-1), 388.
Harvey, W. 1972 'Wanlockhead, lead mine', *Discovery Excav Scot*, 1972, 20, Edinburgh.

Harvey, W.S. and Downs-Rose, G. 1979 'A view of the leadmines at Wanlockhead, 1775', *Trans Dumfriesshire Galloway Natur Hist Antiq Soc*, 3rd, 54 (1979), 90-6.
Hay, G.D. and Stell, G.P. 1986 *Monuments of Industry*. Edinburgh.
HBNC 1907 'Reports of the meetings of the Berwickshire Naturalist's Club, for 1903' *Hist Berwickshire Natur Club*, 19 (1903-5), 18-19. Berwick.
Hewat, K. 1894 *A little Scottish world as revealed in the annals of an ancient Ayrshire parish* [Monkton and Prestwick]. Kilmarnock, 12.
Hewison, J.K. 1912 *Dumfriesshire*. Cambridge.
Hume, J.R. 1976 *The industrial archaeology of Scotland, 1*. London.

Inchcolm Charters 1938 *Charters of the Abbey of Inchcolm*, (eds) D.E. Easson and A. Macdonald. Edinburgh.
Innes, C. (ed.) 1837 *Liber de Melros*. 2 vols, Bannatyne Club, Edinburgh.
Innes, C. (ed.) 1842 *Registrum de Dunfermelyn*. Edinburgh.
Irving, G.V. and Murray, A. 1864 *The upper ward of Lanarkshire described and delineated*, 3 vols. Glasgow, Vol. 1.

Kirk, J. (ed.) 1995 *The Books of Assumption of the Thirds of Benefices: Scottish Ecclesiastical Rentals at the Reformation*. Oxford (Records of Social and Economic History, New Ser 21).
Kirk, J., Tanner, R.J. and Dunlop, A.I. 1997 *Calendar of Scottish Supplications to Rome Volume V 1447-1471*.

Lamb, H.H. 1995 *Climate, History and the Modern World*. London 2nd edition.
Lewis, J. 2000 'Charlestown Limeworks, Fife (Dunfermline parish), lime kiln', *Discovery Excav Scot*, 1 (2000), 40. Edinburgh.
Lewis, J., Martin, C. and P. and Murdoch, R. 1999 '*The Salt and Coal Industries at St Monans, Fife in the 18th and 19th Centuries*' Tayside Fife Archaeol Committee Monograph Ser 2, Glenrothes.
Liber de Melros 1837 *Liber Sancte Marie de Melros* Bannatyne Club. Edinburgh.
Lindsay, W.A., Dowden, J. and Maitland Thomson, J. 1908 *Charters bulls and other documents relating to the Abbey of Inchaffray*. Edinburgh.

Macfarlane, W. 1906-8 *Geographical collections relating to Scotland*, 3 vols. Edinburgh, Vol 1.
MacGibbon and Ross 1887 *Castellated and domestic architecture of Scotland*.
Mackintosh, H.B. 1924 'Fragments of a jet necklace found at Greenhowe, Pluscarden, Morayshire', *Proc Soc Antiq Scot*, 58 (1923-4), 239. Edinburgh.
Mackintosh, H.B. 1924 *Pilgrimages in Moray: a guide to the county*. Elgin.
McDiarmid, W.R. 1895 *Handbook of Colvend and Southwick*, 7, 2nd. Dumfries.
Milne, A. 1743 *A description of the parish of Melrose, in answer to Maitland's queries sent to each parish in the kingdom*. Edinburgh.
Minchinton, W. 1984 *A Guide to Industrial Archaeology Sites in Britain*. London.
Moffat, B. 1989 *The Third Report into Researches into the Medieval Hospital at Soutra, Lothian/Borders Region, Scotland*. SHARP 1989
Murdoch, R. 1997 'Charlestown Limekilns (Dunfermline parish), limekilns', *Discovery Excav Scot* 1997, 36. Edinburgh.

Neilson, G. 1899 *Annals of the Solway Until AD 1307*. (Read at a Meeting of the Glasgow Archaeological Society held on 13th November, 1896.) http://www.stevebulman.f9.co.uk/cumbria/solway_f.html
Newbattle Registrum 1849 *Registrum Sancte Marie de Neubotle*. Bannatyne Club, Edinburgh.
NSA 1845 *The new statistical account of Scotland by the ministers of the respective parishes under the superintendence of a committee of the society for the benefit of the sons and daughters of the clergy*, 15v, Edinburgh.

Oakes, S. 1994 'Siller Holes (Linton parish): medieval pottery, shoes and textile' *Discovery Excav Scot* 1994, 7. Edinburgh.
OPS 1851 *Origines Parochiales Scotiae: The Antiquities Ecclesiastical and Territorial of the Parishes of Scotland*, 1, Edinburgh, 166.
Ordnance Survey Name Book (Ayrshire) 1856.
Ordnance Survey Name Book (Dumfriesshire) 1848.
Ordnance Survey Name Book (Fife) 1855.
Ordnance Survey Name Book (South Lanarkshire) 1851.
Orme, N. and Webster, M. *The English Hospital 1070-1570*
OSA 1791-9 *The Statistical Account of Scotland, drawn up from the Communications of the Ministers of the Different Parishes*, Sinclair, Sir J. (ed), Edinburgh, Vol. 12, 514.

Perry, D. and Bowler, D.P. 1989 'Canmore's Tower, Pittencrieff Park', *Discovery Excav Scot*, 1989, 16. Edinburgh.
Photos Jones, E., Hall, A.J., Pollard, T., Meikle, T.K. and Newlands, A. 1999 '"The manner how it grew was like unto the haire of a mans head." The early 1600's discovery and exploitation of silver at Hilderston, Scotland' in *Metals in Antiquity* Young, S.M.M., Pollard, A.M., Budd, P. and Ixer, R.A. (eds) BAR International Series 792. Oxford.
Pococke, R. 1887 *Tours in Scotland 1747, 1750, 1760*. Edinburgh.
Price, R. and Ponsford, M. 1998 *St Bartholomew's Hospital, Bristol The excavation of a medieval hospital: 1976-8*. CBA Research Report 110.
Pryde, G.S. 1965 *The burghs of Scotland: a critical list*. London.

RCAHMS 1924 *Eighth report with inventory of monuments and constructions in the county of East Lothian*, Edinburgh, 59, No.104.
RCAHMS 1933 *The Royal Commission on the Ancient and Historical Monuments and Constructions of Scotland. Eleventh report with inventory of monuments and constructions in the counties of Fife, Kinross, and Clackmannan*, Edinburgh, 99-100, No 188.
RCAHMS 1956 *An inventory of the ancient and historical monuments of Roxburghshire: with the fourteenth report of the Commission*, 2v, Edinburgh.
RCAHMS 1967 *Peeblesshire: an inventory of the ancient monuments*, 2v, Edinburgh.
RCAHMS 1985 The archaeological sites and monuments of West Rhins, Wigtown District, Dumfries and Galloway Region, *The archaeological sites and monuments of Scotland series* no 24, Edinburgh.
Richards, J. 1971 *The Medieval leper and his Northern heirs*.
Richardson, J.S. 1929 'A thirteenth-century tile kiln at North Berwick, East Lothian, and Scottish medieval ornamented floor tiles' *Proc Soc Antiq Scot*, 63 (1928-9), 281-4. Edinburgh.
Robertson, J. 1979 'Wanlockhead roads', *Trans Dumfriesshire Galloway Natur Hist Antiq Soc*, 3rd, 54 (1979), 161-4.
Rogers, C. (ed.) 1879 *Rental book of the Cistercian Abbey of Cupar-Angus with the Breviary of the Register*, vol 1.
RRS *Regum Registra Scottorum, Vol 2: the acts of William I, King of Scots, 1165-1214*.

Smout, T.C. 1962 'The lead mines at Wanlockhead', *Trans Dumfriesshire Galloway Natur Hist Antiq Soc*, 3rd, 39 (1960-1), 144-58.
Smythe, T. 1843 *Liber Ecclesie de Scon*. Bannatyne Club, Edinburgh.
Snodgrass, C.P. 1953 *The third statistical account of Scotland: the county of East Lothian*. Edinburgh.
Stell, G.P. 1986 *Exploring Scotland's heritage: Dumfries and Galloway*. Edinburgh, 1st edition.
Stephen, W. 1938 *The story of Inverkeithing and Rosyth*. Edinburgh.
Swinbank, P. 1977 'Wanlockhead: the maps, the documents, the relics and the confusion', *Scot Archaeol Forum*, 8 (1976), 23-36. Edinburgh.

Talbot, E. 1976 'A possible Medieval tile-kiln near Melrose', *Glasgow Archaeol Soc Bull*, 2 (1976) Spring, 10. Glasgow.

TDGNHAS 1979 'A select bibliography of the Wanlockhead and Leadhills areas' *Trans Dumfriesshire Galloway Natur Hist Antiq Soc*, 3rd, 54 (1979) Addenda Antiquaria, 173-4.

The Leadhills and Wanlockhead Mines Research Group 1976 *Wanlockhead: Scotland's highest village*. Leadhills.

The Mining Journal 1910 (http://www.crawford-john.org.uk/mining1.htm).

The Mining Journal November 12, 1910.

The Wanlockhead Museum Trust 2002 *The Museum of Lead Mining Wanlockhed*, unauthored; information booklet. Wanlockhead.

Thomson, J.M. et al. (eds) 1882-1914 *RMS Registrum Magni Sigilli Regum Scotorum*, 11 vols 1306-1668. Edinburgh (reprinted 1984).

Thomson, J. 1828 *Northern Part of Ayrshire*, Edinburgh.

Thomson, J. et al. 1882-1914 *RMS Registrum Magni Sigilii Regum Scottorum*.

Torrie, E.P.D. and Coleman, R. 1995 *Historic Kirkcaldy*, the Scottish Burgh Survey, Edinburgh.

Tucker, D.G. 1958 'Millstone making in Scotland', *Proc Soc Antiq Scot*, 114 (1984), 545 553.

University of Edinburgh, Department of Archaeology 1996 *Department of Archaeology, 42nd Annual Report*, 45.

Wade, J.A. 1861 *History of St Mary's Abbey, Melrose, the monastery of Old Melrose and the town and parish of Melrose*, Edinburgh.

Watson, N.D. 1997 *A History of the Pow of Inchaffray, Perthshire*.

Williams, J. 1979 '18th century property lists from Wanlockhead testaments', *Trans Dumfriesshire Galloway Natur Hist Antiq Soc*, 3rd, 54 (1979), 132-46.

Williams, J. 1979 'The Day Book (1742-50) of William Hendry, a Wanlockhead and Leadhills merchant', *Trans Dumfriesshire Galloway Natur Hist Antiq Soc*, 3rd, 54 (1979), Addenda Antiquaria, 167-72.

Wilson, J.A. 1936-7 *A Contribution to the History of Lanarkshire*, 2 vol, Glasgow, Vol.2.

Young, R. 1871 *The Parish of Spynie*. Elgin.

If you are interested in purchasing other books published by Tempus,
or in case you have difficulty finding any Tempus books in your local bookshop,
you can also place orders directly through our website

www.tempus-publishing.com